Urban Citizenship and
American Democracy

Urban Citizenship and American Democracy

Edited by

Amy Bridges and Michael Javen Fortner

Published by State University of New York Press, Albany

Printed in the United States of America

For information, contact State University of New York Press, Albany, NY
www.sunypress.edu

Production, Eileen Nizer
Marketing, Anne M. Valentine

Library of Congress Cataloging-in-Publication Data

Names: Bridges, Amy, editor. | Fortner, Michael Javen, 1979– editor.
Title: Urban citizenship and American democracy / edited by Amy Bridges and
    Michael Javen Fortner.
Description: Albany : State University of New York Press, 2016. | Includes
    bibliographical references and index.
Identifiers: LCCN 2015027114 | ISBN 9781438461014 (hardcover : alk. paper) |
    ISBN 9781438461007 (paperback : alk. paper) | 9781438461021 (e-book)
Subjects: LCSH: Municipal government—United States. | Cities and
    towns—United States. | Citizenship—United States. | Democracy—United
    States.
Classification: LCC JS323 .U73 2016 | DDC 320.8/50973—dc23
LC record available at https://lccn.loc.gov/2015027114

10 9 8 7 6 5 4 3 2 1

Contents

Illustrations

Tables

Figures

Introduction to Cities and Citizenship

Amy Bridges

This volume originated at the "Summer Seminar on the City: American Government as Urban Government," a conference held at Drexel University in 2011. Focusing on politics, the authors consider whether, or when, cities are better, and when they are worse laboratories of citizenship and democracy. Answering that question raises several others long asked about city governments: How can residents secure city governments responsive to public preferences? What can be accomplished by a group empowered in city politics? How limited is city government? When do urban citizens secure the attention of state and federal politicians? When can city government be autonomous of state and federal governments? Beyond the city's limits, the authors explore the potential meaning and consequences of urban citizenship for US politics. In this chapter, I review what scholars of urban politics know about democracy in city politics, the autonomy of cities, their place in US politics, the limits on city government, and a presentation of an active and creative role for cities in the process of globalization. The authors of the chapters here move our understanding of these most basic issues forward, some with cheering information and analysis, and others with sobering evidence and insight.

For those of us who live in a city or grew up in a city, urban citizenship is part of our identity. We commonly recognize urban identities in the character of people we meet, marking them as Angelenos, Chicagoans, Phoenicians, or New Yorkers (or, among New Yorkers, as from the Bronx, Manhattan, Queens, Staten Island, or Brooklyn). There are many ways to identify with, or be proud of, the city in which we live. There might be good weather, great museums, historic sites, strong neighborhood communities, architectural greatness, or equitable public policy. And of course there is politics—an honest and efficient government, an excellent school system, or a tradition of civil service. Some cities are more political than others, and popular culture exhibits this. A simple, unscientific way to discover local political culture is to ask a taxi driver, or a teacher, or a table attendant about an upcoming election. In Chicago or Washington, the answer is likely to be a disquisition on candidates, platforms, misdeeds, and likely popular support. In San Diego, the response is more likely to be "I don't pay much attention to politics." City government, urban politicians, and local political institutions have much to do with how political residents are.

This follows from the ways cities share many of the properties we attribute to nation-states. Writing about nations, Theda Skocpol recognized that national governments have their own sets of electoral, administrative, and service institutions, and they "(and the politics they generate) can operate according to their own logic." The same is true of cities. Like national states, cities impose taxes and fees, distribute jobs, goods, and services, and "matter because their organizational configurations . . . affect political culture, and encourage some kinds of group formation and collective action . . . make possible the raising of [some] political issues" and discourage the appearance of other issues.[1] In addition, city governments have their own political leaders, who lend meaning to particular programs, create policies rewarding some and excluding others, and mobilize voters into coalitions they hope to maintain. Urban leaders can design political rules to make themselves independent of some groups, as they rest comfortably on others.[2] City governments influence the creation of interest groups and offer political lessons citizens may bring to other decisions, as when successful black mayors lower Anglo anxieties about voting for African American candidates. Although it is true that cities are legally creatures of their states, cities also have considerable authority and prerogatives: they raise their own revenues; have monopolies of certain functions for which they preside over employees, policies, and administration; and can be effective on their own behalf.

The authority and scope of city government have made it possible for skillful politicians to improve the well-being of urban residents. The constructive possibilities of city government can be seen in the administrations of the early twentieth-century social reform mayors Hazen Pingree (Detroit), Tom Johnson (Cleveland), and Sam "Golden Rule"

Jones (Toledo).[3] Pingree fought for the three-cent fare and free transfers on public trolleys, campaigns that were closely watched by residents in their cities and brought nationwide attention in the press. Pingree was a very successful businessman, a Republican, pressed by colleagues in his party to run for mayor of Detroit and clean up its corrupt government. In office, Pingree grew to be a strong ally of the city's immigrant working population. It was for their benefit that he championed the three-cent fare and free transfers. It was for their benefit too that he pressed Detroit's utility corporations to lower their fees and became an advocate of municipal ownership of utilities. In the depression of 1893, Pingree initiated the potato patch plan, in which small plots of vacant land were given to indigent families who applied for them. In a few years, nearly 20,000 families farmed on these lands, the value of the crops harvested exceeded the city's poor relief budget, and the plan spread to many other cities. Pingree's efforts to pressure corporations to make them better serve Detroit's population alienated other Republican leaders in Michigan, including many who earlier had been his friends. The governor and state legislature also opposed him and so interfered with his efforts that Pingree ran for governor himself, serving two terms ending in 1901.[4] We can think of comparable efforts and successes at both improving well-being and building community or popular solidarity, Fiorello La Guardia in New York (1934–1945) and Ivan Allen in Atlanta (1962–1970).[5]

More commonly, the authority and domain of city governments have enabled them to establish parks and school systems; supply drinking water and pick up the garbage; create mass transportation in trains, trolleys, and buses; support museums; and innovate in systems of criminal justice. So we know that, for all of our discussion of limits, control of city government conveys wide-ranging powers. Groups empowered by city government have these resources at hand, although, like Pingree and other social reformers, politicians leading their efforts will encounter resistance from several quarters.

What of democracy in cities? In the eighteenth century, it was the great discovery of citizens in the thirteen colonies that elections were an effective way to tie politicians to public sentiment. They came to this by comparing the behavior of colonial governors, who were appointed by the Crown, and members of colonial legislatures, who were elected. In the nineteenth century, residents were keenly aware that they were citizens or residents of a democratic republic, contrasted often by political leaders and the press with the "subjects" who endured monarchs and despots elsewhere. It was the republican government of the United States that informed how residents thought about their prospects in cities. So, amid demonstrations for "work or bread" during the depression of the mid-1850s, Edward Mallon, a tailor, reminded workers that "there was one weapon the [American] workingmen had [that] . . . was more powerful than the gun or the chain behind the barricades of Paris. It was the ballot."[6]

Elections remain the central institutional arrangement for citizens to tie city government to popular preferences. Yet all elections are not equal; rules and institutions matter. Cities make choices in arranging elections and public institutions. They may have mayor-council, city manager, or commission government. Elections may or may not be held concurrently with elections for state or federal offices. Polling places may be open only one day or on several days; they may be open for many hours, accommodating people in the labor force as well as those with more time. Candidates may have party designations, or elections may be nonpartisan. City governments set residence and registration requirements for voters. Each of these choices will influence who votes, how much their votes count, and who is likely to hold public office. Finally, politicians, their supporters, and political party or Nonpartisan Slating Groups activists may walk precincts, knock on doors, and remind people to vote.

The list is elementary, but it is important nevertheless, not least because every choice on that list affects turnout. In cities, turnout matters. Zoltan Hajnal and Jessica Trounstine have shown that the institutional arrangements in cities affect turnout, and turnout affects who is elected. The authors are concerned with racial and ethnic representation. People of color are twice the proportion of urban populations than they are of the nation as a whole. In 61 percent of US cities with populations greater than 100,000, non-Hispanic whites were less than half of the population. Propensity to vote is similar among Anglo Americans and African Americans; Latinos and Asian Americans are less likely to vote. Higher aggregate turnout in local elections results in more Latino and Asian Americas on city councils. Specific institutional changes to increase turnout—changing from at-large elections to district elections and changing from nonconcurrent to concurrent elections—increases the proportion of blacks on city councils by about 6 percent. More surprising, racial and ethnic differences in who turns out to vote in mayoral elections affect who wins. Hajnal and Trounstine simulated mayoral elections in the ten largest US cities to show who would have won if the same proportion of registered voters in each group had voted. In three of those elections (Houston, New York, and San Diego), equal turnout would have resulted in a different winner. The key voters in each of the three cities were Latinos. In each city, Latinos in the actual election supported the loser; if the proportion of Latinos voting had matched the turnout of other groups, the candidate they supported would have won.[7]

My own research suggested that cities with district elections and descriptive representation, parties, and high turnout distributed benefits more equitably than cities without those traits. In *Morning Glories*, I compared seven reform cities (San Diego, San Jose, Phoenix, Albuquerque, Austin, San Antonio, and Dallas) with three I called "machine descendants" (New Haven, Chicago, and New York), in 1960. The reformed cities had citywide, nonconcurrent, and nonpartisan elections. The machine descendants had strong parties, concurrent elections, and representation by districts. The machine descendants distributed libraries and parks more equitably than the cities with reform government. Cities with district elections and descriptive representation had higher turnout and greater citizen satisfaction than residents in cities without them.[8] Of course it would have been infinitely better if I had compared dozens of cities, with measures of more outcomes—educational attainment by race and family income, for example, or descriptive representation among municipal employees, or the incidence of police brutality. That research design would have produced much more information about the substantive and policy outcomes of institutions in city politics. And even more broadly, to know where residents of cities are empowered, we ought to investigate where policy outcomes, especially those most important to residents, match the preferences of the populace, try to identify the institutional arrangements that enable that outcome.

Understanding who gets what and how in cities requires looking beyond formal institutions and party leaders. In 1976, San Antonio residents petitioned the Department of Justice, arguing that the city's annexations, in combination with its voting arrangements, diluted the votes of Latinos, who were about to become a majority of the city's population. In response, the Department found that citywide elections—because they consistently deprived some citizens of ever securing their preferred candidates for political office, "diluting" the votes of Spanish-speaking residents—were discriminatory, violating their civil rights. The demise of citywide elections followed across the Southwest.[9] The crucial actor in events in San Antonio, in both protesting existing political arrangements and mobilizing Latinos once new institutions were in place, was Communities Organized for Public Service (COPS). COPS was brought into being with the assistance of the Industrial Areas Foundation (IAF), founded by Saul Alinsky in 1940.[10] Since that time, IAF has been instrumental in the organization of dozens of community organizations. In the last twenty years, service workers' unions have similarly increased the public visibility of low-wage communities and workers and also raised their wages. Like many community organizations, these unions are politically active, and in many US cities they are a force to be reckoned with.[11] The lesson here is that citizen activism and community and other popular organizations empower citizens to tie elected officials to their will.

Leaders may move some distance from the citizenry, and city governments may formulate and pursue goals that are not reflective of the demands, interests, or ideologies of social groups, classes, or public sentiment more generally. Jessica Trounstine has argued that parties and politicians follow a trajectory in which the most successful can afford to neglect some constituents. In their initial efforts to secure office, politicians seek support from many communities and groups, creating broad coalitions. Once secure in office and confident of victory in future elections, they direct resources to core constituents and curtail benefits to marginal—and so, in their view, possibly superfluous—supporters. The resulting disaffection eventually results in their loss of power.[12]

One reason politicians and other officials may stray from the desires of their constituents is that in the ordinary pursuit of their responsibilities, politicians and municipal employees may operate well under the radar of residents and the press. In this way, low turnout may bear bitter fruit. Widespread withdrawal from politics facilitated the astonishing greed and corruption of public officials in Bell, California, and abuses of authority by an empowered white minority in Ferguson, Missouri. Both cities are small; in 1910 Ferguson's population numbered about 21,000, and Bell counted about 35,000 residents. Residents were also of moderate income. Median household income from 2009 to 2013 was $35,945 in Bell and $38,685 in Ferguson. Bell has a predominantly Latino immigrant population; 67% of Ferguson residents are African American. Small cities are not much studied; Bell and Ferguson offer morality tales of city government gone wrong.[13]

In both cities, police were key partners of elected officials. Like the support armed forces have provided to authoritarian national regimes, police in Bell and Ferguson engaged in repressive and punitive activities. Police also generated funds for government salaries and services by the aggressive use of traffic violations, impounding of cars, and arrests for minor offenses, all targeting the low-income populations. Ferguson officials made both the goals of these activities and their targets clear to the police. The Department of Justice investigation of the Ferguson Police Department reported that "[c]ity and police leadership; pressure officers to write citations, independent of any public safety need, and rely on citation productivity to fund the city budget." Similarly, in Ferguson's municipal court, "staff are keenly aware that the City considers revenue generation to be the municipal court's primary purpose." In Bell, the police chief planned to boost revenue "by aggressively towing the cars of illegal immigrants."[14] In both Bell and Ferguson, elected officials were freed from public scrutiny by low turnout in municipal elections. Officials in Bell were granted more fiscal freedom by an election that turned it into a charter city. In both cities, turnout was kept low by devices known to practitioners and scholars to suppress participation: off-cycle years for elections, elections in the spring rather than the fall, and the depoliticization of government by adoption of the city-manager form.

Corruption in Bell was revealed by the *Los Angeles Times* in 2010. The reaction of the community was immediate. The *Times* revealed that the city manager earned $1.5 million annually; city council members were paid $100,000 per year for their part-time jobs. A new community organization, Basta!, organized in a campaign to recall the city manager, his assistant, and a majority of the city council; the measure was endorsed with 95 percent of votes cast. The same people were convicted of corruption and jailed or fined. Voter registration increased by 10 percent; in 2011 a new city council took office on April 8. Ferguson became the focus of national attention after Michael Brown, an eighteen-year-old black man, was killed by a city police officer. The officer was found innocent of criminal intent. The immediate response was a sustained series of demonstrations. In Ferguson, too, popular response included mobilization to replace city officials with others committed to the community. Local activists were assisted by national nongovernmental organizations (NGOs), including MoveOn.org, the Service Employees International Union's Missouri state council, and the Working Families Party. The election increased black representation on the city council from one to three and, more importantly, brought turnout to 30 percent, almost triple the turnout in the prior election. Here, as in Bell, there was optimism about the city and its government, as well as recognition that "This is the beginning of a long Process."[15] How much change takes place in Bell and Ferguson will depend on how well residents can sustain the organization and energy that brought new officials in these elections.

When have cities and their residents been effective at winning the attention of higher governments and securing policies and funding for them? Scott James has argued very persuasively that the electoral pressures of presidential elections are not confined to the quadrennial event, but continue without end.[16] In the middle of the twentieth century, the presence of African Americans in critical swing states—Illinois and New York most prominently—provoked the Community Action Program and other initiatives of the Great Society intended to cement loyalty and encourage turnout for the Democrats among African Americans.[17] The same dynamics increased the influence of New York and Chicago mayors, whose support was key to Democratic victory in their closely competitive states. Democratic majorities were not African Americans alone, but African Americans and Latinos were central components of a coalition of people of color and Anglos in the nation's cities. The greater inference here is that rules designed for a particular purpose may well serve quite different ends. In this instance, the electoral college, meant to ensure the representation of small population states, and hence their loyalty to the union in 1787, in 2012 reinforced the victory of a popular majority. The meaning was not lost on Republicans, some of whom are now working to change the way electoral votes are counted. What of larger forces—the changing shape of the US economy, and with it the changing roles of cities, and what threats or opportunities might be posed by the international economy? These are indeed towering challenges. Jerome Hodos observed that academic attention to globalization has focused on the "world cities" tasked with managing international enterprises (New York, Tokyo, London). In *Second Cities*, Hodos focused on more common, lesser cities in the world economy and their leaders' efforts to find an economic niche that would support their communities. Looking at Philadelphia and Manchester (England), Hodos shows how nineteenth-century leaders in each city secured a key role in their region, Philadelphia by construction of canals and later railroads tying it to the West, and Manchester by construction of a port that brought it transatlantic commerce in cotton. In this way, Hodos reminds us that regional and world trade were hardly new to the twentieth century. More recently, Philadelphia has rested its hopes in part on the port (landing the enormous coup of winning a large shipbuilding contract, which endowed Philadelphia with a state-of-the-art shipbuilding facility) and, more importantly, its airport's function as a hub for major airlines. Manchester has for the most part abandoned the port and shifted its focus to airlines. Hodos suggests we think of these efforts as urban mercantilism, or municipal foreign policy, emphasizing benefits to the city as a whole on the one hand and the need for connections beyond its immediate region on the other. And he is insistent on the centrality of city governments in this effort. "The local state," Hodos wrote,

> took the leading role in planning, funding, and managing immense transportation infrastructure projects that enhanced the city's position [in the transportation network], reinforced its dominance over its hinterland . . . and spread the city's economy into new leading sectors.[18]

This means that cities were not simply the benefactors of good fortune bestowed by the world system. Rather, "[u]rban agency . . . also constitutes the very process of globalization—it is the stuff of which globalization is made."[19] Urban mercantilism creates the map of trade routes; urban mercantilism charts the flow of commerce; urban mercantilism crafts the ties of globalization.

Any of these claims about the potential for city governments rests on their autonomy. Harold Wolman and Michael Goldsmith define urban autonomy as "the ability of local governments to have an independent impact on the well-being of their citizens."[20] What city government, and hence those empowered by it, can accomplish requires autonomy. *Cities enjoy autonomy when they have adequate resources they control.* New York Democrats learned this in the 1850s. From the founding of the republic, mayors sent envoys to Washington after each presidential election, seeking patronage and resources from the Oval Office. In 1856, politicians realized that city government's own patronage positions outnumbered those available from the federal government in the Customs House, a federal institution central to balancing the federal budget and employer of many citizens. One Tammany politician declared their liberation: "No man should have power in this state if that power is to be swayed by authorities in Washington."[21] Those resources and the fealty of a majority of the city's voters empowered New York's Democrats for decades.[22]

What of the limits on city governments—the restraints imposed by the threat of exit by residents and employers; the legal confines of their status, which subordinates them to their states; and the costs and compromises imposed by the federal government? These are frequently complained of in academic writing, including authors in this book, and the press. Yet before we let our politicians and ourselves off the hook, it is worth listing a few possibilities within reach of local governments, political leaders, and citizens willing to work for them. Housing provides an example. Some cities require that all multifamily housing set aside a portion of units for low-income families, as happened in Oceanside, California, and the more affluent Montgomery County, Maryland. Cities might work harder at enforcing building codes. Equally pressing, we continue to have towering problems of inequity in education, from absence of Head Start and pre-kindergarten to the school-to-prison pipeline. Although it is certainly true that more plentiful resources enable greater efforts, I do not think the fundamental problems here are financial. Alas, teachers are sometimes part of the problem; even lifelong supporters of unions, especially public-sector unions, have been disappointed, disheartened, and angry about the prerogatives claimed by public schoolteachers. And parents can be disappointed, disheartened, and angry about the abandonment of public schools by politicians and by their more affluent neighbors, abandonment both in policy and by where they choose to send their own children to school. In the criminal justice system, we also have problems that are not fundamentally financial. There are the continuing problems of harassment and worse of people of color, especially young men, by police, and their differential treatment by the courts. However high up these systems may be faulty, discriminatory, or white supremacist; for the hapless resident they happen in school, on the sidewalk, and in the streets.

The chapters in this collection provide arguments and evidence that help us understand cities, citizenship, and democracy. Students of cities have long recognized their subordinate legal status, of which the most extreme case is Washington, DC. Nevertheless, cities have at times been home to more, and at other times to less, effective citizenship and democratic government. Sometimes cities have made progress toward these goals when left to their own devices; at other times their path was encouraged by state or federal government. The stakes of city politics are hardly trivial to their citizens. Those high stakes made cities the province of a street-fighting pluralist politics for many years and in some cities still does.

Michael Javen Fortner offers answers to questions about effective citizenship and democracy. Fortner counterposes a centuries-old understanding of cities—more precisely, city-states—as the ideal type of democracy, with the evisceration of urban possibilities by Paul Peterson's declaration that, because cities have for generations not been city-states, but simply cities scattered across the vast expanse of the United States, their governments are very limited in what they can accomplish. The enforcers of those limits are those residents and employers who, should they find the balance of costs and benefits of being in a particular city negative, will not hesitate to exit.[23] It follows from that insight that city governments will be punished if they pursue—and so will be reluctant to engage in—redistributive policies, which the public and employers are likely to reject. As a result, Peterson argued, politicians are likely to pursue policies that benefit the city's economy as a whole. Fortner's response is, in brief, that Peterson's insight was time limited. It is only a quite recent possibility that firms or families will move outside their home city to lower costs; exit only became a possibility practiced by business in the 1950s.[24]

Fortner's larger concern is citizenship. Here he raises the bar, seeing effective citizenship as "individual engagement with city politics" on the one hand and "the capacity of residents to determine the fate of their communities," more particularly to "use the urban state to achieve outcomes they value," on the other. Even if city residents could live up to the standard Fortner sets for them, under what conditions might their city governments be able to deliver? Here Fortner's strongest case for cities to overcome the limitations of law and local resources is for their leaders to leverage, though political parties, their political support of national politicians. Like many other things, that leverage is a product of "big structures and large processes" not under the control of cities. Following Scott James, if we recognize that winning presidential elections is ever the driving force of national politics, then cities will have leverage when their votes are considered critical to success in presidential elections. Sure enough, the most compelling examples of urban leverage within the party system come at those moments when presidents and their parties recognized city votes as critical to election outcomes. For twentieth-century Democrats, that meant the 1960s (as described above), 2012, and 2016.

Tom Hulme shows that long before Mr. Rogers appeared on television, adult immigrants to the United States, and schoolchildren, were taught that cities created beautiful days in their neighborhoods. From World War I through the 1930s, civics textbooks taught that citizens' well-being was the product of the work of municipal employees, who cleaned the streets, ensured that the milk left on the front step was pure and unadulterated, provided clean and safe running water, collected the garbage, and taught in city schools. Civics textbooks presented urban life as peaceful, clean, and orderly—a veritable utopia—and the product of municipal employees. For Hulme, the key insight is that in the interwar period it was urban rather than national citizenship that formed the basis of belonging in the United States. Although Hulme concedes that city dwellers "may not have necessarily seen themselves primarily as Bostonians, Philadelphians, or Chicagoans rather than Americans," residents first learned about, and began the practice of, democracy and government in their cities.[25]

Marion Orr and colleagues turn their attention to contemporary public schools, showing how public schools have functioned to build political participation by Latino parents. The importance of Latino political participation is enhanced by the rapidly increasing size of the Spanish surnamed electorate in the United States, particularly in swing states. Orr and colleagues carefully trace the relations between parent involvement in schools and their political activity. The authors found a significant relationship between participation in school activities and an interest in politics and public affairs. Participation in school activities increased the likelihood that Latino parents contacted a public official and, even more compelling, that participation in school activities was strongly associated with political and civic engagement, joining with others to solve problems.

Schools are especially influential when they offer welcoming, multilingual environments. The process can be seen today in even earlier grades than the ones Orr and colleagues discuss. Immigrant families may have children in Head Start (three-year-olds) or pre-kindergarten (four-year-olds) in public schools. For the parents, especially those not in the labor force, the school provides a US community different from, and likely more diverse than, their own neighborhood. In those ways, schools can provide entry into contemporary American life for parents as well as their children.

There are other readings of cities and city politics that focus on the ways opportunities for effective politics in cities have been diminished, or enhanced for some residents and diminished for others. Richard Harris presents a new urban regime now in place in Camden, New Jersey. Camden's major employers—Campbell Soup, Esterbrook Pen, RCA Victor, and others, have abandoned the city, leaving high unemployment and impoverished government in their wake. Camden is 52 percent African American and 38 percent Hispanic; its unemployment rate is 20 percent, and half of all households in Camden have income no higher than $25,000 per year. In addition, subsequent to the authors' completion of their essay, Camden lost its police force—because it could not pay them—to county government.

In place of the business-government regime presented by Clarence Stone, Camden has seen the rise of a community development regime. In place of business leaders, Harris finds foundations, nonprofits, and sometimes health sector institutions setting the course for urban communities and likely their governments as well. Whereas the old regime joined politicians and business, the new regime hardly consults with politicians or government. This is possible in part because Camden's government became so weak and incapacitated that the community development regime was able to step in to take its place. Camden is not alone. Benton Harbor, Michigan, is a similarly economically distressed city, now "subject to . . . state intervention that effectively prorogues its elected government." East St. Louis (Illinois) too has become a ward of its state. Although organizations in the community development regime "work with activists" in their cities, as happened in urban renewal in the 1950s and 1960s, the decisions of the new regime are presented to the public as faits accomplis rather than propositions for public debate. Harris concludes that, although not tainted by venal interest in the outcomes (as were some of their business predecessors), central actors in the new urban regime are confident that they know best about public policy for their cities. African Americans and Latinos are the majority in cities like Camden and Benton Harbor, communities stripped of gainful employment, good schools, and effective local government. If residents of those cities are beneficiaries of community development regimes, Harris argues, they are nevertheless not effective citizens in those cities, and so are only the beneficiaries of the regimes, not architects of their own future.

Despite the muting of resident voices in Camden and Harris's disparagement of citizenship under community development regimes, his chapter offers grounds for hope. A major redevelopment project to which the mayor and the city council acceded was derailed by popular opposition, supported from two important actors in the community development regime, the Ford and Annie E. Casey Foundations. It seems likely that, absent the foundations, opposition would have been managed one way or another and defeated. As it happened, however, the coalition of popular groups and their wealthy supporters was successful. This suggests that, if nothing else, popular civic participation in Camden may be down, but it is not out. Equally important, partners in the community development regime can be open to, and supportive of, popular input and activism in ways their predecessors were not.

It may also be that community development regimes are quite different in intent and motivation than the business regimes of the past. The Web site describes the Annie E. Casey Foundation as "devoted to developing a brighter future for millions of children at risk of poor educational, economic, social and health outcomes." The Ford Foundation's Web site explains that its "goals for more than fifty years" are "to strengthen democratic values; reduce poverty and injustice, promote international cooperation, and advance human achievement." The Ford Foundation has a long and storied history of promoting progressive liberal reform. The Casey Foundation has chosen two cities, Atlanta and Camden, for community-building assistance. If Harris sees Casey and Ford as directive big brothers, Casey's own description of their efforts in Atlanta has an Alinsky-ish tone:

> Community building, the practice of working with residents and community-based organizations to strengthen civic life and develop community-driven responses to common challenges, has been foundational to this work.

It is obvious, reading the foundation's description of its work in Atlanta, that the initiative is built on years of sometimes painful experience (for example, one lesson of their experience is "the importance of [the foundation] staying out of implementation as a place-based funder"), and that the foundation and its employees are driven by their desire to help residents of Atlanta communities make their lives better. There is much emphasis on "transparent dialogue, participatory planning resident organizing, and organizational capacity building." On the other hand, the document cautions that "more important than strategies . . . is not to get ahead of the community as the Foundation charts its way forward."[26] So I do not doubt that Harris is onto something about the demeanor and intent of foundation representatives in Camden, and I am confident that Camden would be different if the Industrial Areas Foundation had been there instead of Casey and Ford. On the other hand, when push came to shove, Casey and Ford cast their lot with popular opposition to the proposed development, not with the developers, surely a different stance than their business predecessors would have taken, a stance that made all the difference.

Khalilah Brown-Dean investigates the insidious role of prisons in federal and state elections, creating their own peculiar malapportionment and thus draining resources away from poor communities, African Americans, and cities. This is indeed important. The communities in which prisons have been built are a world unto themselves, and their residents want to preserve that status. Although residents of communities that house prisons recognize their economic importance, one wonders how aware they are of the increased power of their own votes. County and town leaders in places with prisons are perfectly clear about the advantages that accrue to their communities and themselves from prisons. Certainly politicians are alert to the dynamics of elections to state legislatures. Interest groups reliant on prisons, especially prison guards, are active on behalf of their own prison-related economic and political interests.

For the general public and in academia, recognition of these dynamics is sparse. On the one hand, there is considerable awareness of the disproportionate imprisonment of people of color, especially black men. Brown-Dean reminds us that African Americans are 12 percent of the US population but 60 percent of all Americans behind bars. Latinos, too, are overrepresented among those in prison. Many people are also aware that the disproportionate number of blacks among convicted felons has also resulted in their permanent disfranchisement, even in states where, according to law, their disfranchisement should end with their prison terms.[27] On the other hand, in addition to political losses to individuals are collective losses, and these are less recognized. Communities of color and cities suffer politically from the rules for counting prisoners in the census. Brown-Dean, retrieving a term that dates to the Middle Ages, denominates the decline in the power and influence of cities that follows from these rules "civil death."

The census counts prisoners not in the places they lived before they were jailed, but as residents of the places where they are incarcerated. Were prisons close to their original residences, this would not be so consequential for their communities and for cities. Prisons are neither close to home nor urban. Rather, prisons are in rural areas, bringing the political weight of their populations with them. The result is that counties and towns take part in "fierce battles to win [prison] construction projects." More remunerative for their locales than Wal-Mart, prisons are a surefire growth strategy. Because federal monies for many programs are allocated on the basis of population, the profits of prisons for their locales are from the public sector as well as the firms that supply food, uniforms, telephones, and many other amenities to prisons and their inmates.

The other side of this coin is the loss to cities of the same industries and federal monies that have moved to the countryside with former city residents. Prisoners have been moved not only from urban to rural areas, but also from one state to another. Sometimes representation in state legislatures is gained or lost by the location of prisoners. In this roundabout way, Brown-Dean argues, counting bodies and ballots results not only in the disfranchisement of individuals, but also in civil death for cities and their residents. As a resident of the District of Columbia, which has jails but no prisons, I add to the pain inflicted by these rules the extreme and entirely unnecessary cruelty of housing prisoners hundreds and sometimes thousands of miles from their communities, their friends, and their families. The costs of counting bodies and ballots in the way we do, and placing prisoners where we do, marks the bottomless perversity of our system of criminal justice.

Lisa Miller argues that "the political arrangements of federalism" create "racially stratified access to power" in the United States. Federal government limits the power, prerogatives, and resources of cities and so limits the power and influence of African Americans, who are predominantly urban. There are examples of African American power and influence in large, prosperous cities: Los Angeles, New York, Philadelphia, and Chicago, for example. Even in these cities, however, citizen efficacy is diminished by the inability of city governments to control the fate of their own communities. Miller's case study of gun control efforts in Philadelphia provides persuasive evidence. There was tremendous public unhappiness about and mobilization against gun violence in Philadelphia. Active community groups hoped to diminish gun violence through policies that would restrict access to guns, especially for young people. Activists emphasized the victimization of individuals and communities and the goal of increasing security. Their efforts were stymied by gun rights advocates, who persuaded the legislature to pass a preemption law. The law precluded localities from taking actions to restrict gun ownership that were more severe than laws enacted by state government. Although gun rights activists lobby for more severe sentencing of criminals, they oppose restrictions on gun ownership.

The continued colonial status of the District of Columbia presents an even more striking example of limited city government. DC residents enjoy neither their chosen gun control policy nor the women's reproductive policy passed by their city council. The Supreme Court found the District's gun control policy unconstitutional. Congress overruled the freedom to choose once championed by the Supreme Court.[28] Congress even failed to enact legislation that would have relieved DC government from budget review and revision by Congress. And at committee hearings, DC Representative Eleanor Holmes Norton was not permitted to testify on behalf of DC's policies. Taxation without representation creates many burdens.

Miller is certainly correct to argue that political rules shape political outcomes and that the limits on urban governments especially constrain

African Americans. Yet there is something to be said about a political arena in which communities of color have more influence—because they are a greater proportion of the population and the electorate—than they do in states or the national government, where their presence is diminished by their relatively smaller numbers. Cities have been settings in which African Americans and other people of color have implemented policies and fueled organizations that serve their interests, sometimes initiated by others and sometimes of their own devising, for example, community control of schools, Head Start and pre-kindergarten, charter schools, community development corporations, neighborhood health centers, police review boards, and the growth of service workers' unions.

Furthermore, political presence in cities enables influence beyond the city's boundaries. African America urban communities have long been a strategic element of presidential politics. As Woodrow Wilson ran for his second term in 1916, worried Illinois Democrats downstate in Jackson County wrote to Wilson's campaign manager that "trainloads" of African Americans were arriving from the South. These were described as simple "excursions" by the railroads, but the chairman of the County Democratic Central Committee wrote that "this is hardly probable . . . We fear that these negroes are being taken to some of the large cities where they will register their vote against our party,"[29] thereby causing Wilson to lose Illinois and with it, reelection.

Later, the presence of African Americans in critical swing states—Illinois and New York, for example—provoked the community action program and other parts of the War on Poverty (some of which, like Head Start, are still with us), and the Legal Services Administration—intended to ensure their turnout for the Democrats.[30] And in the most recent presidential contest, anyone with the stamina to watch hours of John King on CNN saw over and over again that the votes of swarms of red counties voting Republican were overwhelmed by the votes of tightly packed blue counties voting for the Democrats.[31]

The greatest victories for urban citizenship and democracy are not in national elections, but accomplished within their own borders. Successful cities create inclusive collective identities that project character and pride. Those were the accomplishments of Pingree in Detroit, La Guardia's administrations in New York, Atlanta under Allen, and San Antonio under Cisneros. None of those cities was without fault, or without exclusion, but they did not boast about them. They were not—before or after—without fights to change rules, institutions, and leaders, but the fights made for progress. My colleagues and friends will testify that I am not much of a Pollyanna, but the more I study the history of cities, the more I see evidence that they remain the great hope of democracy.

Or we can simply look at Camden—or Bell or Ferguson—down but not out.

Notes

1. Theda Skocpol, "Bringing the State Back In: Strategies of Analysis in Current Research," in Peter B. Evans, Dietrich Rueschemeyer and Theda Skocpol, *Bringing the State Back In* (Cambridge: Cambridge University Press, 1985), 21.

2. On this last point, see Jessica Trounstine, *Political Monopolies in American Cities: The Rise and Fall of Bosses and Reformers* (Chicago: University of Chicago Press, 2008). Similarly, Janet Abu-Lughod has offered a sustained argument about the importance of attention to the particularities of urban communities. Janet Abu-Lughod, *New York, Chicago, Los Angeles, America's Global Cities* (Minneapolis: University of Minnesota Press 1999).

3. Jones was succeeded in office by Brand Whitlock. Whitlock, who served four terms as mayor of Toledo, championed a less harsh system of criminal justice. For this, he was attacked by Toledo's Federation of Churches. Whitlock responded in a long public letter, *On the Enforcement of Law in Cities* (Indianapolis: Bobbs-Merrill, 1910).

4. Melvin G. Holli, *Reform in Detroit: Hazen S. Pingree and Urban Politics* (New York: Oxford University Press, 1969). Holli also contributed the terms "social reform" and "structural reform" to urban studies. Social reform mayors were animated by a commitment to benefit low-income residents; structural reformers sought to reshape urban political institutions, often favoring nonpartisan elections, city managers, and commission government.

5. Ivan Allen Jr., *Notes on the Sixties* (New York: Simon and Schuster, 1971). Allen and Atlanta city government more generally were pilloried in Floyd Hunter, *Community Power Structure, A Study of Decision Makers* (Chapel Hill: University of North Carolina Press, 1953). The same years are chronicled in Clarence N. Stone, *Economic Growth and Neighborhood Discontent: System Bias in the Urban Renewal Program in Atlanta* (Chapel Hill: University of North Carolina Press, 1976), later theorized by Stone in *Regime Politics: Governing Atlanta, 1946–1988* (Englewood Cliffs, NJ: Prentice-Hall, 1979).

6. Quote is from Carl N. Degler, "Labor in the Economy and Politics of New York City, 1850–1860: A Study of the Impact of Early Industrialism" (PhD diss., Columbia University, 1962, 276–277).

7. Zoltan Hajnal and Jessica Trounstine, "Where Turnout Matters: The Consequences of Uneven Turnout in City Politics" *Journal of Politics* 67, no. 2 (2005): 515–535; city councils, 535–536; mayoral elections, 521–522.

8. Amy Bridges, *Morning Glories, Municipal Reform in the Southwest* (Princeton: Princeton University Press, 1997), chapters 7 and 8.

9. Charles L. Cottrell and R. Michael Stevens, "The 1975 Voting Rights Act and San Antonio, Texas: Toward a Federal Guarantee of a Republican Form of Government," *The Public Interest* 8, no. 1 (Winter 1978): 79–89. 86; Bridges, *Morning Glories*, chapter 8, The Politician and the Crowd.

10. Saul Alinsky, *Reveille for Radicals* (New York: Vintage, 1969 [1946]).

11. Leo Fink and Brian Greenberg, *Upheaval in the Quiet Zone, A History of Hospital Workers' Union Local 1199* (Urbana: University of Illinois Press, 1989); Karen Brodkin, *Making Democracy Matter, Identity and Activism in Los Angeles* (New Brunswick, NJ: Rutgers University Press, 2007); Ruth Milkman, *LA Story: Immigrant Workers and the Future of the US Labor Market* (New York: Russell Sage Foundation, 2006).

12. This is the argument of Jessica Trounstine, *Political Monopolies in American Cities, the Rise and Fall of Bosses and Reformers* (Chicago: University of Chicago Press, 2008).

13. J. Eric Oliver has studied governments in small cities for many years. In *Democracy in Suburbia* (Princeton: Princeton University Press 2001) and *Local Elections and the Politics of Small-Scale Democracy* (Princeton: Princeton University Press, 2012), Oliver presents a measured appraisal of politics in small cities. Although Oliver has reservations about those governments, he mostly sees them as benign. Hogen-Esch, cited below, argues that small suburbs of Los Angeles are commonly governed by corrupt administrations. Tom Hogen-Esch provides a good account of politics in Bell in "Predator State: Corruption in a Council-Manager System—the Case of Bell, California," paper presented at the City of Bell Scandal Revisited Conference, Chapman University, February 19, 2015.

14. U.S. Department of Justice Civil Rights Division, "Investigation of the Ferguson Police Department," March 4, 2015, "fund the city budget," 10; "primary purpose," 14. Hogan-Esch claims that Los Angeles suburbs are commonly governed by corrupt administrations; "Southeast Los Angeles County: Corridor of Corruption," op cit, 7–9.

15. For Bell, *Los Angeles Times*, "Timeline Bell." For Ferguson, *New York Times*, "Election in Ferguson, Watched Nationwide, Carries Hope of 'New Tomorrow'" April 5, 2015, A14; "Ferguson Elects 2 Blacks but Snubs Protest Slate," April 8, 2015, A16; Council Vote in Ferguson Brings Promise and Pause," April 9, 2015, A18.

16. Scott James and Brian Lawson, "The Political Economy of Voting Rights Enforcement in America's Gilded Age: Swing States, Partisan Commitment, and the Federal Election Law," *American Political Science Review* 93, no. 1 (1999): 115–131.

17. Frances Fox Piven, "The War on Poverty as a Political Strategy," in *The Politics of Turmoil, Essays on Poverty, Race, and the Urban Crisis*, ed. Richard Cloward and Frances Fox Piven (New York: Vintage Books, 1975), 271–283.

18. Jerome I. Hodos, *Second Cities, Globalization and Local Politics in Manchester and Philadelphia* (Philadelphia: Temple University Press, 2011), 178.

19. Hodos, *Second Cities*, 185.

20. Harold Wolman and Michael Goldsmith, "Local Autonomy as a Meaningful Analytic Concept, Comparing Local Government in the United States and the United Kingdom," *Urban Affairs Quarterly* 25, no. 1 (1990): 3–27.

21. Amy Bridges, *City in the Republic, Antebellum New York and the Origins of Machine Politics* (Cambridge: Cambridge University Press 1984), 137.

22. Readers see, in the essay by Harris, how resources are key to urban autonomy or its absence. Weak economies have deprived Camden, New Jersey, and other cities of self-government and so, Harris argues, of opportunities for participatory democracy and effective citizenship. Brown-Dean and Miller have shown how political forces outside cities, as well as higher governments, have chipped away at the autonomy and power of city residents and their governments, limiting possibilities for urban residents and possibly eroding possibilities for effective urban representation in state and federal politics and government.

23. That observation was the insight of economist Charles Tiebout. Charles Tiebout, "The Pure Theory of Local Expenditures," *Journal of Political Economy* 64 (1956): 416–424.

24. In the 1940s, a few large production sites were constructed for war material in rural areas. Automobile manufacturers began moving production outside Detroit in 1950s. Thomas Sugrue, *Origin of the Urban Crisis, Race and Inequality in Detroit* (Princeton: Princeton University Press, 1996), chapters 5 and 7. In my view, Peterson does not provide persuasive evidence for his second claim, about politicians' choices. The history of urban renewal suggests that the pursuit of improvement of the economy of the city as a whole can be disastrous for politicians; see John Mollenkopf, "The Politics of Post-War Urban Development," *Politics & Society* 5, no. 9 (1975): 247–295.

25. Full disclosure requires me to state my father was a carpenter for New York City, and I worked at several campuses of the City University of New York before it was absorbed by the State University of New York.

26. "Community Building to Drive Change, Strategies for the Atlanta Civic Site," Annie E. Casey Foundation, April 4, 2014, 1, 6, 15, 16. On the foundation's Web site, www.aecf.org. The site does not have a comparable account of Camden.

27. The *New York Times* estimated that there would be 5.85 million disfranchised convicted felons on the day of the midterm elections on November 5, 2014, nearly half of whom had completed their sentences. Editorial, Sunday, November 7, 2014, http://takingnote.blogs,nytimes.com/2014/11/07/florida-leads-the-pack-in-felon-disenfranchisement.

28. According to several media sources, Congressman Rand Paul was a key player in these losses (*DC Wire*, a *Washington Post* blog, June 26, 2012; *Huffington Post*, July 31, 2012; *Politico*, 7/31/12.

29. Letter from William Blair, Chair of the Jackson County Democratic Central Committee (Murphysboro, IL), to Thomas Walsh, manager of Wilson's

western campaign October 20, 1916. Thomas J. Walsh Papers, Library of Congress, Box 363.

30. Frances Fox Piven, "The Great Society as a Political Strategy," in Richard A. Cloward and Frances Fox Piven, *The Politics of Turmoil—Poverty, Race, and the Urban Crisis* (New York: Random House, 1975), 271–283.

31. And so Obama won, despite the overrepresentation of low population Western states in the electoral college. This has led to Republican efforts to reconfigure how electoral votes are counted. Albert R. Hunt, "Changing the Path to the Presidency," *New York Times* January 28, 2013, A1.

1

Urban Autonomy and Effective Citizenship

*Michael Javen Fortner**

In his famous funeral oration, Pericles extolled the virtues of Athenian citizenship and democracy. The general declared, "Our constitution is called a democracy because power is in the hands not of a minority but of the whole people."[1] He added, "No one, so long as he has it in him to be of service to the state, is kept in political obscurity because of poverty . . . We give obedience to those whom we put in positions of authority, and we obey the laws themselves, especially those which are for the protection of the oppressed."[2] For Pericles, citizenship—individual civic engagement, political equality, rule of law, and the people's capacity to rule and defend the oppressed—distinguished Athens from its neighbors and defined the greatness of his city-state.

Many have shared these sentiments. From Aristotle to Robert Dahl, cities have been central to the study of politics and democracy. But in 1981, Paul Peterson fundamentally reconfigured the debate about cities and democracy and reshaped how we understand the substance and worth of city politics. Exploiting the theoretical implications of public choice theory, he finds that urban areas are no longer the city-states Aristotle

*I would like to thank Amy B. Bridges, Richardson Dilworth, Jennifer L. Hochschild, Harvey Mansfield, Rogers M. Smith, and two anonymous reviewers for very helpful comments on earlier drafts. I would also like to thank Jason D. Rivera and Zachary Wood for excellent research assistance.

studied and Pericles praised. "Too often cities are treated as if they were nation-states," he writes. "Local politics," Peterson declares, "is not like national politics. . . . City politics is limited politics."[3] He stresses that urban democracy functions within a broader political economy, which generates specific interests and imposes certain constraints on cities. Peterson posits: "Local government leaders are likely to be sensitive to the economic interests of their communities."[4] He sees the reasons as follows: "First, economic prosperity is necessary for protecting the fiscal base of a local government . . . Second, good government is good politics. By pursuing policies which contribute to the economic prosperity of the local community, the local politician selects policies that redound to his own political advantage."[5] According to Peterson, both the ability of cities to pursue their own notion of the good and the fate of local politicians rest on the economic health of urban communities. Consequently, local political leaders will primarily pursue developmental policies that maximize their city's advantage in the national and global competition for scarce, mobile resources (e.g., jobs, businesses, and residents) rather than redistributive polices.

Its considerable insights notwithstanding, Peterson's framework requires reexamination. Critical questions remain: Did cities and their elected officials face similar constraints when economic resources (e.g., jobs, businesses, and residents) were less mobile? If so, what does this historical variation imply about Peterson's theory of city politics and urban citizenship in the United States?

By urban citizenship, I mean something more than legal residence in cities or individual loyalty and sense of belonging to cities. Urban citizenship certainly encompasses citizen engagement with city politics. "Good citizenship as political participation," Judith Shklar theorizes, "concentrates on political practices, and it applies to the people of a community who are consistently engaged in public affairs."[6] Shklar's theory of citizenship also stresses the autonomy and self-respect that economic security cultivates. Similarly, some critics of procedural theories of justice have advanced a "capabilities approach"[7] that emphasizes the importance of individuals having the ability "to achieve outcomes that they value and have reason to value."[8] What is the virtue of fair procedures or vigorous participation if they do not yield desirable results? Consequently, my notion of *effective citizenship* emphasizes individual engagement with city politics and the *capacity* of residents to determine the fate of their communities, including the ability of residents, especially the poor, to use the urban state to achieve outcomes they value.

The chapters in this volume look beyond city limits to discover urban citizenship and evaluate American democracy. Chapters by Tom Hulme and Marion Orr and colleagues excavate the relationship between city government and urban citizenship. They add empirical substance to Pericles's praise of urban democracy and Shklar's notion of "good citizenship." Chapters by Richard Harris, Khalilah Brown-Dean, and Lisa L. Miller expose how social forces, economic trends, and political institutions have interacted with race to undercut some communities' ability to determine their own fate. We see from their accounts what American democracy looks like when cities lack autonomy and their residents are deprived of effective citizenship.

This chapter provides a theoretical basis and historical background for the urban state at the center of our chapters. Drawing on urban political theories, state-centered approaches, and historical institutionalism, I argue that urban autonomy and the effectiveness of urban citizenship are primarily contingent on the evolution of the economy, demography, and structure of city government. While legal and resource constraints may limit a city's ability to pursue the collective interests of its residents, these constraints are not insurmountable. Instead, I maintain that the extent to which local officials can overcome them depends on the development of the party organizations and politics that link city politics to state and national politics. Next, I clarify these theoretical propositions. Then I defend them by tracing the evolution of city politics from the antebellum period until the late twentieth century. Finally, I conclude by exploring the normative implications of my analysis.

The Urban State and Urban Autonomy

Urban autonomy has been a central issue in urban political theory for quite some time. For nearly three decades, Clarence Stone's scholarship on urban politics and policy has drawn attention to the resources available to urban governments or, more importantly, the lack thereof.[9] Instead of focusing on electoral politics within cities, Stone's approach to urban politics highlights the capacity of local actors to achieve collective goals.[10] He writes, "Even though the institutions of local government bear most of the formal responsibility for governing, they lack the resources and the scope of authority to govern without the active support and cooperation of significant private interests."[11] Stone formulated "urban regime theory" to delineate the ways in which resource constraints on government shaped local policy development. Urban regime theory "assumes that the effectiveness of local government depends greatly on the cooperation of nongovernmental actors and on the combination of state capacity with nongovernmental resources."[12] Given this, urban actors, the theory proposes, must forge coalitions with private interests to build the capacity necessary to achieve collective goals.

Stone's immense contribution to urban political theory cannot be emphasized enough. While Dahl and other pluralists struggled to identify the ways in which economic elites directly or indirectly shaped urban policy making through local elections,[13] Stone discovered other ways that business exerted its power within city politics.[14] He suggests that, "in a liberal order, many activities and resources important for the well-being of society are nongovernmental and that fact has political consequences."[15] The productive capacities of industry make them a necessary partner in the development of local government initiatives and give business interests a significant voice in the formulation of these plans. While Peterson identified the limits of local politics, Stone found the conditions under which urban political actors could overcome the constraints of market forces by building coalitions with nongovernmental actors.

Stone is not the only urban scholar to notice the urban state and to place city politics within a broader political economy. Uniting the analytic tools of history with the theoretical tools of political science, Amy Bridges unravels the complex relationship between city politics and the American polity.[16] She rightly acknowledges the constraints the American polity and economic systems impose on urban politics: "The political life of cities is shaped by their lack of autonomy from their political and economic environments. City governments are dependent on the state governments of which they are, legally, the creatures, and local politics bears the marks of federal policies and politics."[17] At the same time, Bridges underscores the historical contingency of these constraints: "city governments thrive and decline with local economies, as connected to the national and even international economy as local governments are to higher governments."[18]

My theory of the urban state builds on the work of both Stone and Bridges. Like Stone, my understanding of city politics spotlights urban state capacities. I also recognize that the liberal order disperses resources across public and private sectors. I contend, however, that the ramifications of this distinction depend on the urban state's ability to coerce resources from the private sector. Like Bridges, I emphasize the contingency of city politics, specifically its relationship to the "rise and decline" of local and global economies and their link to federal and state politics and policies.

I add to these propositions an institutional vision of urban politics. Of course, at the center of city politics and the broader economic and political forces that surround it stands an urban government with statelike properties. The urban state, the administrative and policing organizations that constitute local political units claiming authority over residents and territory within cities, may formulate and pursue goals that are not simply reflective of the demands, interests, or ideologies of social groups, classes, or society; leaders gain some distance from the citizenry.[19] This autonomy emerges from several sources.[20] First, urban governments are "functionally specialized" and operate according to "explicit rules."[21] Consequently, once created, urban governments (and the politics they generate) can operate according to their own logic.[22] Second, the organization of local offices—the rules that define their duties and the institutionalized partial separation from forces that might seek to control them[23]—allows urban officials to be "actors in their own right, enabled and constrained by the political organizations within which they operate."[24]

Third, urban governments extract resources from society and deploy them to establish and maintain their own coercive and administrative organizations. The independent extraction of resources and the independent creation and support of administrative organizations can sometimes extricate urban governance from state and federal entanglements. The urban state's ability to capture and exploit societal resources varies over time, depending on several factors. Key among them is the mobility of individuals and capital. Within liberal democratic orders, individuals and businesses exert substantial control over their property. Even so, the urban state may command and use these resources for its own purposes. In these instances, individuals and firms have two options: "voice" or "exit."[25] As Dahl suggests, individuals and firms can use their "voice" to directly or indirectly sway elections and policy. As Peterson suggests, individuals and firms can "exit" and take their resources with them. Exit, however, is not preordained. The likelihood that individuals or firms will depart cities is related to the organization of economic systems—the structure of production and the social relations it begets and the spatial location of resources—as well as technology and transportation, which determine individual and business demand for particular locations and the cost of departure from or movement to those locations.

The legal position of cities within the federal polity also matters. Bridges argues that "the boundaries of the urban polity are highly permeable. The dependence and permeability of the urban polity mean that things happen not only *in* cities, but also *to* cities."[26] She adds, "The limited capacity of city government and the potential interventions of state (and national) government force political actors in the city to go outside the city itself to achieve their goals, and this changes the configuration of political forces in the city."[27] The permeability of the urban polity and the legal position of city government need not mean that things *always* happen *to* cities. How the federal government and state governments interact with local municipalities, specifically city governments and officials, at any particular moment is a political outcome structured by historical social, economic, and institutional variables. For example, a city's delegation within a state legislature can shield it from state interference and place state capacities in the service of local priorities. This influence is contingent on the size of a city's delegation within a state legislature, its partisan cohesion, party rule of state governments and the dynamics of state-wide electoral competition, legislative norms and rules, the cultural imagining of cities,[28] and the political salience of local issues.[29]

Furthermore, local officials can develop their own autonomy. They can "take actions consistent with their own wishes, actions to which [politicians and bureaucrats in other levels of governments] defer even though they would prefer that other actions (or no action at all) be taken."[30] By institutionalizing a link between city officials and politicians at the state and federal levels, parties provide local politicians access to capacity and authority otherwise unavailable to them. Of course, party ties do not guarantee that local actors will acquire these assets. City officials must exert some control over resources that politicians operating at other governmental levels require to achieve their own goals. Under these conditions, city officials can leverage their local influence to place federal and state authority and capacity in the service of the urban state.

Given this discussion, one might question the analytic utility of the "urban state" and "urban autonomy." The coincidence of factors needed to achieve urban state autonomy might make such autonomy seem almost chimerical. Even so, the key factors that foster urban autonomy—economic organization, demography, and national partisan alignments—represent "big structures" and "large processes" that define historical periods. The potential for urban autonomy is greater during some historical periods than others. The next two sections trace and compare urban autonomy in United States from 1830 until 1990 to clarify and defend the theoretical propositions outlined above.

I begin when modern cities begin to take shape. I end at 1990 because a different set "big structures" and "large processes," including globalization, new waves of immigration, and different party alignments, have redefined city politics over the last twenty-five years.[31] Describing and exploring the implications of these forces is beyond the scope of this chapter. Additionally, many of the chapters in this book take up where I leave off and provide incisive examinations of urban autonomy and effective citizenship in the context of contemporary economic, social, and political forces.

Although this chapter studies the evolution of urban politics in the United States from 1830 until 1990, the narrative focuses on the transformation of politics and policy in New York City. I study one city over time to isolate the specific mechanisms driving general trends. I do not claim that policy development in New York City is representative of policy development across the United States. Instead, I demonstrate that variation in policy development across cities and across time is contingent on four key variables: 1) the organization of capitalism; 2) demography (i.e., population size and racial and ethnic composition); 3) the structure of local government; and 4) the position of cities within national and state-level partisan conflict.

I selected New York City because of its centrality to debates over *City Limits*. For some, the city's fiscal crisis in 1975 illustrates the significance of politics and political institutions and, as a result, challenges Peterson's account.[32] In his defense, Peterson argued that such assessments ignored the conceptual difference between long and short-term economic and political factors. He suggested that taking a long-term view of the city's fiscal policies exposes structural economic constraints: the fiscal crisis was precipitated by short-term political responses to long-term economic forces. Finding Peterson's rejoinder extremely compelling, I extend the temporal lens and trace politics and policy in New York City across systematically different economic contexts: industrialization and deindustrialization.

Urban Autonomy and Effective Citizenship in the United States, 1830–1950

Contemporary city residents would probably not recognize the colonial city. Crowded for their time, they hardly resemble the bustling metropolises of today. In many ways, politics in the colonial city seems unimaginable today. Public goods were administered by the private sector, and political power rested in private hands. Dahl even calls New Haven's political order during this period an oligarchy. Men of means held a tight grip on political offices and public policy, and paternalistic norms governed their obligations to everyone else.

By the 1830s, however, broader economic, social, and political forces
had fundamentally altered urban life. The arrival of the industrial system,
mass immigration, and the expansion of suffrage to nonpropertied white
males produced new, complex forms of social and political organization in the antebellum city. Industrialization shattered the personal ties,
loyalties, and obligations that defined the colonial city of patricians, arti-
sans, and shopkeepers. The reorganization of the economy—not just the
growth of manufacturing but also the ways in which products were mar-
keted and distributed—reconfigured social relations. Ira Katznelson notes:
"Commercial enterprises grew increasingly specialized, as they came to
deal exclusively in a specific genre of goods—china, glass, hardware, dry
goods, watches, wines, clothing. Market forces replaced personal contact
in the management of the growing volume and complexity of trade. And
in finance and transportation the joint-stock finance company superseded
more traditional family and partnership forms of ownership."[33]

Pushed by social and political challenges in Europe and pulled by
the urban labor market, immigrants further complicated life in the antebellum city, changing the cultural composition and class and ethnic relations in many American cities. The number of immigrants in the United
States climbed from 100,000 between 1820 and 1829 to a half-million
between 1830 and 1839 to 1.4 million between 1840 and 1849 and to 2.7
million between 1850 and 1859.[34] The Irish dominated these early waves of
mass immigration: they constituted 40.2 percent of individuals immigrating from 1820 to 1829, 31.7 percent of those immigrating between 1830
and 1839, 46 percent of those immigrating between 1840 and 1849, and
36.9 percent of those immigrating between 1850 and 1859.[35]

Additionally, these shifts reconfigured class structures and relations
in the antebellum city. In 1840, four of ten Irish workers were hod carri-
ers, laborers, draymen, and stevedores in Philadelphia. In Boston, 48 percent of the working Irish population were laborers compared with fewer
than 10 percent of Germans and fewer than 5 percent of the native-born
population in 1850. In New York City, a quarter of the Irish population
worked as servants in 1855.[36] Thus, while economic forces segmented
the urban class structure, ethnic differences solidified these boundaries.

These developments had profound policy and political implications.
Increasingly crowded and dirty streets produced a host of public safety
and health problems, and private, voluntary services no longer sufficed.[37]
From complexity, insecurity, and crisis, the urban state emerged to restore
order and assert its local monopoly on violence. Dennis Judd teaches us
that "[p]ublicly-financed municipal services were organized in response to

the breakdown of informal community norms and the consequent chaos of urban life. Services were expanded out of practical necessity . . . [and] [t]he development of organized city government was a slow, painful process. When the urban community became too complex to be governed informally, urban leaders were forced to invent new institutions."[38]

To confront its problems, cities extracted capital from the private sector and deployed it to create and support new policies and administrative forms. Specifically, city governments levied property taxes and issued public bonds to finance this new urban state. In New York City, the government increased taxes from $.97 per $100 to $1.23 in 1853, to $1.56 in 1857, and to $2.03 in 1863. Additionally, the city government increasingly relied on bonds to fund large capital projects as well as to finance city expenditures. In 1844, taxes covered 67 percent of operational expenditures. That number fell to 49 percent in 1853 and to 32 percent in 1856.[39] New York was not unique. Charles N. Glaab and A. Theodore Brown report: "In the decade after the end of the Civil War, when the fifteen largest American cities saw their aggregate population rise by about 70 per cent, the debts of the same cities rose by 271 per cent."[40]

Revenues and expenditures fueled and were fueled by a new political animal: the career politician. The new urban state and the bureaucratic entities that constituted it generated stable new positions that allowed entrepreneurial individuals to pursue their ambitions, namely power and prestige, outside of the traditional social structure. Moreover, organizational differentiation meant that selection to these offices and remaining in these offices depended on processes that operated according to their own logic, one independent of—even if influenced by—the social structure. While a city's wealth remained in the hands of business owners and professionals, a city's political power rested in the hands of the much larger and largely immigrant majority. And ambitious politicians needed to secure popular support to maintain their offices. The backing of the working class, however, was not assured. This period of "rapacious individualism"[41] did not feature the well-organized, disciplined Democratic machines that appeared by century's end, and factionalism among local Democratic groups made the local political market even more competitive and city politics intense.

Career politicians' need for mass support; the substantial size of the working class, largely immigrant electorate; and factionalism among Democratic groups had profound effects on antebellum city politics. Entrepreneurial politicians used tax revenue and debt to not only finance basic social services and build infrastructure but also expand their base of support within working-class, immigrant populations. Second, taking from those with means and jeopardizing their investments to woo working-class immigrants cultivated ethnically inflected class conflict. The tax burden fell on a small proportion of the population. Few people owned homes and were subject to property taxes: in 1900, only 22 percent of residents owned their own homes in Philadelphia; almost 19 percent of Boston residents owned their own homes; and fewer than 6 percent of New Yorkers owned their own homes.[42] At the same time, beginning in the 1840s, substantial numbers of the Irish were becoming naturalized and becoming voters. In New York City and Boston, for example, the number of Irish voters tripled from 1850 to 1855. By the 1880s, Irish voter turnout was high in New York, Philadelphia, Chicago, Boston, San Francisco, Pittsburgh, Jersey City, and Albany.[43] Cognizant of this demography, many opportunistic Democratic politicians appealed to immigrants rather than business leaders and middle-class taxpayers. Regarding New York City, Bridges writes that "rapidly expanding and precariously financed municipal budgets, unobtainable franchises, and rising tax rates testified to elite loss of control of municipal governance."[44] She adds: "Little wonder that businessmen sought to regain control of the city government."[45]

As Bridges intimates, wealthy and middle-class citizens did not sit back while ambitious politicians enlarged government, dispensed patronage, and accumulated debt. They mobilized on behalf of "retrenchment and reform."[46] Jon C. Teaford reports that "[t]axpayer revolts were common as early as the 1850s, with angry citizens in New York City, Chicago, Philadelphia, and Milwaukee complaining of public extravagance and corruption and already urging a more frugal, businesslike administration of municipal government."[47] Initially, the middle class attempted to shape urban policy through local elections. Yet these efforts only occasionally yielded systematic policy shifts. Consequently, middle-class activists turned their energy to lobbying state legislatures in the hope that state actors would use their authority to reverse local policies and impose fiscal restraint. The success of reform movements in New York City and other cities depended on the partisan climate in state legislatures. Retrenchment and fiscal constraint were usually imposed by Republican-dominated legislatures. In 1858, New York's Republican-controlled legislature took control of the New York City police department away from the mayor. The state also established an independent Board of Supervisors to regulate taxation in the city.[48] By 1868, the city council, which had been dominated by Democrats, controlled fewer than 17 percent of city expenditures.[49]

Democratic legislatures, on the other hand, offered local Democratic politicians important opportunities. New York City's Boss Tweed effectively leveraged his local electoral influence, achieved through patronage, charity, and graft, to secure state resources and authority.[50] A. C. Bernheim complained in 1894:

> For a decade after the first interference [New York City's] charter was still respected and changes were infrequent; but, under the inspiration of William M. Tweed, legislative action placed millions at the command of Tweed and his associates. An act of 1868, chapter 853, authorizing the comptroller to adjust claims against the city, and a modest little clause stowed away in the tax levy of I 870, authorizing the mayor (A. Oakey Hall), the comptroller (Richard B. Connolly) and the president of the board of supervisors (William M. Tweed) to audit all existing liabilities of the County of New York, were the means through which more than ten [million] were secured by the Tweed Ring. Moreover, seeing the increasing wrath of the citizens of New York, this ring actually purchased a new charter, which contained many novel and desirable administrative features. It abolished the state commissions and gave to the mayor increased power and corresponding responsibilities. But it provided that the terms of all heads of departments should end five days after the passage of the charter, and conferred upon the mayor (A. Oakey Hall) the power to fill all these offices, not merely for the remainder of his term, but for a period of five years. This provision was unsound in principle as it was dishonest in motive. It was devised in order to perpetuate the power of the Tweed Ring, even if it should be overthrown by the people at the polls. In depriving the incoming mayor of the power to select his own heads of departments, it made responsibility for corrupt administration impossible.[51]

Tweed transformed the legal position of cities from a constraint into an opportunity, and he exploited this opportunity to expand public works and extend substantial charity to the city's poor.[52] Tweed also exploited this opportunity to make himself a very wealthy man. Tweed's corruption eventually caught up with him. He went to jail. The "Tweed Ring" ended. Still, Tweed's demise marked the beginning of more sophisticated, well-organized political machines. In New York City and throughout the country, urban Democratic machines traded votes for patronage and power. They benefited themselves, expanded the urban state, and improved the capabilities of working-class immigrants.

Antebellum social and economic transformations and the political conflicts they generated continued through the Gilded Age and the Progressive Era. The pace of urban modernization quickened toward the end of the 1800s. As John Mollenkopf reminds us about cities in the mid to late twentieth century, "the industrial revolution transformed the thinly settled agrarian and small town landscape of the United States into a series of large, dense, smoky, and brawling cities. The factories of these new cities brought together great concentrations of labor and capital."[53] Indeed, American manufacturing dramatically expanded during this period. Before the Civil War, manufacturers rarely employed more than 50 employees and those in cities averaged between 8 and 20 employees. Between 1860 and 1910, the number of employees per establishments in agricultural implements and machinery increased from 7.5 to 79. The number increased from 5 to 39 in malt liquor breweries and increased from 54 to 426 in iron and steel.[54] Overall, the number of manufacturing workers increased by 440 percent and the value of manufacturing products increased between 1869 and 1929. By 1900, manufacturing represented 50 percent of the nation's total output of commodities.[55]

Urban population growth was equally astounding. Big cities grew bigger. From 1870 until 1900, the populations of New York City, Boston, Baltimore, and Philadelphia increased by 20 percent to 40 percent each decade. On average, Chicago's population doubled during this period.[56] Smaller cities grew big. During the 1880s, 101 cities with populations of 8,000 and above doubled in size. From 1860 to 1910, the number of cities with populations larger than 100,000 rose from 9 to 50, and the number of cities with populations between 10,000 and 25,000 surged from 58 to 369.[57]

As American cities expanded, urban governments continued to exercise their autonomy and implemented policies to meet collective needs. Moreover, these new policies went beyond basic services (e.g., police, fire, and sanitation), which both helped the public and housed plum patronage appointments used by party leaders to maintain and grow their organizations. These new initiatives also went beyond developmental policies (e.g., building infrastructure) promoted by business elites, who believed such policies would enhance their competitive advantage, and by party bosses, for whom large projects meant more jobs for their allies and working-class constituents. City governments began to institute programs to improve

Table 1.1. Per Capita Expenditures by Level of Government, 1880–1929

	Total Expenditure ($)				Annual Increase (%)	
	1880	1890	1913	1927	1880–1913	1890–1927
United States (Total)	5.34	5.05	9.98	29.68	2.6	13.2
United States (domestic)	1.26	1.72	5.22	13.22	9.5	18.1
State and Local	8.00	9.09	21.21	65.61	5.0	16.8
State only	1.25	1.22	3.99	17.20	6.6	35.4

Source: Adapted from Ballard C. Campbell, "Federalism, State Action, and 'Critical Episodes' in the Growth of American Government," Social Science History 16, no. 4 (1992): 561–577, 569.

the social welfare of the poor and working class. Ann Shola Orloff and Theda Skocpol tell us that "before the 1930s most social policies were enacted at local and state levels, not at the level of the federal government. During the Progressive Era, cities and states were the major sites of policy innovation, and such 'national' changes as occurred—including the laws establishing workers' compensation and mothers' pensions—did so in the form of waves of similar legislation across many states."[58] Public finance data compiled by Ballard Campbell help corroborate Orloff and Skocpol's observation and help us grasp the substantial growth of the urban state from 1880 to 1929 (see Tables 1.1 and 1.2). First, per capita state and local expenditures consistently outpaced per capita federal expenditures from 1880 until 1927, and state and local expenditures consistently dwarfed per capita domestic federal expenditures during this period. Second, per

Table 1.2. Per Capita Expenditures for Selected Cities, 1880-1915

	Total Expenditure ($)				Annual Increase (%)	
	1880	1890	1915	1927	1880–1915	1890–1929
Baltimore	21.96	25.32	36.42	67.73	1.9	4.3
Birmingham	5.31	8.58	9.49	43.62	2.3	10.5
Boston	50.51	47.82	76.48	143.99	1.5	5.2
Chicago	12.00	17.54	33.95	74.0	5.2	8.2
Detroit	13.57	21.79	41.37	112.64	5.8	10.7
Providence	17.13	35.78	28.52	70.87	1.9	2.5

Source: Adapted from Ballard C. Campbell, "Federalism, State Action, and 'Critical Episodes' in the Growth of American Government," Social Science History 16, no. 4 (1992): 561–577, 569.

capita local expenditures represented the lion's share of state and local expenditures. Third, big cities had the largest per capita spending rates in the country. Based on these data, Campbell concludes, "[W]hen gauged by dollars, the federal role before 1933 was considerably smaller than the responsibilities undertaken by state and local government. Complaints about profligate spending before the New Deal were best directed to officials in Baltimore, Birmingham, and Boston, not in the nation's capital."[59]

After the turn of the century, cities continued to finance new services and projects with taxes and debt. A vast majority of cities relied mostly on taxes. In 1902, taxes constituted 74 percent of revenue for cities with populations greater than 30,000. That number only dropped slightly to 65.1 percent in 1921. Many larger cities accumulated sizable debt over this period. In 1902, 146 cities sampled by Ernest S. Griffith accumulated a combined net debt of $900 million. That number nearly doubled by 1910, climbing to $1,707 million. As earlier, the tax burden fell predominately on the middle class, as the poor did not own property and wealthy individuals were able to use savings, securities, and the like to minimize their tax burden.[60] For their part, business elites worried about excessive spending and mounting debt, viewing the former as an impediment to economic growth and considering the latter a potential threat to the health of the financial system.[61] Of course, this was not always the case. C. K. Yearley writes: "Real estate interests . . . almost invariably in the van of fiscal reform movements, faced and succumbed to tempting speculations which public indebtedness could and did abet; the roads, sewers, utilities, schools, and other public improvements useful to increasing the value of existing realty and attracting even larger populations to particular areas could thereby come more swiftly." He also noted: "Men of substance, realtors, bankers, construction men, contractors, manufacturers, and suppliers of the varied equipage essential to urban growth . . . first acceded to municipal indebtedness and then encouraged it."[62] "Men of substance" clearly did not oppose municipal debt in itself. Even so, they frequently felt that Democratic machines went too far: spent too much and accumulated too much debt in order to doll out patronage.[63]

Business elites and middle class activists used their voices to counter the perceived inefficiencies and corruption of urban political machines. Teaford observes:

> During the last decades of the nineteenth century, members
> of the upper middle class recognized the emerging power of
> the working-class wards and realized that immigrants and the

"unwashed majority" were gaining ground in the city councils
and the party organizations. To counter this erosion of authority and guarantee that the social balance of power continued
to tip toward the "better elements" of society, business leaders
and professionals turned to extralegal organizations as alternate
organs of expression and influence.

He continues: "Such groups as the chamber of commerce, the board
of trade, and the good-government club became instruments for ensur-
ing the voice of the 'respectable' citizens was heard as loud and clear
as ever."[64] As before, middle-class activists tried entering local politics.
When that failed, they tried state legislatures and occasionally achieved
some victories. The policy successes of the middle and upper classes at
the state level were not guaranteed by their class or capital: their victories
resulted from the absence or weakness of urban political machines and
the presence of federated progressive organizations, such as the Municipal
League, that could simultaneously leverage their influence at multiple governmental levels.[65]

These struggles lasted into the New Deal era with one significant
change: the arrival and growth of new ethnic groups. In 1860, only 26,522
individuals immigrated to the United States from Southern, Central, and
Eastern Europe between 1860 and 1869.[66] That number continued to climb
dramatically for the next several decades. From 1890 to 1899, 1.7 million
people emigrated from Southern, Central, and Eastern Europe. Between
1900 and 1909, 5.8 million immigrated. That number declined to a still
considerable 3.9 million between 1910 and 1919.[67] The mass migration
of blacks from the South further transformed the cultural milieu of cities
in the Midwest and Northeast. From 1870 to 1880, 71,000 blacks left the
South. That number rose to 195,000 between 1890 and 1900. From 1910
to 1920, that number climbed to 522,000, and it hit 872,000 between 1920
and 1930.[68] As a result, the black proportion of New York City's total
population increased from 1.8 percent in 1900 to 4.7 percent in 1930. In
Chicago, the black proportion of the total population increased from 1.9
percent in 1900 to 6.9 percent in 1930.[69]

Furthermore, the concentration of these groups within specific wards
intensified the political repercussions of their presence.[70] The ballooning
size of the Jewish, Italian, and black electorate within cities upset the
long-standing political battle between Irish-dominated political machines
and native white, upper and middle-class voters. Population change and
new civic and labor organizations opened opportunities for new alliances,

particularly for anti-machine reform coalitions.[71] Irish-dominated political machines, however, were not without a response to these shifting conditions. At first they tried to incorporate the new ethnic groups on terms
favorable to them by offering token patronage appointments and symbolic
rewards.[72] When that failed, they found another strategy. Stephen P. Erie
explains: "Unwilling to share the core resources of power and patronage,
yet recognizing the limited appeal of welfare serves and 'recognition,' Irish
bosses turned to collective benefits as a way both of securing the new
immigrant vote and of maintaining the Irish monopoly over divisible
benefits."[73]

In New York, Tammany was extremely aggressive in this regard. For
example, after the Triangle Shirtwaist Company fire killed more than a
hundred mostly Jewish and Italian female garment workers, Tammany
decided to use this horrific event as an opportunity to address the
grievances of Jewish and Italian immigrants. Tammany's Al Smith, the
Assembly's majority leader, and Robert Wagner, the Senate majority leader, "secured passage of workmen's compensation, stricter tenement laws,
a widows' pension plan, state utility and insurance regulation, and educational scholarships for the poor."[74] During the debate over workmen's
compensation legislation, Smith gave a stirring defense of the policy. His
words were well received: "Up in the high galleries that overlooked the
floor, the reformers stood and cheered. The compensation law might be
lost but they knew the Republicans would never dare to touch the other
[reforms now]. Great advances had been secured. And, more important, at
last they had their champion. Smith, the Tammany man, had made their
dreams come true."[75] Jewish and Italian immigrants had endured dangerous workplace and living conditions and being shut out of patronage jobs
by the Irish-dominated Democratic machine, both of which frustrated
their pursuit of the American dream. Although the organization of city
offices and party structures permitted Tammany to ignore the voices of
their new immigrant constituents for a time, the growth of new immigrant populations and their concentration within particular wards forced
Tammany to respond. So Tammany leveraged its influence within state
politics and used state authority and resources to protect workers and
improve the capabilities of the poor.

Maintaining the machine's influence proved to be extremely expen-
sive, and Democratic organizations decided to spend their way to political
prosperity. For a time, the booming economy of the 1920s helped sustain
these efforts. The assessed value of property in New York City doubled
between 1921 and 1932. Yet the depression, tax delinquency, and expen-

sive financial obligations, including the sizable city payroll, education costs, and servicing the debt, precipitated a fiscal crisis.[76] Because their political interests were linked to government spending, Democratic leaders, specifically Mayor James "Jimmy" Walker, initially resisted dramatic spending cuts.[77] As the crisis loomed in 1931, the city's administration boosted spending on municipal employment and social welfare.[78]

The following year, the municipal bond market collapsed, and the business community pressed Walker for retrenchment. The *New York Times* reported: "In a statement issued yesterday through Thomas W. Lamont of J.P. Morgan & Co., the eight banking houses with whom Controller Charles W. Berry is negotiating for a loan of upward of $90,000,00 in effect warned Mayor Walker and his associates in the city administration that the city's ability to borrow money under present conditions rested largely upon the determination of its officials to adopt a strict economy program which would warrant the confidence of bankers and investors that municipal affairs would be handled prudently."[79] Soon, Walker succumbed to business pressure, and the Board of Estimate passed his retrenchment resolution, capitulating to the demands of the city's business community. One section declared: "our citizens must recognize that economic conditions throughout the world have recently undergone great change resulting in the current industrial and financial depression . . . [B]ecause of radically altered economic conditions, we are compelled to curtail and retrench in numerous measures directly designed for the public benefit . . ."[80]

Following through with this strategy proved easier said than done. The three Democratic mayors who ran the city between 1932 and the election of Republican Fiorello La Guardia in 1934 were caught in a tightening political vice being turned by their constituencies and the city's business community. The conflict eventually produced a negotiated settlement: the "Bankers Agreement." In exchange for financing and credit, the city agreed to a four-year plan that segregated tax revenue to pay down past and future debt, created a $50 million reserve as a hedge against possible delinquent property taxes, revised the property tax collection schedule, froze property tax rates from 1934 to 1937, and dropped its taxes on stocks, savings banks, and life insurance companies.[81]

New York City was not the only urban state to lose substantial capacity during the Great Depression. In early June 1932, the leaders of twenty-eight cities, including Mayor Walker, attended a national conference of mayors in Detroit to discuss their common fiscal problems and to push for federal support.[82] In June 1932, a group of mayors, led by Detroit Mayor Frank Murphy, petitioned President Hoover to support a $5 million bond issue to help cities take care of the unemployed.[83] In February 1933, this group formed an official organization, the "United States Conference of Mayors," to serve as a vehicle for mayors across the country to share information and resources and to lobby the federal government for unemployment relief and loans.[84] T. Semmes Walmsley, mayor of New Orleans, later commented, "Mayors are a familiar sight in Washington these days . . . Whether we like it or not, the destinies of our cities are clearly tied in with national politics."[85]

In September 1933, President Roosevelt sent a telegram to a meeting of the conference that encouraged them to take advantage of funds available through the Public Works Administration (PWA).[86] The president's missive was not greeted warmly. The mayors complained that Roosevelt did not fully appreciate the law's problem. Mason B. Williams explains: "Even as they sought to draw upon the strengths of local governments, the New Dealers had designed a program that bumped up against its weaknesses, for the exhaustion of local finances and the constraints of municipal debt ceilings all but ensured that local governments would choose not to invest in public works, even on the comparatively favorable terms the PWA offered (Federal officials had exacerbated this flaw by making federal loans contingent on the sound credit of recipient governments)."[87] Given this, the 180 attendees were much more concerned about the fiscal crises they were facing and pushed for a federal municipal bankruptcy act. Capturing the sentiments of the conference, John W. Smith, acting mayor of Detroit, remarked, "Today, in the stark realism of the time, Detroit is no different from the unwilling, unhappy, disillusioned petitioner in the bankruptcy courts." He groused: "Stripped of all its legal and financial verbiage, the great city of Detroit, the victims of Babbittry, the victims of selfishness, the victims of vanity, are today called upon to face their banker—their banker is the bondholder. The prosperity chickens have come to roost." The mayor then clarified his position: "The city of Detroit asks only that it be given that which the oldest nations in the world have already availed themselves of, the right to adjust with creditors an unbearable, an impossible, a staggering debt charge."[88]

Eventually, city officials used the Civilian Works Administration (CWA) and other New Deal programs to repair the fiscal situation of their cities, expand employment, and pursue their political goals. Certain administrative schemes placed control over the distribution of the resources in the hands of urban machines. Others did not. Erie notes that "[i]n faction-torn Boston . . . welfare-state assistance and national public works projects were channeled through federal, not local, officials," while in Chicago, the "emerging local machine coalesced with the New Deal, capturing federal offices and programs in the process. The machine controlled the postwar selection of congressmen and retained control of federal benefits."[89] Therefore, urban autonomy during the New Deal Era no longer depended on a city's ability to independently extract and deploy societal resources. Now it was largely contingent on the influence city officials wielded within national politics.

During this period, politics and policy in New York City were defined by the constraints of economic forces, the ethnic composition of the population, and the organization of local political institutions and the opportunities offered by federal policies. In these instances, dissatisfaction with the Democratic organization and the growing assertiveness of non-Irish white ethnics and African Americans propelled Republican Fiorello La Guardia to city hall in 1934. Unlike Walker, La Guardia managed to square a political circle. He successfully cut spending that nourished the Democratic machine while swelling spending that benefited the members of his fusion coalition, particularly Jews. In his first year as mayor, La Guardia slashed the city's payroll by 6 percent and raised several taxes.[90] Because FDR desired to blunt Tammany's influence and cultivate ties with the city's progressive community, La Guardia proved to be a useful ally. The mayor took advantage of this relationship, steering significant New Deal funds toward the city to build public works and enlarge social service agencies.[91] Moreover, the mayor instituted several civil service reforms that made it difficult for members of the Democratic machine to discriminate against non-Irish job seekers.[92]

The city's fiscal crisis did not weaken La Guardia or city government. He expanded the urban state and left office a hero. When he died in 1947, the *New York Times* published the following eulogy: "[H]e took over a discredited city government and directed and inspired it. He did not find us brick and leave us marble, but he rescued our public credit, put nonpartisan experts in charge of city departments, expanded parks and playgrounds, developed clinics, public markets, housing projects, airports." The editorial ended: "We say farewell to him now with gratitude for the reformation of city government and the renaissance of civic pride . . . The achievements of those days will be remembered long after the tumult of battle has died down."[93]

La Guardia's capacity was contingent on his unique relationship with FDR. In general, the ability of city officials to place federal resources in the service of their political ends depended on their influence within state and national party politics, and the electoral prominence of cities grew dramatically during the first half of the twentieth century. In 1949, Samuel J. Eldersveld, based on his analysis of New York, Chicago, Philadelphia, Pittsburgh, Detroit, Cleveland, Baltimore, St. Louis, Boston, Milwaukee, San Francisco, and Los Angeles, observed: "Since the twenties, tremendous political change in the orientation of our national politics has taken place. It is a significant political fact that metropolitan party pluralities have played a major role in this change. The metropolitan vote may well have become the balance-wheel in our political system."[94]

Few things bear Eldersveld's assessment out more than the development of civil rights. From the birth of the nation until the Civil War, Southern and Northern politicians had forged a series of compromises on slavery to maintain the union.[95] Fearing the destabilizing force of civil rights, the parties reached a détente on the issue after the Civil War. Yet President Harry Truman overturned this consensus by advocating for a strong civil rights plank at the 1946 Democratic Convention.[96] Excavating the origins of this decision, Edward G. Carmines and James A. Stimson write: "[The Democratic Party's] success in maintaining a majority coalition depended critically upon its electoral fortunes beyond Dixie. And winning the electoral vote of northern states depended upon winning central cities by large margins, which, in turn, depended upon appealing to increasing numbers of northern black voters."[97] They add: "The logic of the New Deal coalition, in short, was forcing Democrats to begin to confront racial issues to an extent that they had not had to do since Reconstruction."[98]

Clark Clifford's civil rights memo to Truman adds texture to Carmines and Stimson's analysis by exposing how political activists interpreted the political implications of urban demography. Outlining the general rationale behind the pro–civil rights approach, Clifford wrote: "A theory of many professional politicians is that the northern Negro voter today holds the balance of power in Presidential elections for the simple [mathematical] reason that the Negroes not only vote in a bloc but are geographically concentrated in the pivotal, large and closely contested electoral states as New York, Illinois, Pennsylvania, Ohio and Michigan."[99] Substantiating this theory, Clifford noted, "In great measure, this explains the assiduous and continuous cultivation of the New York Negro vote by Governor Dewey and his insistence that his controllable legislature pass a state anti-discrimination act."[100] Then, after warning that urban blacks might soon return to the Republican Party because of the intransigence of Southern democrats, Clifford insisted, "Unless the Administration makes a determined campaign to help the Negro (and everybody else) on the problems of high prices and housing—and capitalized politically on its efforts—the Negro vote is already lost."[101] He explained, "Unless there are new and real efforts (as distinguished from mere political gestures that are today thoroughly understood and strongly resented by sophisticated Negro leaders), the Negro block, which certainly, in Illinois and probably in New York and Ohio, *does* hold the balance of power, will go Republican."[102] All in all, Clifford's memo helps us comprehend how urban actors operating through party organizations and politics can take advantage of the resources and authority of the federal government. Although party organizations attempted to control the burgeoning black electorate at the beginning of the twentieth century,[103] the urban African American electorate continued to grow, and African American activists parlayed this clout into significant civil rights gains at the local, state, and federal levels.[104]

Teaford praises city government between 1870 and 1900, calling it "the Unheralded Triumph." I agree and would go a step further: the triumph began in the 1840s and ended with the New Deal. In fits and starts, a potentially autonomous urban state emerged to "[balance] the elements within society and [provide] the services vital to citizens in the industrialized world of the late nineteenth century."[105] A conjuncture of big structures and large processes fundamentally reordered and complicated social life in the American city. Industrialization concentrated people and problems within urban areas, and, by reorganizing economic systems and driving immigration, industrialization broke down the mutualistic relationships and norms that defined the colonial city. It instigated new forms of social conflict, and the organizationally diverse urban state and the ambitious politicians who inhabited it commanded private resources to solve social problems and resolve social conflict. The greatest triumph of city government during this period is that it frequently sided with the working-class, largely immigrant majority. Conflicts over the urban state's extraction and deployment of societal resources fostered a "streetfighting pluralism."[106] In response to electoral pressures, clever officials implemented social programs and services (e.g., relief, widow's pensions, public schools, and hospitals) and built public works (e.g., sewers, bridges, parks, and subways) to achieve collective aspirations and enhance the capabilities of working-class immigrants.

Contrary to many contemporary theories of urban politics, a "power elite," the wealthy, or business interests did not control city politics during this period. Contrary to Peterson's account and Stone's regime theory, the needs and desires of business interests did not always figure prominently in the development of urban public policy. The clustering of people and industry within cities and their immobility meant that the fear of losing people and capital did not define local policy. Instead, the ability of city governments to command private resources meant that urban policy was shaped by the goals of local political officials and the needs and preferences of the majorities who elected them.

Therefore, the critical question is *when* rather than *whether* business elites governed American cities. Excessive spending and the accumulation of debt prompted the middle class, on whom the tax burden fell, and financial interests, who fretted about the potential effects of debt on the business climate, to attempt to shape urban policy. When the working-class, immigrant composition of cities created challenging electoral environments for advocates of retrenchment, business leaders and middle-class taxpayers built and expanded civic organizations to influence local policy *outside* urban democracy, lobbying other levels of government, particularly state capitals, to use their legal authority over cities to reverse previous policies or implement new ones. They succeeded *when* the office of the governor and the legislature were in the hands of allies. They also succeeded *outside* urban democracy *when* immediate or looming debt crises granted a city's creditors and other financial interests extraordinary power to demand policy change. As La Guardia's election suggests, economic elites and the middle class succeeded *within* urban democracy *when* factionalism among Democratic organizations or tensions among ethnic groups opened up opportunities for new viable electoral coalitions. As La Guardia's tenure suggests, the need to build and maintain loyal constituencies among the city's polyglot, working-class population halted retrenchment efforts and reintroduced a redistributionist fervor. Ultimately, because of the inconstancy of business power, the messiness, at times ugliness, and promise of "street-fighting pluralism" distinguished urban citizenship in the industrial city.

Urban Autonomy and Ineffective Citizenship in the United States, 1950–1990

Soon the triumphant city fell into crisis. From the 1950s onward, the big structures and large processes that sustained the autonomy of city politics and frequently shielded local government from the undue influence of economic elites evolved in a manner that slowly eroded the independence of the urban state and diminished the effectiveness of urban citizenship.

Specifically, the evolution of capitalism and migration patterns undercut the ability of city officials to extract and deploy societal resources to benefit urban residents and advance their own goals. Furthermore, changes in state and national party politics frustrated attempts by city officials to exploit partisan ties and place federal and state authority and capacities in the service of local interests.

Technological advances (e.g., computers) and global trade transformed a labor-intensive, manufacturing-driven economy to an information-based service economy. In New York City, the proportion of individuals working in manufacturing fell from 30 percent in 1950 to 10 percent in 1989. Services, finance, and the government were the only sectors in New York City to witness significant growth. The proportion of individuals employed in the financial sector jumped from 9.7 percent in 1950 to 14.7 percent in 1988. The proportion of individuals employed in the public sector climbed from 10.8 percent in 1950 to 16.7 percent in 1989. The proportion of individuals working in the service sector rose from 14.6 percent in 1950 to 31.8 percent in 1989.[107]

Other old, industrial cities experienced similar shifts. In Philadelphia, the proportion of total employment devoted to manufacturing declined from 45 percent in 1953 to 18 percent in 1985. Philadelphia lost more than two-thirds of its manufacturing jobs. Over the same period, the number of Boston's manufacturing jobs fell from 114,000 to 49,000. In Baltimore, the number declined from 130,000 to 55,000. In St. Louis, that number dropped from 194,000 in 1953 to 66,000 in 1985. Data on the percentage of jobs in information-processing industries (with more than 60 percent of individuals working in executive, managerial, professional, and clerical occupations) reveal dramatically different trends. In Philadelphia, the number increased from 208,000 to 263,0000. In Boston, it grew from 189,000 to 269,0000. In Baltimore, the number increased from 92,000 to 129,000. In St. Louis, that number rose slightly from 92,000 to 100,000.[108]

Following departing jobs and encouraged by federal policies that improved transportation and expanded defense-related industries in the South and the Southwest, millions of people moved from cities in the Northeast and Midwest to suburbs and the Sunbelt. Detroit, Cleveland, and Buffalo each lost approximately 20 percent of its population between 1970 and 1980. Like many other big, industrial cities, Chicago and Baltimore lost about 10 percent of their populations. Unlike their counterparts, the larger metropolitan areas surrounding Chicago and Baltimore witnessed modest population gains. At the same time, large cities in the Sunbelt experienced very different demographic shifts. The

populations of Houston, San Diego, Phoenix, El Paso, and Tucson experienced growth rates between 25 percent and 36 percent from 1970 to
1980. Though remarkable, the growth rates for the larger metropolitan
regions surrounding these cities are even more impressive. They witnessed
growth rates between 33 percent and 55 percent. Interestingly, Dallas/
Ft. Worth's population rose by only 4.1 percent, while the population of
its metropolitan region increased by 25.1 percent.[109] Denver's population
actually declined by 4.5 percent, while the population of its metropolitan
region grew by 30.7 percent.

    While economic forces are crucial to these transformations, the racial
origins of these trends cannot be ignored. The Second Great Migration
and the local struggle for racial equality placed African Americans and
working-class whites in competition for increasingly scarce resources (e.g.,
housing, jobs, and political power).[110] This competition, race riots, and
declining quality of life in cities caused "white flight."[111] Moreover, discrimination within local housing markets and federal housing policy allowed
whites to depart central cities and trapped many African Americans in
them.[112] The black proportion of central cities of the twelve largest metropolitan areas jumped from 7.6 percent in 1930 to 30.8 percent in 1970.
By 1970, the black proportion of the populations of Baltimore and St.
Louis was 47.0 and 41.3 percent, respectively. The black proportion of
Washington, DC's population hit an astonishing 72.3 percent.[113]

    The racial consequences of these social and economic shifts are also
worth noting. The economic organization of the industrial city, specifically the prevalence of labor-intensive manufacturing jobs, offered poorly
educated, working-class white ethnics steady work. The economic organization of the postindustrial city, specifically the rise of information-
based service jobs, and the spatial movement of manufacturing jobs to the
Sunbelt and overseas created a very challenging labor market for poorly
educated, working-class black males. The proportion of black men born
between 1941 and 1949 working in manufacturing and construction
declined from 40 percent in 1970 to 27 percent in 1987. The proportion
of black men born between 1950 and 1955 working in manufacturing and
construction declined from 72 percent in 1970 to 31 percent in 1987.[114]
William Julius Wilson reports even more despairing trends: "Seven out of
ten of all black men worked full-time, year-round, in eight out of ten years
in the 1970s, but only half did so in the 1980s. The figures for those who
reside in the inner city are obviously even lower." He also notes: "Among
prime-age nonwhite males, the share of those who had no jobs at all in a
given year increased from 3 percent to 17 percent during the last quarter

century."[115] Making matters worse, the concentration of the chronically jobless within inner cities created fertile grounds for various social problems, including teenage pregnancy, drug addiction, and violent crime.[116]

These broader social and economic changes and the organization of city politics posed significant challenges for urban political officials. New York City in the 1960s and 1970s epitomizes these difficulties. As before, ethnic change and newly invigorated labor organizations, municipal unions in this instance, undercut local Democratic machines and introduced uncertainty into city politics. African Americans pressed for their share of patronage and power even as they also urged city governments to confront the mounting social problems in minority neighborhoods. For their part, municipal unions lobbied for more jobs and better benefits. Mayor John Lindsay, like La Guardia before him, marshaled the resources of the urban state to advance his political interests and address the concerns of newly empowered white ethnic populations. Consequently, the proportion of the city's operating expenditures devoted to wages, pensions, and fringe benefits rose by 313.6 percent from 1961 to 1975, and the proportion devoted to social welfare expanded by 828 percent over that same period.

Financing this spending was an arduous task. A late 1960s economic downturn reduced tax receipts, and raising taxes was a difficult proposition. While the city's businesses and white middle-class homeowners in the outer boroughs could not tame a mushrooming budget, they aggressively opposed tax hikes. Martin Shefter indicates that "[the politicians representing citywide constituencies] found it politically useful to increase municipal expenditures, whereas [politicians representing many neighborhood constituencies] found it increasingly difficult to vote for revenue measures sufficient to finance these expenditures."[117] Consequently, Mayor Lindsay relied on debt—short-term notes and long-term bonds—to close the city's budgetary gaps. As a result, per capita short-term debt increased from $115.4 in 1965 to $618.58, a 437.2 percent increase. The per capita long-term debt jumped from $843.38 in 1965 to $1,255.11 in 1975, a 48.8 percent increase.[118] Finally, in March 1975, banks refused to bid on municipal bonds, plunging the city into another fiscal crisis.

This crisis consumed Abraham Beame's mayoralty. Although he survived, the office of the mayor was severely weakened and urban autonomy unceremoniously compromised. An embattled Beame agreed to several proposals that he either doubted the feasibility of or outright opposed. Against his wishes, Governor Hugh Carey and legislature formed the Municipal Assistance Corporation (MAC) to issue bonds on behalf of the city. Beame also opposed the Emergency Financial Control Board (EFCB), which was given authority over the city's budget. The seven-member EFCB included Governor Carey, Mayor Beame, the state controller, and the city controller. Carey also appointed three businessmen: William M. Ellinghaus, the president of the New York Telephone Company; Albert Vincent Casey, chairman and president of American Airlines; and David I. Margolis, president of Colt Industries, Inc. The law authorizing the board required the city to balance its budget within three years, revise its accounting procedures, and submit a three-year plan. The legislature also empowered the board to review and reject the city's plan and make other financial decisions. The governor, legislature, and the new entities they established forced Beame to make some tough decisions. He closed schools, police stations, and firehouses. He dismantled city bureaucracies. He laid off 25,000 workers, retired another 11,000, and instituted a wage freeze on the rest.[119] The mayor was also forced to fire close aides and as well as many other political appointees.[120]

In October 1975, the *New York Times* asked Beame, "Who's running the city?" He answered: "[S]ure, they've taken away powers from me. I've made my point that I felt it was more important to me that the city get its services—the people get it—[than] for me to have that power."[121] By the end of the year, the mayor sounded exhausted and nearly defeated. Reflecting on the events of 1975, Beame remarked, "I am the Mayor . . . I manage the city. I run the city. I determine the priorities. I hire and fire. I'm much the Mayor of the city."[122] The facts, however, belied these pronouncements. Beame may have been "much the Mayor," but the mayor wasn't much. During the fiscal crisis of 1975, the center of political gravity in New York City shifted from City Hall to the state capital and to boards in which the voices of the business community spoke loudly.

Despite its seriousness, this crisis was not unique. The city had been here before. Likewise, these reforms were not unusual. Many of these policy ideas had been in the repertoire of middle-class activists and business elites since Boss Tweed governed New York with reckless abandon. Beginning in antebellum New York, business elites seized every opportunity supplied by propitious partisan environments within state capitals to impose some of them on unreceptive local Democratic machines. Yet these moments of retrenchment did not last. Local Democratic organizations frequently regained their hold on state capitals and reversed many of these reforms. Taxes, debt, and spending flourished. Patronage flowed. But not this time.

Similarly, Beame's anguished remonstrations sound familiar. One can easily imagine Jimmy Walker or mayors of other big cities during the early 1930s expressing similar frustrations with the economic perils of their cities and the heavy-handed way business communities imposed their policy preferences on city governments. Nevertheless, while Beame appeared feckless, La Guardia is remembered as a valiant champion of the urban state and the people it served. With the help of FDR and New Deal funds, La Guardia, despite the city's fiscal woes and deteriorating position within the economy, was able to expand social services.

And there's the rub. Unlike La Guardia, after the 1970s Beame and other mayors no longer possessed access to substantial federal funds. The famous 1975 *New York Daily News* headline "Ford to City: Drop Dead"[123] not only succinctly captured President Ford's reluctance to bail out New York City from its fiscal crisis, but also powerfully symbolized the systematic shift in federal-city relations from the late 1970s onward. Although Ford never actually uttered those words, his hostility to the city was unmistakable.[124] In a speech outlining his own approach to the city's fiscal crisis, the president castigated local officials for "bad financial management." "And when New York City now asks the rest of the country to guarantee its bills," Ford declared, "it can be no surprise that many other Americans ask why." Expressing antipathy toward the city, Ford pressed, "Why, they ask, should they support advantages in New York that they have not been able to afford for their own communities? Why, they ask, should all the working people of this country be forced to rescue those who bankrolled New York City's fiscal policies for so long—the large investors and big banks?"[125] Eventually, Ford relented, telling aides, "I hope they understand this is it. Come hell or high water, this is it."[126] Ford's position was not an aberration. It signaled a fundamental shift in the political power of cities.[127]

For a time, Eldersveld's prediction held. The value of the urban vote within the national political marketplace allowed some urban officials, like Chicago's Richard Daley, to place federal and state resources in the service of local ends for a time. From 1957 to 1977, federal aid to states and local governments increased by 1,500 percent and state aid to local governments increased by 750 percent. Over this same period, the amount of direct aid to cities—revenue not funneled through state governments—increased by 4,892.7 percent.[128] David R. Berman observes: "Organizations representing local officials helped produce the flurry of federal activity in the 1960s and 1970s. Although local officials were not completely happy about the initial results—they complained about meddlesome conditions attached to federal programs—they continued to press for more programs."[129]

Substantial federal aid to cities, however, did not last. The proportion of city revenue coming from federal and state sources rose dramatically from 1962 to the late 1970s. Federal aid constituted $.05 of every $1 of revenue received by cites in 1962. That number climbed to a high of $.26 before dropping to $.15 in 1983. State aid constituted $.21 of every $1 of revenue received by cites in 1962. That number rose to a high of $.42 in 1975 before declining and remaining around $.32 from 1980 to 1983.[130] Intergovernmental transfers in New York City and Chicago confirm these aggregate trends. Between 1975 and 1985, federal aid to New York City and Chicago fell by 23 percent and 26 percent, respectively.[131]

To understand the political origins of these revenue shifts and the weak strategic position of cities within national partisan politics after the 1970s, it is important to examine how demographic shifts altered the geographical terrain of partisan competition in national politics. Population shifts to the suburbs and the Sunbelt shifted political power away from the Northeast and Midwest to the South and West.[132] Figure 1.1 traces regional influence within the electoral college from 1860 until 1988. It documents the declining electoral dominance of the Northeast and Midwest. In 1860, the Northeast and the Midwest controlled 61 percent of votes in the electoral college. That number rose to 63 percent in 1876 but declined to 58 percent in 1928. Between 1932 and 1952, that number fell from 56 percent to 54 percent. It dropped again from 54 percent in 1952 to 50 percent in 1972. It fell once more from 50 percent in 1976 to 47 percent in 1988. Figure 1.1 also reveals the burgeoning electoral influence

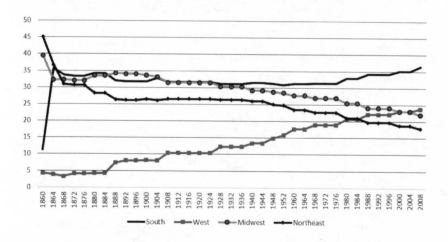

Figure 1.1. Regional Proportions of the Electoral College Vote, 1860–1988.

of the South and the West. In 1952, the South and the West controlled 46.2 percent of the electoral college. That number hit 53.4 percent in 1988.

On the surface, these movements appear relatively small. However, these relatively small trends interacted with partisan shifts within these regions to reconfigure the strategic position of cities within American politics. The "Solid South" made the Democratic party a formidable force in national politics from 1876 until 1948 and buttressed the power of urban political machines in the Northeast and Midwest. Similarly, the end of the "Solid South" hastened the demise of Democratic machines. Demographic shifts made the Republican Party more competitive in the South, upturning the map and math of the New Deal coalition.[133] In 1952, 78 percent of southern white voters identified as a Democrat. Only 11 percent identified as a Republican. As the latter half of the twentieth century progressed, this pattern had reversed itself. Southern white Republican voters have consistently outnumbered southern white Democratic voters in every presidential election since 1984.[134] Although urban Democratic organizations in the Northeast and Midwest used presidential politics to their advantage from 1876 to 1948, the electoral map began to turn against them after the 1950s. Partisan ties no longer mitigated the perils of deindustrialization.

The racial features of these transformations are unmistakable. The calculations of two key Republican strategists, Kevin Phillips and Lee Atwater, unmask the racial and geographical components of national partisan competition after the 1970s. Kevin Phillips, a strategist for Richard Nixon, stated in 1970: "From now on, the Republicans are never going to get more than 10 to 20 percent of the Negro vote and they don't need any more than that . . . but Republicans would be [shortsighted] if they weakened enforcement of the Voting Rights Act. The more Negroes who register as Democrats in the South, the sooner the Negrophobe whites will quit the Democrats and become Republicans. That's where the votes are. Without that prodding from the blacks, the whites will backslide into their old comfortable arrangement with the local Democrats."[135]

In 1981, Lee Atwater, advisor to President Reagan and George H. W. Bush, was a bit more explicit. He reasoned:

> You start out in 1954 by saying, "Nigger, nigger, nigger." By 1968 you can't say "nigger"—that hurts you. Backfires. So you say stuff like forced busing, states' rights, and all that stuff. You're getting so abstract now [that] you're talking about cutting taxes, and all these things you're talking about are totally

economic things and a by-product of them is [that] blacks get hurt worse than whites. And subconsciously maybe that is part of it. I'm not saying that. But I'm saying that if it is getting that abstract, and that coded, that we are doing away with the racial problem one way or the other. You follow me—because obviously sitting around saying, "We want to cut this," is much more abstract than even the busing thing, and a hell of a lot more abstract than "Nigger, nigger."[136]

Both Philips and Atwater outline a strategy dramatically different from the one Clifford proposed to President Truman. Whereas the concentration of African Americans within cities once made the black vote a valuable commodity in the national partisan marketplace from the 1940s until 1970s, now it was a liability. Although African Americans and other minorities replenished the dwindling rolls of urban Democratic organizations, the white "taxpayer" had become the holy grail of American politics.[137]

Obviously, this new partisan climate had adverse consequences for cities. The racial makeup of urban communities and the ascendency of suburban white voters in the South and West impaired city officials' access to federal resources, and declining federal aid hastened the first of two democratic paradoxes of the postindustrial city. Despite the rising needs of working-class and poor urban residents, city officials shifted the benefits of the urban state toward middle-class residents and businesses. The proportion of local government expenditures from its own sources (as a percentage of local, state, and federal expenditures) devoted to welfare declined from 8.5 percent in 1962 to 4.3 percent in 1973.[138] In New York City, the proportion of expenditures, excluding servicing debt and pensions, devoted to redistributive programs (health, social services, and housing) fell from 40.9 percent in 1978 to 39.1 percent in 1983 and to 34.8 percent in 1989.[139]

Additionally, poor and working-class residents also endured higher fees for services, such as transportation. For example, while all New Yorkers benefit from the subway, fares constitute a necessary expense for poor and working-class residents, for whom it is their main source of transportation. It is no coincidence that Democratic mayors fiercely resisted raising fares during economic downturns. Given this, fare changes over the twentieth century speak volumes about the transformation of city politics. As Figure 1.2 reveals, the forty-four years between 1904 and 1948 only saw one fare increase. During the twenty-six years between 1949 and 1975, New Yorkers endured five fare hikes. During the fourteen years between 1976 and 1990, subway fares rose five more times.

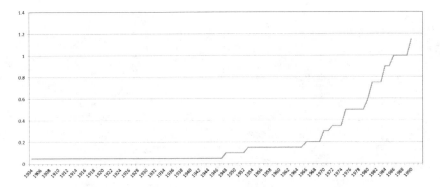

Figure 1.2. New York City Subway Fares ($), 1904–1990.

While local officials under pressure from the federal government, state governments, and business shifted more of the costs of the urban state onto the poor and the working class, the tax burden on the middle class and businesses fell. The number of states offering state and local tax abatements climbed substantially from the 1960s to the 1980s. For example, the number of states offering corporate tax exemptions rose from eleven in 1966 to thirty-three in 1986. The number of states offering a sales/use tax exemption on new equipment increased from sixteen in 1966 to forty-two in 1986. The number of states offering a tax exemption or moratorium on land and capital improvements increased from ten in 1966 to thirty-four in 1986. The changing composition of tax revenue in New York City is also revealing.[140] While taxes on business income as a percentage of local taxes dropped slightly from 12.9 percent to 12.3 percent in 1990, real estate taxes as a percentage of total local taxes in New York City declined from 62.7 percent in 1960 to 43.5 percent in 1990.[141]

It is in this political moment that the theories of Peterson and Stone ring true. Although cities were once able to command private resources and isolate themselves from the pressures of business interests, cities could no longer do so after the 1970s. As Peterson proposes, the mobility of capital and people during this period made the economic interests of the city primary, as the urban state required resources to meet the collective needs and desires of city residents. Given these dynamics, businesses no longer needed to exercise their influence *within* urban democracy. The threat of exit alone worked wonders. Additionally, corporate interests control resources of great value to political entrepreneurs (i.e., campaign contributions), especially those isolated from regular party organizations, and, as Stone argues, the inability of the city to command resources from the private sector compelled local political entrepreneurs to join coalitions with business to develop the capacity to govern.[142]

The economic and political forces that conspired to constrict the fiscal capacity of cities interacted to remove the leverage that local actors, acting primarily through party organizations and politics, once held in state and national politics. Despite the concentration of African Americans within cities and the concentration of black votes within the Democratic Party, urban African American activists were unable to fully exploit the American party system to their advantage in the post–civil rights era.[143] This led to the second tragic democratic paradox of the postindustrial city: greater representation arrived with the loss of urban autonomy, which dramatically decreased the effectiveness of African American citizenship. Working-class African Americans and the urban black poor were limited in their ability to use, like poor and working-class white immigrants before them, the urban state to reverse their employment woes, better their neighborhoods, and improve their capabilities. In the end, politics in the postindustrial city featured all the messiness of early twentieth-century "street-fighting pluralism" but offered none of its promise.[144]

Conclusion

In his presidential address delivered at the annual meeting of the American Political Science Association in 1967, Robert Dahl explored what ought to be the "appropriate unit [of analysis] for a democratic political system."[145] He admitted that the "approved school-solution is, of course, the nation-state."[146] Then Dahl opined: "Yet the bare possibility that the question has not been so much answered by this solution as ignored is hinted at by the troubling recollection of a simple historical fact: accepting the nation-state as the appropriate unit for democracy required the flat negation of an older conventional view that prevailed for some two thousand years."[147] Describing the "older conventional view," he stated:

> The vision of democracy in the city-state that prevailed, by and large, from the Greeks to Rousseau is surely one of the most seductive ever generated in the Western world. Its [millennial] appeal draws its force, I think, from the vision of man living in a genuine human community of man-sized proportions. In this vision, the city-state must be small in area and in population. Its

dimensions are to be human, not colossal, the dimensions not of an empire but of a town, so that when the youth becomes the man he knows his town, its inhabitants, its countryside about as well as any of us knows his own college or university. Given these human dimensions, at its best citizenship would be close to friendship, close even to a kind of extended family, where human relations are intense rather than bland, and where the eternal human quest for community and solidarity can be wholly satisfied within the visible and comprehensible limits of the polis. If the city-state is democratic—and it is this particular vision I have in mind—it would be small enough to insure extensive opportunities for direct participation by all free (male) citizens in the management of the community; and in the best of circumstances policies and decisions would reflect wide discussion and a pervasive consensus.[148]

Dahl concludes this part of his speech by claiming, "Above all, the city-state would be autonomous, in the sense that no one who is not a citizen of that community would possess any legitimate right or power to interfere in the management of the affairs of the city."[149]

On the surface, Peterson's theory of city politics seems like a complete repudiation of Dahl's propositions. Not so. Dahl and his critics were at cross-purposes. Dahl's presidential address and *Who Governs?* focus on the ways in which local government promotes "good citizenship" and is responsive to the preferences of city residents. He does not fully consider the implications of nonresidents (e.g., actors at other levels of government and mobile capital) having the "legitimate right or power to interfere in" city affairs. Specifically, while illuminating the power of "voice," Dahl does not scrutinize the potency of "exit." On the other hand, Peterson does not fully evaluate the position of "voice" within his political economy or temporal variation in its effect.

Looking historically, I have attempted to reconcile these theoretical and normative tensions. I have suggested that both perspectives are too stark. Contrary to Dahl, cities are not always autonomous. Contrary to Peterson, cities are not always weak. The independent ability of city governments to extract and deploy resources and establish organizationally differentiated bureaucratic structures establishes the potential for urban autonomy, and the increasing dependence on mobile resources curbs this potential. Unable to command and coerce, cities tried to coax and cajole businesses and middle-class taxpayers into remaining in cities or moving to them. The legal authority and resources of the federal government and state governments can also limit urban autonomy. These limits, however, are not impassible. Individual actors or groups of local actors can at certain moments exploit their power within party organizations to place state and federal resources in the service of local goals.

Nevertheless, for the last forty years, historical economic, political, and social forces colluded to cripple the capacity of cities and curtail the effectiveness of urban citizenship. Pericles once said, "My own opinion is that when the whole state is on the right course it is a better thing for each separate individual than when private interests are satisfied but the state as a whole is going downhill. However well off a man may be in his private life, he will still be involved in the general ruin if his country is destroyed; whereas, so long as the state itself is secure, individuals have a much greater chance of recovering from their private misfortunes." The general added, "Therefore, since a state can support individuals in their suffering, but no one person by himself can bear the load that rests upon the state, is it not right for us all to rally to her defense?"[150] The historical development of city politics in the United States confirms Pericles's intuition: a secure and robust urban state can benefit the whole while helping the downtrodden recover from their private misfortunes. Given this, perhaps in this moment of vast inequality it is time we rally once more to the defense of cities and their autonomy and strive to cultivate effective citizenship.

Notes

1. Thucydides, *History of the Peloponnesian War* (New York: Penguin, 1972), 145.

2. Ibid.

3. Paul Peterson, *City Limits* (Chicago: University of Chicago Press, 1981), 3–4.

4. Ibid., 29.

5. Ibid.

6. Judith N. Shklar, *American Citizenship: The Quest for Inclusion* (Cambridge, MA: Harvard University Press, 1991), 5.

7. Martha Craven Nussbaum and Amartya Sen, eds., *The Quality of Life* (Oxford: Clarendon Press, 1993).

8. Amartya Sen, *Development as Freedom* (New York: Knopf, 1999), 291.

9. Clarence N. Stone and Heywood T. Sanders, *The Politics of Urban Development* (Lawrence: University Press of Kansas, 1987); Clarence N. Stone, *Regime Politics: Governing Atlanta, 1946–1988* (Lawrence: University Press of Kansas, 1989); Clarence N. Stone, "Urban Regimes and the Capacity to Govern: A Political

Economy Approach," *Journal of Urban Affairs* 15, no. 1 (1993): 1–28; Clarence
N. Stone, Jeffrey R. Henig, Bryan D. Jones, and Carol Pierannunzi, *Building Civic
Capacity: The Politics of Reforming Urban Schools. Studies in Government and
Public Policy* (Lawrence: University Press of Kansas, 2001); Clarence N. Stone,
"Looking Back to Look Forward: Reflections on Urban Regime Analysis," *Urban
Affairs Review* 40, no. 3 (2005): 309–341.

10. Stone, "Urban Regimes and the Capacity to Govern."

11. Stone, *Regime Politics*, 6.

12. Stone, "Urban Regimes and the Capacity to Govern," 6.

13. Robert Dahl, *Who Governs? Democracy and Power in an American
City* (New Haven: Yale University Press, 1961); Nelson W. Polsby, *Community
Power and Political Theory* (New Haven: Yale University Press, 1963); Raymond
E. Wolfinger, *The Politics of Progress* (New Haven: Yale University Press, 1964).

14. Of course, Stone is not the only urban scholar to make these points.
See also Susan S. Fainstein, *Restructuring the City: The Political Economy of Urban
Redevelopment* (New York: Longman, 1983); Todd Swanstrom, *Crisis of Growth
Politics: Cleveland, Kucinich, and the Challenge of Urban Populism* (Philadelphia:
Temple University Press, 1985); Stephen L. Elkin, *City and Regime in the American
Republic* (Chicago: University of Chicago Press, 1987).

15. Ibid., 6–7.

16. Amy Bridges, "Becoming American: The Working Classes in the United
States before the Civil War," in *Working-Class Formation: Nineteenth-Century
Patterns in Western Europe and the United States*, eds. Ira Katznelson and Aristide
R. Zolberg (Princeton: Princeton University Press, 1986); Amy Bridges, *A City in
the Republic: Antebellum New York and the Origins of Machine Politics* (Ithaca, NY:
Cornell University Press, 1987); Amy Bridges, *Morning Glories: Municipal Reform
in the Southwest* (Princeton: Princeton University Press, 1997). Amy Bridges, "The
Sun Also Rises in the West," in *The City, Revisited: Urban Theory from Chicago, Los
Angeles, and New York*, eds. Dennis R. Judd and Dick W. Simpson (Minneapolis:
University of Minnesota Press, 2011).

17. Bridges, *Morning Glories*, 17.

18. Ibid.

19. This definition draws out the implications of Skocpol's conception of
national states for urban states. Skocpol, *Bringing the State Back In*, 9.

20. Harold Wolman and Michael Goldsmith, "Local Autonomy as a
Meaningful Analytic Concept Comparing Local Government in the United States
and the United Kingdom," *Urban Affairs Review* 26, no. 1(1990): 3–27; Lawrence
Pratchett, "Local Autonomy, Local Democracy and the 'New Localism,'" *Political
Studies* 52, no. 2 (2004): 358–375.

21. Theda Skocpol, *States and Social Revolutions*, 48.

22. Paul Pierson, "Increasing Returns, Path Dependence, and the Study of
Politics," *American Political Science Review* 94, no. 2 (2000): 251–267.

23. The periodicity of elections and appointments removes the daily actions
of local officials from the direct control of the electorate or organized interests.

This point revises the conditions Skocpol outlined for the potential autonomy of the old regimes of France, Russia, and China by drawing out their implications for democratically organized institutions.

24. Skocpol, *Protecting Soldiers and Mothers*, 41–42.

25. Albert O. Hirschman, *Exit, Voice, and Loyalty; Responses to Decline in Firms, Organizations, and States* (Cambridge, MA: Harvard University Press, 1970).

26. Bridges, *A City in the Republic,* 14–15. Emphasis in original.

27. Ibid., 15.

28. Michael B. Katz, *The Undeserving Poor: From the War on Poverty to the War on Welfare* (New York: Pantheon, 1990).

29. Nancy Burns, Laura Evans, Gerald Gamm, and Corrine McConnaughy, "Urban Politics in the State Arena," *Studies in American Political Development* 23, no. 1 (2009): 1–22; Margaret Weir, Harold Wolman, and Todd Swanstrom, "The Calculus of Coalitions: Cities, Suburbs, and the Metropolitan Agenda," *Urban Affairs Review* 40, no. 6 (2005): 730–760; Gerald C. Wright and Brian F. Schaffner, "The Influence of Party: Evidence from State Legislatures," *American Political Science Review* 96, no. 2 (2002): 367–379; Peter F. Nardulli, "Geo-Political Cleavages, Conflict, and the American States," in *Diversity, Conflict, and State Politics: Regionalism in Illinois*, ed. Peter F. Nardulli (Urbana: University of Illinois Press, 1989); Gerald Gamm and Thad Kousser, "No Strength in Numbers: The Failure of Big-City Bills in American State Legislatures, 1880–2000," *American Political Science Review* 107, no. 4 (2013): 663–678.

30. Carpenter, *Forging Bureaucratic Autonomy*, 4.

31. For discussions of globalization and the city, see Saskia Sassen, *The Global City: New York, London, Tokyo* (Princeton: Princeton University Press, 1991); Janet L. Abu-Lughod, *New York, Chicago, Los Angeles: America's Global Cities* (Minneapolis: University of Minnesota Press, 2004); Philip Mirowski, *Never Let a Serious Crisis Go to Waste: How Neoliberalism Survived the Financial Meltdown* (New York: Verso, 2013). For discussions of new waves of immigration, see Philip Kasinitz, John H. Mollenkopf, and Mary C. Waters, *Inheriting the City: The Children of Immigrants Come of Age* (New York: Russell Sage Foundation, 2008); Michael Jones-Correa, *Governing American Cities: Interethnic Coalitions, Competition, and Conflict* (New York: Russell Sage, 2001); Taeku Lee, S. Karthick Ramakrishnan, and Ricardo Ramírez, *Transforming Politics, Transforming America The Political and Civic Incorporation of Immigrants in the United States* (Charlottesville: University of Virginia Press, 2006). For discussions of new partisan alignments and conflicts, see Nolan M. McCarty, Keith T. Poole, and Howard Rosenthal, *Polarized America: The Dance of Ideology and Unequal Riches* (Cambridge, MA: MIT Press, 2006); Andrew Gelman, *Red State, Blue State, Rich State, Poor State: Why Americans Vote the Way They Do* (Princeton: Princeton University Press, 2008); Bill Bishop and Robert G. Cushing, *The Big Sort: Why the Clustering of Like-Minded America Is Tearing Us Apart* (Boston: Houghton Mifflin, 2008).

32. Martin Shefter, *Political Crisis, Fiscal Crisis: The Collapse and Revival of New York City* (New York: Basic Books, 1985); Ester R. Fuchs, *Mayors and Money: Fiscal Policy in New York and Chicago* (Chicago: University of Chicago Press, 1992).

33. Ira Katznelson, *City Trenches: Urban Politics and the Patterning of Class in the United States* (New York: Pantheon Books, 1981), 48.

34. Niles Carpenter, *Immigrants and Their Children, 1920. A Study Based on Census Statistics Relative to the Foreign Born and the Native White of Foreign or Mixed Parentage* (Washington, DC: Government Printing Office, 1927), 324–325.

35. Ibid.

36. Noel Ignatiev, *How the Irish Became White* (New York: Routledge, 2009), 136.

37. Blake McKelvey, *The Urbanization of America, 1860–1915* (New Brunswick, NJ: Rutgers University Press, 1963).

38. Dennis R. Judd, *The Politics of American Cities: Private Power and Public Policy* (Glenview, IL: Scott, Foresman, 1988), 36.

39. Ibid., 134.

40. Charles Nelson Glaab and A. Theodore Brown, *A History of Urban America* (New York: Macmillan, 1967), 188.

41. Martin Shefter, "The Emergence of the Political Machine: An Alternative View," in *Theoretical Perspectives on Urban Politics*, eds. Willis D. Hawley and Michael Lipsky (Englewood Cliffs, NJ: Prentice-Hall, 1976).

42. Clifton K. Yearley, *The Money Machines The Breakdown and Reform of Governmental and Party Finance in the North, 1860–1920* (Albany: State University of New York Press, 1970), 27.

43. Steven P. Erie, *Rainbow's End: Irish-Americans and the Dilemmas of Urban Machine Politics, 1840–1985* (Berkeley: University of California Press, 1988), 33–34.

44. Bridges, *City in the Republic*, 144.

45. Ibid.

46. Ibid., 143.

47. Jon C. Teaford, *The Unheralded Triumph: City Government in America, 1870–1900* (Baltimore: Johns Hopkins University Press, 1984), 5.

48. Shefter, "Emergence of the Political Machine," 24.

49. Erie, *Rainbow's End*, 37–38; Bridges, *City in the Republic*, 135–138.

50. John W. Pratt, "Boss Tweed's Public Welfare Program," *New York Historical Society Quarterly* 45 (1961): 396–411; Mandelbaum, *Boss Tweed's New York*.

51. A. C. Bernheim, "The Relations of the City and the State of New York," *Political Science Quarterly* 9, no. 3 (1894): 377–402, 389–390.

52. Kenneth D. Ackerman, *Boss Tweed: The Rise and Fall of the Corrupt Pol Who Conceived the Soul of Modern New York* (New York: Carroll & Graf Publishers, 2006).

53. Ibid.

54. Judd, *Politics of American*, 25.

55. Paul Kantor and Stephen M. David, *The Dependent City: The Changing Political Economy of Urban America* (Glenview, IL: Scott, Foresman, 1988), 85.

56. Teaford, *Unheralded Triumph*, 5.

57. Glaab and Brown, *History of Urban America*, 113–115.

58. Ann Shola Orloff and Theda Skocpol, "Why Not Equal Protection? Explaining the Politics of Public Social Spending in Britain, 1900–1911, and the United States, 1880s–1920," *American Sociological Review* 49, no. 6 (1984): 726–750, 732.

59. Ballard C. Campbell, "Federalism, State Action, and 'Critical Episodes' in the Growth of American Government," *Social Science History* 16, no. 4 (1992): 561–577, 568.

60. Yearley, *Money Machines*.

61. Erie, *Rainbow's End*, 53–54.

62. Yearley, *Money Machines*, 263–264.

63. Erie, *Rainbow's End*; Kantor and David, *The Dependent City*.

64. Teaford, *Unheralded Triumph*, 187–188.

65. Ernest S. Griffith, *A History of American City Government: The Conspicuous Failure, 1870–1900* (New York: Praeger, 1974); Erie, *Rainbow's End*.

66. Excluding Germany.

67. Stanley Lieberson, *A Piece of the Pie: Blacks and White Immigrants Since 1880* (Berkeley: University of California Press, 1980), 20.

68. Doug McAdam, *Political Process and the Development of Black Insurgency, 1930–1970* (Chicago: University of Chicago Press, 1982), 78.

69. Ira Katznelson, *Black Men, White Cities: Race, Politics, and Migration in the United States, 1900–30, and Britain, 1948–1968* (Chicago: University of Chicago Press, 1976).

70. Erie, *Rainbow's End*.

71. Kenneth Finegold, *Experts and Politicians: Reform Challenges to Machine Politics in New York, Cleveland, and Chicago* (Princeton: Princeton University Press, 1995).

72. Harold F. Gosnell, *Negro Politicians; The Rise of Negro Politics in Chicago* (Chicago: University of Chicago Press, 1967); Katznelson, *Black Men/White Cities*; Erie, *Rainbow's End*.

73. Erie, *Rainbow's End*, 103.

74. Ibid., 104.

75. Robert Caro, *The Power Broker: Robert Moses and the Fall of New York* (New York: Vintage, 1975), 126.

76. Fuchs, *Mayors and Money*, 74.

77. Mason B. Williams, *City of Ambition: FDR, La Guardia, and the Making of Modern New York* (W.W. Norton & Company, 2013), 112.

78. Fuchs, *Mayors and Money*.

79. "Banks Warn Mayor City Must Retrench," *New York Times*, January 11, 1932, 1.

80. "Text of the Mayor's Resolution for City Economy and for Plan to Make Enterprises Pay Own Way," *New York Times*, January 21, 1932, 1.

81. Fuchs, *Mayors and Money*, 70; "Chief Points in the Financial Agreement Reached by City Officials and Bankers," *New York Times*, September 29, 1933, 1.

82. "U.S. Relief for Idle Is Urged by Mayors," *Washington Post*, June 2, 1932, 2.

83. "Mayors Urge President to Support Bond Issue," *Washington Post*, June 9, 1932, 4.

84. "Parley of 50 Cities Urges R.F.C. Loans," *Washington Post*, February 18, 1933, 2.

85. Quoted in Williams, *City of Ambition*, 132.

86. "Roosevelt Urges Municipal Works," *New York Times*, September 23, 1933, 4.

87. Williams, *City of Ambition*, 146.

88. "Roosevelt Urges Municipal Works," *New York Times*, September 23, 1933, 4.

89. Erie, *Rainbow's End*, 224.

90. Erie, *Rainbow's End*, 122; Fuchs, *Money and Mayors*, 71.

91. Sidney M. Milkis, *The President and the Parties: The Transformation of the American Party System Since the New Deal* (New York: Oxford University Press, 1993), 58; Erie, *Rainbow's End*.

92. Williams, *City of Ambition*, 137–140.

93. "A Warrior Takes His Rest," *New York Times*, September 21, 1947, E10.

94. Samuel J. Eldersveld, "The Influence of Metropolitan Party Pluralities in Presidential Elections Since 1920: A Study of Twelve Key Cities," *American Political Science Review* 43, no. 6 (1949): 1189–1206, 1206.

95. Joseph J. Ellis, *Founding Brothers: The Revolutionary Generation* (New York: Vintage Books, 2002); David Morris Potter, *The Impending Crisis, 1848–1861* (New York: Harper & Row, 1976); Eric Foner, *Reconstruction: America's Unfinished Revolution, 1863–1877* (New York: Harper & Row, 1988).

96. Harvard Sitkoff, "Harry Truman and the Election of 1948: The Coming of Age of Civil Rights in American Politics," *The Journal of Southern History* 37, no. 4 (1971): 597–616.

97. Edward G. Carmines and James A. Stimson, *Issue Evolution: Race and the Transformation of American Politics* (Princeton: Princeton University Press, 1989), 33.

98. Ibid., 34–35.

99. Memo, Clark Clifford to Harry S. Truman, November 19, 1947, Political File, Clifford Papers, Truman Library, Independence, MO.

100. Ibid.

101. Ibid.

102. Ibid.

103. Harold F. Gosnell, *Negro Politicians; The Rise of Negro Politics in Chicago* (Chicago: University of Chicago Press, 1967); Katznelson, *Black Men, White Cities.*

104. Martha Biondi, *To Stand and Fight: The Struggle for Civil Rights in Postwar New York City* (Cambridge, MA: Harvard University Press, 2003); Thomas J. Sugrue, *Sweet Land of Liberty: The Forgotten Struggle for Civil Rights in the North* (New York: Random House, 2008).

105. Teaford, *Unheralded Triumph*, 313.

106. Douglas Yates, *The Ungovernable City: The Politics of Urban Problems and Policymaking* (Cambridge, MA: MIT Press, 1977).

107. John H. Mollenkopf, *A Phoenix in the Ashes: The Rise and Fall of the Koch Coalition in New York City Politics* (Princeton: Princeton University Press, 1992), 54.

108. Bruce J. Schulman, *From Cotton Belt to Sunbelt: Federal Policy, Economic Development, and the Transformation of the South, 1938–1980* (Durham: Duke University Press, 1994), 152.

109. John Hull Mollenkopf, *The Contested City* (Princeton: Princeton University Press; 1983), 214.

110. Isabel Wilkerson, *The Warmth of Other Suns: The Epic Story of America's Great Migration* (New York: Random House, 2010); James R. Grossman, *Land of Hope: Chicago, Black Southerners, and the Great Migration* (Chicago: University of Chicago Press, 1989); Nicholas Lemann, *The Promised Land: The Great Black Migration and How It Changed America* (New York: A.A. Knopf, 1991).

111. Thomas J. Sugrue, *The Origins of the Urban Crisis: Race and Inequality in Postwar Detroit* (Princeton: Princeton University Press, 1996); Kevin Michael Kruse, *White Flight: Atlanta and the Making of Modern Conservatism* (Princeton: Princeton University Press, 2005); Jonathan Rieder, *Canarsie: The Jews and Italians of Brooklyn against Liberalism* (Cambridge, MA: Harvard University Press, 1985); Howard Gillette, *Camden After the Fall: Decline and Renewal in a Post-Industrial City* (Philadelphia: University of Pennsylvania Press, 2006).

112. Douglas S. Massey and Nancy A. Denton, *American Apartheid: Segregation and the Making of the Underclass* (Cambridge, MA: Harvard University Press, 1993); Arnold R. Hirsch, *Making the Second Ghetto: Race and Housing in Chicago, 1940–1960* (New York: Cambridge University Press, 1983; Ira Katznelson, *When Affirmative Action Was White: An Untold History of Racial Inequality in Twentieth-Century America* (New York: W.W. Norton, 2005).

113. Edward G. Carmines and James A. Stimson, *Issue Evolution: Race and the Transformation of American Politics* (Princeton: Princeton University Press, 1989), 33.

114. William J. Wilson, *When Work Disappears: The World of the New Urban Poor* (New York: Knopf, 1996), 249.

115. Ibid., 26.

116. Kenneth Bancroft Clark, *Dark Ghetto: Dilemmas of Social Power* (New York: Harper & Row, 1965); Lee Rainwater, *Behind Ghetto Walls: Black Families*

in a Federal Slum (Chicago: Aldine Transaction, 1970); William J. Wilson, *The Truly Disadvantaged: The Inner City, the Underclass, and Public Policy* (Chicago: University of Chicago Press, 1987); Michael Javen Fortner, *Black Silent Majority: The Rockefeller Drug Laws and the Politics of Punishment* (Cambridge, MA: Harvard University Press, 2015).

117. Martin Shefter, *Political Crisis, Fiscal Crisis: The Collapse and Revival of New York City* (New York: Basic Books, 1985), 123.

118. Fuchs, *Mayors and Money*, 38.

119. Fred Ferretti, "Beame and Fiscal Crisis," *New York Times*, September 7, 1975, 1.

120. John Darnton, "Unions and Banks Will Get Role in Governing of City," *New York Times*, November 19, 1975, 89.

121. "Mayor Beame's Observations on the Crisis," *New York Times*, October 5, 1975, 52.

122. Fred Ferretti, "After Difficult Year, Beame Says He's Still in Charge," *New York Times*, December 28, 1975, 1.

123. *Daily News*, October 1, 1975.

124. Lou Cannon, "Ford Pledges Post-Default Aid to N.Y.C.," *Washington Post*, October 30, 1975, A1.

125. Lou Cannon, "Ford Pledges Post-Default Aid to N.Y.C.," *Washington Post*, October 30, 1975, A1; Martin Tolchin, " 'Bailout' Barred," *New York Times*, October 30, 1975, 81.

126. John Robert Greene, *The Presidency of Gerald R. Ford* (Lawrence: University Press of Kansas, 1995), 9.

127. Roger Biles, *The Fate of Cities: Urban America and the Federal Government, 1945–2000* (Lawrence: University Press of Kansas, 2011).

128. Kantor and David, *The Dependent City*, 512.

129. Berman, *Local Government and the States*, 25.

130. Ibid., 515.

131. Fuchs, *Mayors and Money*, 159.

132. Margaret Weir, "Central Cities' Loss of Power in State Politics," *Cityscape* 2, no. 2 (1996): 23–40.

133. Earl Black and Merle Black, *Politics and Society in the South* (Cambridge, MA: Harvard University Press, 1987).

134. Earl Black and Merle Black, *Divided America: The Ferocious Power Struggle in American Politics* (New York: Simon & Schuster, 2007), 37–38.

135. James Boyd, "Nixon's Southern Strategy: 'It's All in the Charts,' " *New York Times*, May 17, 1970.

136. Quoted in Alexander P. Lamis, "The Two-Party South: From the 1960s until the 1990s," in *Southern Politics in the 1990s*, ed. Alexander P. Lamis (Baton Rouge: Louisiana State University Press, 1999).

137. Paul Frymer, *Uneasy Alliances: Race and Party Competition in America* (Princeton: Princeton University Press, 1999).

138. Peterson, *City Limits*, 80.

139. Mollenkopf, *Phoenix in the Ashes*, 132.

140. Kantor and David, *The Dependent City*, 231.

141. Charles Brecher and Raymond D. Horton, *Power Failure: New York City Politics and Policy Since 1960* (New York: Oxford University Press, 1993), 192.

142. Mollenkopf, *Phoenix in the Ashes*.

143. Adolph Reed Jr., "The Black Urban Regime: Structural Origins and Constraints," in *Power, Community and the City: Comparative Urban and Community Research*, ed. Michael Preston Smith (New Brunswick, NJ: Transaction, 1988).

144. Frederick F. Siegel, *The Future Once Happened Here: New York, D.C., L.A., and the Fate of America's Big Cities* (New York: Free Press, 1997); Jim Sleeper, *The Closest of Strangers: Liberalism and the Politics of Race in New York* (New York: W.W. Norton, 1990).

145. Robert A. Dahl, "The City in the Future of Democracy," *American Political Science Review* 61, no. 4 (1967): 953–970, 954.

146. Ibid.

147. Ibid.

148. Ibid.

149. Ibid.

150. Thucydides, *History of the Peloponnesian War*, 158–159.

2

Putting the City Back into Citizenship

Civics Textbooks and Municipal Government in the Interwar American City*

Tom Hulme

In the previous chapter, Michael Javen Fortner showed how city governments can maintain considerable autonomy by raising revenue, building bureaucracies, and governing social welfare. In this chapter, I connect the representations of such urban administration in civics education to the attempt to make urban citizens in the interwar period. I show how one aspect of citizenship was an identity discourse tied explicitly and strongly to this notion of the city and its autonomous government, expressed through the educational materials of "community civics." While urban inhabitants may not have necessarily *seen* themselves primarily as Bostonians, Philadelphians, or Chicagoans instead of Americans, the *idea* of urban citizenship, meaning here the collective benefits received through the membership of an urban community and the engendered consequent responsibilities, was still used as a tool of governance to inculcate and encourage loyalty in schoolchildren and immigrants. This loyalty was

*My thanks to Simon Gunn and Douglas Tallack for their comments on an earlier version of this chapter; Amy B. Bridges, Michael Javen Fortner, and the anonymous reviewers for more recent feedback; the delegates of the Summer Seminar on the City at Drexel University for providing the arena of debate that made these observations relevant; and the Economic and Social Research Council UK for funding this work.

based strongly on the relationship between municipal government and the health of the citizen, with the former providing the structure and the latter consequently embodying certain types of social, economic, and political behavior. Specifically, citizens were envisioned as interlocking parts of local communities that inhabited a municipal utopia, realized through egalitarian social service provisions, such as public baths and parks or electricity and water. While this discourse declined in the post–World War II years, I conclude that, in the language of civics and citizenship, a large part of interwar American government was still its urban element.

This may seem a counterintuitive argument to make when we con-sider the more typical categorization of citizenship in the period during and after the First World War as distinctly "national." Certainly, under the conditions of war and the home front effort, a wave of popular patrio-tism had emerged as associational culture and government cooperated to instill a sense of togetherness and national identity.[1] Christina A. Ziegler-McPherson has traced the cause of this cooperation to the mass immi-gration of the first two decades of the twentieth century, when federal and state governments sought "to more clearly shape American national identity by aggressively lobbying aliens to naturalize and assimilate into a culture pre-defined by the country's British heritage."[2] In the wartime citizenship output of the Committee on Public Information, there was little reference to the city or the municipal, with the focus instead on democracy as realized through American cultural values, practices, and an ethnically homogenous population.[3] Conservative organizations such as the Sons and Daughters of the American Revolution, the National Security League, and the American Legion actively worked to inculcate a notion of citizenship based on English literacy, the mechanics of American government, patri-otic rituals, and "a reverential, unquestioning view of American history."[4] These cooperative strands led to what Ziegler-McPherson has termed a "poisonous atmosphere of paranoia and hyper-patriotism."[5] Following the cessation of hostilities, demands for "100 percent Americanism" continued as signs of cultural or economic nonconformity—such as labor strikes and fears of communism—were displayed as contrary to the idea of what it meant to be a "true" American.[6] As Roosevelt famously wrote in 1919, "We have room for but one flag, the American flag. We have room for but one language, and that is the English language . . . and we have room for but one sole loyalty to the American people."[7]

Yet to declare the death of local citizenship in the interwar period is simplistic. Recent research by Daniel Amsterdam, for example, has challenged the historiographical view of 1920 marking the close of the

Progressive Era and beginning of a period of social reform stagnation before the intervention of the New Deal. Rather than being a decade of retrenchment and reaction, Amsterdam has used a study of Atlanta, Detroit, and Philadelphia to reveal a period of "aggressive governmental expansion" and the consolidation of what he has termed "the civic welfare state."[8] Importantly for the arguments presented here, Amsterdam highlighted that the greatest investment was in policies that had a "common emphasis on fostering specific visions of citizenship through moral, physical and cultural reform," such as schools, parks, playgrounds, museums, libraries, and the construction of roads, sewers, and water mains.[9] While perhaps in retreat on the national stage, progressivism in the local arena was very much alive. Indeed, as Julia Reuben has argued, the educators who designed community civics believed that industrial, urban society was incompatible with older political ideas of minimal government and maximum individual liberty. Community civics therefore aimed to "wean students from individualistic philosophies and build support for government activism."[10]

An analysis of civics textbooks then is a timely contribution to this rethinking of the local state and citizenship. It is in these materials that the "civic welfare state" in its ideological state was found, in descriptions of clean water, durable pipes, and friendly-but-efficient street cleaners. It is also in these texts that the municipal and the local rose to prominence alongside the national dimension outlined above. In the first section, I draw on a wider literature to discuss the methodological issues of using civics texts as historical sources before locating the specific moment at which "community civics" emerged. In section 2, I use a sample of these texts to draw out the municipal focus in its various forms, paying particular attention to the functions and technologies of urban government. In the final section, I concentrate on the specific example of Chicago to show how these discourses had been absorbed into syllabi and teaching materials of adult education in the 1920s and 1930s. While Ziegler-McPherson may be correct that "Americanization as a social movement and public policy faded from public consciousness" after immigration restriction in the 1920s, the formative ideas of community civics that I discuss remained deeply embedded in the discourse of citizenship throughout the interwar years.[11]

Civics Textbooks as Sources

Civics textbooks ranged from short publications of fifty pages to weighty tomes of more than four hundred and could be purely text based or also contain diagrams, maps, and images. Such form depended, naturally, on their aim and intended audience, taking into consideration age, language, gender, and social class. Many used simplified and direct language, others highly specialized expert terminology, while some extensively used literary forms such as allegory and metaphor. In texts aimed at children especially, authors approached the reader with a "friendly" tone that sought to present the book as a benign adviser. The majority delivered their knowledge as objective and wholly scientific. It is worth differentiating, as have Alain Choppin and Chris Stray, between books that were not primarily intended, but nonetheless used, for educating, such as literature, and books that were "designed to provide an authoritative pedagogic version of an area of knowledge"—the latter clearly being textbooks.[12] Though they may now be seen as historical sources, it is unlikely that educators considered the long-term durability of their work at the time of writing; textbooks were employed by teachers to communicate (historically relative) knowledge and morals in a particular context. Structurally, each chapter usually corresponded to a different topic that would likely form the basis of a lesson, and the books were arranged so that chapters would be studied in a sequence.[13] Each chapter was often followed by a set of questions, homework tasks, or bibliographic information for further reading. Above all, textbooks were practical and period-specific tools for teaching.

Reflecting the masses of teaching materials that could be categorized as textbooks, and the multitude of styles within this, theirs has unsurprisingly proved to be a fruitful endeavor for both social scientists and historians across a range of subjects and periods.[14] Because of this scholarship, a series of methodological issues have been raised about their usefulness as primary sources for research. Johanne Lebrun, summarizing François Richaudeau, noted four areas of potential research through textbooks:

> contents (analyzed for their sociocultural, ideological, scientific, and pedagogical dimensions), communication (communicative meanings, forms of the message, readability, density), method (organization, method of use, and adaptability), and textbooks as material objects (sturdiness, manipulability, cost).[15]

It is strictly with the content of textbooks that this chapter is concerned. There are some obvious problems specific to treating civics textbooks content as a representative source of what pupils and adult immigrants were taught in this period. First, such an assertion would require extensive comparative research across all the varying educational units of the country—city, state, private, religious—both before and after the development of the "community civics." While the United States Bureau of Education, the National Education Association, and the American Political Science Association endorsed the "community civics" course, the scope for implementation remained in local hands, and many civics texts were written with particularly local audiences in mind. Without such investigation, it is impossible to verify that these newly published books penetrated educational culture to a comprehensive extent, regardless of the intent of their authors. Even if ascertaining this were feasible in a study of this size, it only raises two more concurrent questions: how did teachers use these materials, and how did students respond to civics more generally?[16] As Stray has suggested with regard to both teachers and pupils, some would follow the book blindly, whereas others would use it as a reference tool.[17]

Civics textbooks therefore are useful perhaps not so much in trying to gauge how and what the pupil was taught, but more in reflecting the social conditions in which they were produced. In this sense, the textbook is what Stray has termed a "composite cultural commodity . . . standing at the crossroads of culture and pedagogy, publishing and society."[18] Textbooks, while not ordinarily representing an outlet for new knowledge, nonetheless gave "an indication of the state of the field's development" at the time of publication.[19] Bearing this in mind, civics texts in particular, rather than history or geography texts, are the most useful source to discover how the developing ideas of the city and the municipal had become ingrained in the discourse of citizenship, because the notion of citizenship was the explicit purpose of their publication. For citizenship discourse they reflected the range of opinion that was deemed to be a legitimate field of political thought, suitable to be used in the transmission of ideas and morals to students.[20] From the late nineteenth century and into the 1920s, there was a substantial rise in the number of these books, written by historians, librarians, politicians, school directors, or administrators, targeted both to inform teachers as well as to be used directly as a classroom aid. This rise was primarily a response to the late nineteenth-century population explosion coupled with the multiethnic nature of the migrants and calls for a coordinated American curriculum.[21]

Many authors stressed a departure from older forms of citizenship instruction, with titles frequently referring to a "new" form of instruction. Roscoe L. Ashley, for example, author of *The New Civics: A Textbook for Secondary Schools*, first published in 1918, saw this movement as "naturally different from that of a generation ago" and even "from that of a decade ago."[22] Rather than simply detailing government and its machinery to inform voters, which was the focus of previous civics texts, Ashley now saw citizenship as "social" inasmuch as it detailed how the citizen placed and lived within and benefited from the hierarchies and structure of society.[23] Similarly, in *Our Community: Good Citizenship in Towns and Cities,* the authors described how the new interest in civics had superseded the limited study of government and replaced it with two clearer questions: what is the community doing for the citizen, and what does the citizen owe the community?[24] Much of the same point was made in *Community Civics* (1921), which proclaimed: "The old order changeth" as the "old methods of teaching the science of government, outworn and laid aside, give place to a wider interpretation of the subject and a wider application of its principles." In practice, the best "tool" for this was "the study of the relationship of the individual to his fellow man and to the government instituted for his benefit."[25]

While this may sound suspiciously like pedagogic rhetoric, contemporaries and historians alike have recognized the distinctiveness of this new field of civics texts. The Report of the Commission on the Social Studies by the American Historical Association in 1935 traced the point of departure primarily to *The Community and the Citizen* by Arthur W. Dunn, published in 1907.[26] Dunn's book was described as "revolutionary" for several reasons, including its emphasis on participation in community life by pupils and on citizenship as something to be lived rather than memorized and recited from a textbook. Most important was his emphasis on "the physiology rather than the anatomy" of government.[27] This development had the effect of making community civics texts distinctly urban based, as the location in which most government functions were carried out. Dunn later expanded on the importance of government to his account of civics in a 1915 essay:

> Community civics by no means minimizes the importance of government. It describes and emphasizes government at every step as the chief means by which the citizens of a community co-operate . . . It approaches the mechanism of government through its relation to the immediate interests of the citizen.[28]

The notions catalyzed by Dunn's civics text spread into wider educational currents. At a meeting of an association of history teachers in 1913, for example, two of three resolutions passed directly encouraged the teaching of the new civics: that the focus should be on the functions of government and not just the machinery, and that work should be based on pupils' experience of their immediate surroundings.[29] When this "community civics" was endorsed by the United States Bureau of Education, the National Education Association, and the American Political Science Association, it became the core of civics education.[30]

Civics texts were used mainly in two distinctive ways. First, in the school—a place the University of Chicago political scientist Charles E. Merriam dubbed in the 1930s "the outstanding agency in civic instruction."[31] This emphasis on the school and citizenship extended nationally, with President Hoover, against a backdrop of severe economic depression, insisting that "we must not encroach upon the schools or reduce the opportunity of the child through the school to develop adequate citizenship."[32] The second way civics texts were used was in adult citizenship classes tied to the naturalization of immigrants, usually given by a combination of civic associations, the local board of education, industrial employers, and, in the 1930s, as part of the New Deal program. Peter Roberts, the author of *Civics for Coming Americans* in 1920, highlighted the importance of targeting the immigrant especially, stating, "In the last three years 37,715 failed to pass the examination for naturalization. Half a million are now in training for citizenship, and of them 100,000 will not pass unless a sympathetic person will give them the help they need . . . It is good neither for them nor for us to have them remain aliens."[33] While there was a continuance of a form of citizenship education based around notions of workplace efficiency, realized predominately in factory classes and serving the needs of industrial employers, community civics was different; this was targeted education to create citizens loyal to the community, city, state, and nation—and the governments that ensured the life of the individual and his or her community.[34] This was achieved through the presentation of information about the city and its governance, presented in an objective, nonpolitical, and accessible format, and through statistics, maps, diagrams, pictures, and above all description. It is this relationship in civics texts between the city, municipal government, and citizen that I wish to further explore in the next two sections.

It is not, however, my intention to totally obscure either the national patriotic element or the role of the federal government in citizenship. Certainly the idea of the national was prominent too; civics texts celebrated national achievements and national government and spoke of the American spirit, and there were of course more specifically national-based civics texts too that detailed voting, taxation, and the justice system.[35] When we consider the prominent notion of citizenship as a national identity, with all its corresponding cultural and legal sustainers, this is not surprising. City and national pride complemented and reinforced each other in an essential way. But, as Julia Reuben has also argued, the authors of the new civics "rejected the traditional focus on the national government" and "began with the students' local community rather than the state or national government."[36] As *Community Civics* recognized, "the laws of the town or city in which we live come closest to us," and so it made sense for this to be the starting point of any civics study, because "we can see how these laws work."[37] Concentrating on the city and its government was a logical approach to take, and I now build on Reuben's work by highlighting the ways in which this municipal community was presented to the student of civics.

Representations of Municipal Government in Civics Texts

Through an enabling structure provided and maintained by the municipality, it was emphasized that the citizen could live a safe, healthy, and virtuous life. Of course, this was a highly idealized image of perfect government that did not relate to the "messiness" and uncertainty of urban systems.[38] Civics texts were not unlike the ambitious or "fantastical" city plans that imposed a "distinctive way of seeing the city, whereby key urban functions were highlighted and other uses were deliberated occluded."[39] This "imagined urban scene that was in excess of the socially possible or politically acceptable"[40] attempted to create citizens by then showing "what is being done for them" and consequently "what they are expected to do for themselves and for their fellows."[41] *Civics for New Americans* (1915) was particularly interesting in the way it recognized the opportunities of vice in the modern city for both parents and children but showed the choice of virtue as offered by the municipal as well. Admitting that "young people develop bad habits which they acquire in back alleys and on city streets,"[42] and "American city and factory life have dangers which must be guarded against,"[43] the text proceeded to detail the publicly run amenities like schools, public gymnasiums, playgrounds, and public libraries that provided an alternative solace from the street, workplace, and saloon. Advanced civilization was now portrayed, by comparison, as a set of governmental functions that structured physical and social life and "helped citizens meet their basic needs."[44]

Significantly, the administrators of these functions were shown not to be partisan politicians. They were instead the efficient municipal employees, impartial and outside the sphere of politics, and often the first point of contact between the subject and the state. As Roberts asked and answered:

> Why does a city need a government? Because the health of the people, the enforcement of law, and the improvements needed for the comfort and enjoyment of the citizens must be looked after by a group of men specially assigned to the task.[45]

Perhaps more interesting, however, was the way that focus was often transferred away from the mayor, councilor and aldermen and toward the more familiar urban characters who actually carried out the functions of government. In *Civics for Coming Americans*, it was the role of the health officer in combating the "many people" who "sell milk that is adulterated, ice that is filthy, and meat and vegetables that are not fit for use" or the "cases of smallpox, scarlet fever, diphtheria, and measles" that was emphasized. Against all these "evils," the board of health officers "protect the health of the people of the city."[46] In *Community Civics*, the role of health officers was also highlighted:

> How government comes into the home—Early in the morning the milkman leaves at your city home your daily supply of milk . . . If you buy your milk off the milkman, he must have it examined to see that it is clean and free from harmful germs, and that it has a proper amount of nourishment in it. Your local government looks after this, sending out inspectors who, under the orders of the local health officers, attend to these duties.[47]

This importance given to health officers in the community reflected the prerogatives of the neighborhood health center movement, which had begun in 1910, targeting the environment and lifestyle of new immigrations especially.[48] Perhaps surprisingly, another of the most frequently cited municipal representatives is the street cleaner, "aided with mechanical street flushers to wash the streets and sweepers that brush up the dirt" to make "it possible to breathe pure air, and to keep our bodies clean, two prime necessities for good health."[49] In *A Community Civics: A Textbook in Loyal Citizenship*, the children were told to look out of the window and see the street cleaners, "aiding us so that we may have clean streets."[50] Other city employees, such as firemen, teachers, and policemen, were often referred to in similar ways: they were fundamental parts of the urban environment maintained apolitically to ensure the safety of the citizen. The street cleaner represents one facet of the extensive attention given by civics texts to the streets of the city. As the author of *Community Civics* explained: "streets are of great importance to a community . . . It is along these streets that much of the community life is centered. Many of the laws passed have to do with the streets and the protection of the people in them."[51] Likewise, in *Civics for Coming Americans,* the author emphasized that "the people" own the streets, and it is in this part of the urban environment that people communicate with one another. For this reason, every city needed "good streets, well planned, well paved, and well kept. They should be clean, smooth, and durable. They should be free from disorder and obstruction; and well lighted at night. . . ."[52] Importantly, though the people may have "owned" the streets, it was the municipal that maintained them and made sure that "no privileges" were "given to corporations which would cause discomfort to, or increase the danger of, the people."[53]

Most important and worth stressing is the continual occurrence of the idea that government provided egalitarian "welfare." As Ashley stated,

> our governments frequently and usually *promote the welfare of the citizen* [Ashley's italics]. Free public schools, parks, and playgrounds exist for his benefit . . . Public utilities, such as municipal water plants and the national Post Office, give service without making profit the first and chief consideration. The individual citizen benefits directly or indirectly from these activities of our government.[54]

In *Community Civics*, the author was equally explicit about the reasons for government action:

> Government is interested in recreation because of the effect it has in bettering citizenship. To provide attractive playgrounds for boys and girls where they will get beneficial exercise and wholesome enjoyment in the form of games, is to lessen idleness and the evils which go with it . . . To provide public baths and wholesome entertainment in which people's bodies and minds may be re-created is to lessen the evils which are in every crowded city.[55]

As Reuben has convincingly argued, this was a fundamental change in how citizenship was conceptualized from the nineteenth century. It was no longer a "primarily political status" tied strongly to the notion of exercising democracy at the ballot box, but rather a character-based identity. To be a good citizen was now to be clean, neat, obedient, respectful, helpful, honest, thrifty, and above all healthy.[56] It was through technologies and structures of urban government that these character traits could be realized, and thus it was urban government that was shown to have the largest impact on citizens' lives. In *Elementary Civics: The New Civics*, the author used storytelling techniques to display the influence of the municipal through technology on the everyday life of a Bostonian:

> Our Bostonian begins the day by bathing in water supplied by the public through an elaborate system of public pumps and reservoirs and pipes. After it has been used, the water escapes through the citizen's own plumbing systems; but this private plumbing system has been constructed in accordance with public regulations, is liable to inspection by public officials, and empties into sewers constructed and managed by the public . . . he steps out upon a sidewalk constructed in accordance with public requirements, crosses a street paved and waters and swept by the public, and enters a street car whose route, speed, and fare are regulated by the public . . . When finally all the business of the day is finished, this imaginary Bostonian walks through the Common and the Public Garden, and soon enters the Public Library, a building that is the latest and most striking expression of the public's interest in the individual . . . and at last he hastens home through streets that public servants are now beginning to light.[57]

Water provision and regulation was also highlighted as "one of the most important duties of local government" in *Community Civics* because of the necessity of water for good health. Again, it was the man-made flow of water that was highlighted:

> Reservoirs are built to hold back a sufficient supply, which is piped to the town or city and then into our homes. Great care is taken that all the water which drains into a reservoir is pure and that all the land surrounding the water supply is kept in a sanitary condition.[58]

Civics for Coming Americans is particularly interesting in the way it extended the jurisdiction of municipal technology far outside the city, right into the untamed natural environment. The text first described the "mountain streams miles away, where the water is pure and the watershed is free from contamination." For this water to "be made serviceable," city government had to fulfill several technical responsibilities:

> [R]eservoirs must be built, and often the water must be pumped to a high tower in order to give the pressure needed, either for high buildings or in case of fire. In some instances, cities must pump water from a polluted river, purify it in a plant specially built for the purpose, and protect the people from diseases due to contamination of rivers by cities on their banks.[59]

In these stories, municipal and state government had "conquered" the urban environment for the citizen. References were made to the "before" situation; in *Civics for New Americans*, the author described the amount of work that went into maintaining the streets before asking "What kind of pavements have you in your community? Do you remember the kind of pavings you had in the old country?"[60]

Systems also worked symbolically. Maria Kaika and Erik Swyngedouw, drawing on Marx's ideas relating to the fetishization of commodities in the market, have argued that, during the nineteenth century, urban technological networks and their urban dowry of pumping stations, power stations, and water towers became prominently located in the city and celebrated as "phantasmagorical" symbols of modernity and progress. Rather than just carrying water or electricity into the city, they also "embodied the promise and the dream of a good society."[61] Crucially, this was a society of universal justice under the "equalizing and totalizing powers of technology."[62] Into the twentieth century, however, these "glorious icons" increasingly began to disappear from both the cityscape and urban imagination, as it "became abundantly clear that, although the networks did deliver the promised material in the form of commodified goods, they somehow failed to deliver in their wake a better society . . . The fetish character of the networks and technological artifacts collapsed under the weight of unfulfilled promises."[63]

Though an interesting and persuasive argument, it is perhaps fair to say that, while inequalities remained, city government did go a considerable way to abolishing plague and disease.[64] Furthermore, perhaps the "urban dowry" did not disappear in the interwar period so much as relocate. While it may be true that many technological systems were buried underground, other schemes, like civic airports and distant reservoir pumping stations, by necessity took place outside the immediate urban environment. Civics texts represented one way to visually bring utilities back to the city, now pictorially celebrated as symbols of municipal and urban progress. Kaika and Swyngedouw further argued that the promise of "emancipation and freedom resided in the intimacy of the disconnected house" as the domestic became clear, pure, functional, and safe for the subject.[65] Again, while true, passages and pictures in civics texts linked this vision back to technological systems by clearly describing the methods used to create such an "emancipated" space.

What really stands out in these books is the way in which government was presented as a benign background force, making sure what William B. Munro termed "the humdrum data of routine civic life" ran smoothly.[66] In this narrative it provided the structure for living, but it did not make the citizen live in a certain way. Instead, this was deemed to be an inherent and obvious citizenship responsibility. These everyday routines were presented as questions of administration, outside politics, and carried out by impartial material systems and public regulations. Now accepted and engrained in everyday life, these systems were then shown to the city's inhabitants and celebrated to strengthen the relationship between government and citizen, as good citizenship became a responsibility because of the promise of effective and egalitarian government.

Case Study: Chicago and Civics

By concentrating on the teaching advice produced in one city, it is possible to gain an understanding of how the municipal images propagated in the textbooks of the war period and immediately after had become crucial to the way in which a sense of "citizenship of the city" was cemented. Increasingly, as school enrollment levels rose, civics materials found their way into classes; in Chicago, 91 percent of schools reported that such texts were used in assemblies and English classes by the mid-1930s.[67] In a 1921 publication prepared for the Chicago board of education and tailored toward adults with "little command of English" who were applying for naturalization, three interlinked aims were laid out clearly.[68] First, government (city, county, state, and nation) was planned, effective, and a "good" system. Second, government was both indispensable and convenient, and "the only workable device to attain these objects." Finally, it highlighted the role of "the people" as a "silent partner," with the products or achievements of the government being spread across all citizens.[69] As a

publication that was for instructors only, the authors were direct in what
they saw as the quickest route to citizenship:

> These men are not accustomed to learn about things through
> abstract ideas, or by formula. The subject of civics is, therefore,
> to be presented from the standpoint of the concrete evidence
> of the benefits it insures, beginning with the city government
> and proceeding by connected steps to the county, state and
> national government . . . presented entirely from the standpoint
> of its *products* [original italics]; not from the standpoint of
> its machinery or mechanics, a method that has been all too
> prevalent.[70]

From the first lesson, instructors were advised to encourage their students
to link their citizenship to the geography of the urban environment in
which they lived, such as recognizable areas of North/South/East/West,
and more specific neighborhoods and streets. By lesson 6, the material
got decidedly more patronizing and explicitly civic:

> Gentlemen, we are now ready to begin a study of our *Home
> City*. What is the name of our home city? (Secure correct
> pronunciation: Chicago, not Tchicaggo, nor Chi-cah-go!) Will
> you all please repeat: Chicago is my home city? What is home?
> "There's no place like home."[71]

Further into these instructions, the recognized importance of the material
environment created by urban government took center stage, particularly
concentrating on one of its greatest triumphs over nature: the provision
of a clean water supply. In this narrative, the situation before municipal
ownership was presented negatively, with private companies delivering
little water, in opposition to the city council's egalitarian goal of "millions
of streams for every emergency."[72] A concerted effort was made to stress
the infallible expert opinion on which the water system was based: the
physician who understood water's relationship to health, the scientist, the
"political genius with the welfare of the city at heart," the skillful engineers,
the craftsmen, and the "strength and good will of the laborer."[73] Reflecting
social instability since the end of the war, the author noted that, in "these
days of frenzied discussion of Class consciousness," it was "a good time
to emphasize at every opportunity the ideas of interdependence and the
solidarity of all classes and not the solidarity of a single class; that we are

all partners; that we must all "hang together, or we will hang separately."[74] It went on to describe the literal structures that made this possible, tracing the water flow in reverse order from the faucet, water pipe, street water mains, pumping station, concrete water tunnels that went from the city into the lake, and the source: "the Cribs which stand out there in the lake, some two miles and others four miles from shore."[75] Through these municipal technologies, the citizens benefited from "a good many baths, plenty of clean clothes, clean streets, fresh lawns and parks."[76] This concentration on health and cleanliness reflected the continued importance of such bodily attributes as a cornerstone of respectability in the interwar period.[77]

By 1932, those interested in citizenship in Chicago thought it was time for a comprehensive Chicago-specific civics text. So far as my research has gathered, *Local Government in Chicago* seemingly never made it past the "tentative draft of an outline"[78] to press and into schools, but it certainly picked up techniques from other civics texts in the period. Though the reality of municipal ownership was evidently less secure in the city than in other places,[79] there was a concerted effort to draw attention to how local government "builds its own bridges, constructs harbor facilities, builds and cares for public edifices, furnishes street lights, paving, sidewalks, street name plates, cleaning of streets and alleys, including the disposal of garbage and ashes."[80] While there was no mention of the contentious issue of the tramways, there was pride shown for the other large concerns in the city, like the sewage system of the Sanitary District, which was the "largest publicly owned utility in the Chicago area . . . valued at four and one half billion dollars . . . ," and the Public Works Department, which "spends about thirty-five million a year."[81]

Interestingly, there was a direct acknowledgement that the regulatory functions of municipal government were a direct responsibility to the citizen; "not a matter for dispute, but an accepted commonplace:"[82]

> The city dweller expects the water which runs from his faucet to be tested chemically by experts each day. He expects to have streets cleaned and the garbage taken out of his way. He expects that the city will keep the factories and railroads, over which he as an individual has no control, from shutting off the sunlight by smoke. He expects the milk left at his door every morning to be free from disease, and his neighbors to be quarantined when their children have scarlet fever. He wants a competent life guard on a safe beach in the summer heat. He takes for

granted that the city will complement the meager chance for
recreation offered by small homes and crowded streets, with
parks, playgrounds, museums and libraries.[83]

Civics education in Chicago was given a large boost with the establishment
of federal funding for adult education under the terms of the New Deal,
first through the Civil Works Education Service from December 1933,
to September 1935, then through the Works Progress Administration
(WPA) from December 1935 to after the Second World War.[84] By 1937,
the Citizenship Department of the Adult Education Program had grown
to 147 centers, 194 classes, and 63 teachers, with a weekly attendance of
4,654 in 1937.[85] From the beginning, the organization of classes was a
cooperative exercise; the organizers and supervisors were appointed by
representatives of municipal authority, who had educational control; the
money to pay the teachers was provided by the federal government, who
retained administrative control; and the classes took place in and with the
cooperation of churches, YMCAs, and settlements, who provided "the heat
and light."[86] In the mid-1930, students had a wide geographical choice;
on the North Side, for example, students could use Christopher House,
Eli Bates House, and Lincoln-Belmont House; on the Northwest Side,
Association House and Northwestern University Settlement; on the West
Side, Logan Square Branch Library, Chicago Commons, Austin Branch
Library, Hull House, Maxwell Street YMCA, and Garibaldi Institute; on
the Southwest Side, the University of Chicago Settlement and House of
Happiness; and on the South Side, the Hyde Park Baptist Church, Beverly
Community YMCA, Church of the Good Shepherd, and the Chicago
Urban League.[87] By 1940, there were classes and study groups in 500 locations throughout the city.[88] Teachers were encouraged to make themselves
familiar with the community in which they were to teach to best "meet
the general interests and needs of the people."[89] The WPA understood
the importance of using this network, stating its purpose as integrating
the program with "the established agencies of public education of state,
county and school districts."[90]

    Of the classroom material disseminated to teachers that has sur-
vived, it is possible to ascertain a clear municipal focus, again stressing the
themes of egalitarianism, community, and services.[91] In a pamphlet of the
Social Studies Conference held in Chicago in 1937, reference was made to
the fact that "community civics" texts were to be used in the adult education classes.[92] In a lesson on taxes from the 1930s, for example, pupils
were taught that their money was used "to take care of the streets, the

parks, [and] the water-works." It was emphasized that everyone paid taxes. Again, it was the depoliticized municipal employee, or "public servant," who was the familiar point of reference: the fireman, the policeman, and the street cleaner.[93] The following lesson was titled "Civic Responsibility" and drew attention to functions of the municipal that "belong to the citizen," such as schools, libraries, and parks.[94] Importantly, good behavior of schoolchildren was seen as the responsibility of the adult because of these amenities: "we must teach them to obey the laws, protect public property, help keep our city clean"; "we must teach them to do their part"; "we can only have a good country when everyone helps."[95]

Outside civics classes, the emphasis on the city, its communities, and its government also remained in other venues of adult education. The Free Chicago Tours program used the actual site of the city as a pedagogical tool by visiting areas of educational, historical, and contemporary interest such as Chinatown, Hull House, the "Halsted Street Melting Pot," and the Municipal Airport. According to the Adult Education Annual Report for 1937, there were 744 tours held that year, with a total attendance of 52,931 and—alarmingly—as many as 3,000 people on some tours.[96] It is clear from these teaching materials that the "new" civics approach had lasted throughout the interwar period in Chicago. Municipal government and its functions were still seen worthy of study and adulation for the benefits they brought to the individual citizen.

Conclusion

Extrapolating the typicality of Chicago's experience in this period is problematic. Certainly the civics narrative was produced first through textbooks that had a wide purview, produced by educators across the country. Furthermore, as the American Historical Association stated, community civics "completely dominated" civic education after 1915.[97] In 1929, therefore, Armand J. Gerson could summarize that "[i]n none of the social studies have the changes of the last twenty years been so marked as in the field of civics" after its previous incarnation as "a simplified study of government . . . restricted to the upper grades . . . [, which] took the form of verbatim memorization of the Constitution of the United States."[98] At minimum, it is evident that community civics was not confined to Chicago. Yet Chicago was undoubtedly a city in need of a cohesive sense of citizenship because of the social problems it was experiencing as a result of its magnetism for immigrants—the primary target of citizenship education.[99] Widespread and obvious political corruption in the city further encouraged a form of citizenship education that painted the city government in a positive, depoliticized light.[100] More local case studies could ascertain if this general movement passed as prominently into the teaching materials of other local cities not necessarily experiencing similar levels of civic strife and changing demographics. It is also worth discussing the extent to which these municipal utopian visions were accepted or uncontested. School textbooks were, by their very definition, "expressive of the social and political ideologies of particular vested interests" and were open to both criticism and even censorship.[101] The author had the ability to use an unbalanced selection, distort the content that was chosen, or not include contentious material at all.[102] The changing of the law by the Mississippi state legislature in 1940 to make sure democracy, rights, and civic responsibilities were absent from textbooks used in black schools provides one apt example.[103] If the descriptions of local government and infrastructure presented here seem biased and idealized in favor of the municipal, this issue was not missed by all contemporaries. While the civics textbook is the ideal place to look for citizenship discourse, it must be balanced with the reaction its publication engendered from contemporaries. The municipal bias was of particular concern to the proponents of private ownership, who made their living from selling utilities to urban dwellers. One public relations director asserted that "97 per cent of all the textbooks used in the public schools affecting public utilities are written by socialists and advocates of public ownership."[104] A combative publicity campaign was devised in order that "future generations of Americans will be staunch friends of the public utilities" by learning that "the utility men are neither bugaboos nor bandits, but public servants supplying the essentials of the modern home and business . . . that the progress of the community depends upon the development of its utilities."[105]

In Chicago, and Illinois more widely, this was particularly vociferous; instructed by utilities magnate Samuel Insull to "get busy and do something," the executives of his companies in 1919 formed the Illinois Committee on Public Utility Information.[106] As well as taking lectures and talks to the schools delivered by men trained in public speaking and giving prizes to students who wrote the best essay on the nature of the utility business, the committee was quick to release its own assessment of private ownership.[107] In *Chicago's Genii, The Public Utilities* (1921), the narrative presented used the same language of modernity and classless duty to describe privately run gas, electricity, telephones, and transport: "A wonderful transformation—a miracle—has happened in the last half century, that has placed all men and women, rich or poor, on the same level in relation to the fundamental conveniences of life."[108] In response to these campaigns, a Save-Our-Schools-Committee was organized in 1928 "to establish upon yet firmer foundations . . . that American schools and colleges are not to be considered as subjects for propaganda by special interests, groups, or causes."[109] There was clearly a battle to present the supposed "real" image of municipal ownership, which often crossed business and government lines. The *Chicago's Genii* pamphlet, for example, was produced for the Chicago Boosters' Publicity Club, an organization of businessmen and key municipal figures such as William Hale Thompson, also a sometimes friend of municipal ownership when it suited his political interests.[110]

As Amy Bridges points out in the introduction to this volume, it is when cities have adequate resources under their control that they gain autonomy. It was this relative power in the interwar period, especially before the rapid rise of federal government in the 1930s, that enabled city governments—despite the challenges of men like Insull—to construct elaborate civics stories about the roles they played in the life of the urban inhabitant. This was a particular type of "cultural imagining," a process of attaching to the city stories of dominant and shared symbols of social and economic activity. As Fortner's chapter suggests, the bureaucratization of local policy provided the basis for urban citizenship by making millions of Americans loyal to the authority of the urban state. When federal bureaucracy increased, therefore, the administrative capacity of urban government was crippled, threatening the independence and vibrancy of urban citizenship. As the federal state demanded obligations and sacrifices from the nation's citizens during the Second World War, it was consequently to national rather than local governments that citizens looked for the fulfilling of the benefits of citizenship.[111]

Local citizenship also declined for reasons that had been developing since the Great Migration of southern blacks to urban areas in the previous thirty years. As Jennifer L. Hochschild notes in Chapter 7, the boosterism and urban optimism of civics contrasts sharply with the current urban despair and hollowing out of a city's ability to self-control or to right the wrongs of its residents. Indeed, this was an aspect of the 1930s, and one that irrevocably damaged the ability of this particular urban citizenship discourse to endure. While civics texts proclaimed egalitarian provision and an ideal city, the reality of Chicago was a racially stratified environment with unequal service provision.[112] It was the inability of civics textbooks to capture, or indeed even try to engage, with ethnic and racial identities in relation to provision, in a similar manner as Chapter 3 by Marion Orr, Kenneth K. Wong, Emily M. Farris, and Domingo Morel and Chapter 8 by Lisa L. Miller have discussed, that meant they eventually had little realistic purchase. In talking of "community" and "the people," they ignored black ghettoization—a hypocrisy that cannot have escaped adult education students using civics materials in segregated classes during the 1930s.[113] As Rogers Smith summarizes in the final chapter of this volume, it was the growing presence of urban African Americans, and the choices about the different paths of further discrimination or greater acceptance as civic equals, that helped fuel the activism of the civil rights movement.[114] Certainly the city was the site of many of these paths.[115] Yet with the rise of the civil rights movement, segregation and racism were tackled, if only partially, through recourse to national legal legislation.[116] Postwar citizenship discourse therefore was less interested in the "street-fighting pluralism" that Fortner describes and more concerned with establishing civil rights through legal measures.

Citizenship discourse in the interwar period therefore stands at the apex of several themes of this volume; an expression of the administrative and autonomous power of city government before further deindustrialization, centralization, and suburbanization, eventually superseded by the narrative of equal rights. Certainly, ideas of what the "good" municipal government actually "meant" remained unclear and contested. Calls for municipal ownership sometimes grew in strength, sometimes weakened. But the idea of the municipal as infallible, egalitarian, and benign—even if the reality of Chicago government in the interwar period was somewhat different—maintained a consistently popular way of linking the citizen to his or her environment. It has not been the aim of this chapter to obscure the other topics of civics textbooks beyond the municipal focus; rather, I have attempted to draw out the mundane and quotidian from the more expected accounts of national pride, the president, Ben Franklin, and the Constitution to show that, in one arena at least, urban government was at the forefront of public consciousness.

Notes

1. Christopher *Capozzola, Uncle Sam Wants You: World War I and the Making of the Modern Citizen* (Oxford: Oxford University Press, 2008). See also John F. McClymer, "The Federal Government and the Americanization Movement, 1915–1924," *Prologue: The Journal of the National Archives* 10:1 (Spring 1978).

2. Christina A. Ziegler-McPherson, *Americanization in the States: Immigrant Social Welfare Policy, Citizenship and National Identity in the United States, 1908–1929* (Gainesville: University of Florida Press, 2009), 1–2.

3. Ziegler-McPherson, *Americanization in the States*, 88.

4. Ziegler-McPherson, *Americanization in the States*, 10. See Bessie L. Pierce, *Citizens' Organizations and the Civic Training of Youth* (Chicago: C. Scribner's Sons, 1933) for a good description of the multitude of groups working in this vein.

5. Ziegler-McPherson, *Americanization in the States*, 91.

6. For a Chicago-centric analysis of the calls for 100 percent Americanism, see Robin F. Bachin, "At the Nexus of Labor and Leisure: Baseball, Nativism, and the 1919 Black Sox Scandal," *Journal of Social History* 36:4 (2003). For a wider-ranging study, see Capozzala, *Uncle Sam Wants You.*

7. *The American Citizen* 1, no. 4 (February 1927): 2. See also Cecilia E. O'Leary, *To Die For: The Paradox of American Patriotism* (Princeton: Princeton University Press, 1999).

8. Daniel Amsterdam, *The Roaring Metropolis: Business, Civic Welfare and State Expansion in 1920s America* (PhD diss., University of Pennsylvania, 2009), v.

9. Amsterdam, *The Roaring Metropolis,* vi.

10. Julie A. Reuben, "Beyond Politics: Community Civics and the Redefinition of Citizenship in the Progressive Era," *History of Education Quarterly* 37, no. 4 (Winter 1997): 416.

11. Ziegler-McPherson, *Americanization in the States,* 19.

12. Chris Stray, "Paradigms Regained: Towards a Historical Sociology of the Textbook," *Journal of Curriculum Studies* 26, no. 1 (1994): 2. See also Alain Choppin, "The *Emmanuelle* Textbook Project," *Journal of Curriculum Studies* 24, no. 4 (1992).

13. Foster McMurray and Lee J. Cronbach, "The Controversial Past and Present of the Text," in *Text Materials in Modern Education: A Comprehensive Theory and Platform of Research,* ed. Cronbach (Urbana: University of Illinois Press, 1955).

14. Ruth Firer, "Human Rights in History and Civics Textbooks: The Case of Israel," *Curriculum Inquiry* 282 (1998); Stephen Heathorn, "Let Us Remember That We, Too, Are English": Constructions of Citizenship and National Elementary School Reading Books, 1880–1914," *Victorian Studies: A Journal of the Humanities, Arts and Sciences* 383 (1995); David Tyack, "Monuments between Covers: The Politics of Textbooks," *American Behavioral Scientist* 426 (1999); Frances FitzGerald, *America Revised: History Schoolbooks in the Twentieth Century* (Boston: Little Brown and Co., 1979); Robin Richardson, "The Hidden Messages of Schoolbooks," *Journal of Moral Education* 151 (1986); Meenaz Kassam and Bernd Baldus, "Make Me Truthful, Good, and Mild": Values in Nineteenth Century Ontario Schoolbooks," *Canadian Journal of Sociology* 21, no. 3 (1996); Michael V. Belok, "Forming the American Character: Essayists and Schoolbooks,"

Social Science 431 (1968); Thomas J. Davis, "Images of Intolerance: John Calvin in Nineteenth Century History Textbooks," *Church History* 652 (1996). See also in particular the specialist journal *Paradigm*, which was the journal of the Textbook Colloquium.

15. François Richaudeau quoted in Johanne Lebrun, "Past and Current Trends in the Analysis of Textbooks in a Quebec Context," *Curriculum Inquiry* 32, no. 1 (Spring 2002): 55.

16. Ibid., 55. Lebrun quotes Robert M. Anderson and George S. Tomkins, who argue that while we must not forget that "materials may well be powerful determinants of the curriculum," it is nevertheless the teacher who adapts the materials and determines how they are used. Anderson and Tompkins, *Understanding Materials: Their Role in Curriculum Development. A Discussion Guide* (Vancouver: University of British Columbia, 1983).

17. Stray, "Paradigms Regained," 5.

18. Ibid., 4.

19. David Klein and William L. Smith, "Historical Trends in the Marriage and Family Textbook Literature, 1887–1980," *Family Relations* 34 (1985): 211.

20. Brindle and M. Arnot, "England Expects Every Man to Do His Duty": The Gendering of the Citizenship Textbook 1940–1966," *Oxford Review of Education* 25, nos. 1/2 (1999): 119.

21. William E. Marsden, *The School Textbook: Geography, History and Social Studies* (London: Woburn Press, 2001), 16.

22. Roscoe L. Ashley, *The New Civics: A Textbook for Secondary Schools* (New York: Macmillan, 1921), v.

23. Ibid.

24. Samuel H. Ziegler and Helen J. Wilds, *Our Community: Good Citizenship in Towns and Cities* (Chicago: Winston, 1918), xi.

25. Edgar W. Ames and Arvie Eldred, *Community Civics* (New York: The Macmillan Company, 1921), v.

26. Arthur W. Dunn, *The Community and the Citizen* (Boston: D.C. Heath, 1907). For an excellent account of the progressivism context of Dunn's book, see Reuben, "Beyond Politics," 401–404 especially. For further Dunn civics texts, see *Community Civics and Rural Life* (Boston: D.C. Heath, 1920) and *Community Civics for City Schools* (Boston: D.C. Heath, 1921).

27. Rolla M. Tryon, *The Social Sciences as School Subjects* (Report of the Commission on the Social Studies, American Historical Association, part XI) (Chicago: C. Scribner's Sons, 1935), 292.

28. Ibid., 311.

29. Ibid., 292–293.

30. Reuben, "Beyond Politics," 401. The Bureau of Education report in 1915, which presented a national guideline for high school teachers on how to teach civics, was particularly important. United States Bureau of Education, *Report on the Teaching of Community Civics*, Bulletin, Number 23 (1915). In Ziegler and Wilds, *Our Community: Good Citizenship in Towns and Cities*, iii, the authors,

both history and civics teachers in Philadelphia high schools, make reference to preparing their book in the style of the Bureau bulletin.

31. Charles E. Merriam, *Civic Education in the United States* (Chicago: University of Chicago Press, 1934), xiii.

32. *The Phi Delta Kappan* XV, no 5 (February 1933): 129.

33. Peter Roberts, *Civics for Coming Americans* (New York: Association Press, 1920), preface.

34. Gerd Korman, *Industrialization, Immigrants and Americanizers: The View from Milwaukee, 1866-1921* (Madison: State Historical Society of Wisconsin, 1967), 136.

35. See Charles F. Dole, *The New American Citizen* (New York: D.C. Heath & Co., 1918), which, although covering city life and government, also covers a remarkable amount of elements relation to the nation and state structure.

36. Reuben, "Beyond Politics," 405.

37. Ames and Eldred, *Community Civics*, 52.

38. Frank Trentmann, "Materiality in the Future of History: Thing, Practices, and Politics," *Journal of British Studies* 48 (April 2009): 306.

39. Frank Mort, "Fantasies of Metropolitan Life: Planning London in the 1940s," *Journal of British Studies* 43 (2004): 125.

40. Ibid., 124.

41. Mabel Hill and Phillip Davis, *Civics for New Americans* (Boston: Houghton Mifflin, 1915), iii.

42. Ibid., 33

43. Ibid., 27.

44. Reuben, "Beyond Politics," 405.

45. Roberts, *Civics for Coming Americans,* 50–51.

46. Ibid., 54.

47. Ames and Eldred, *Community Civics*, 26.

48. See George Rosen, "The First Neighborhood Center Movement," *American Journal of Public Health* 61 (1971) and Michael M. Davis, *Immigrant Health and the Community* (New York: Harper and Brothers, 1921).

49. Ames and Eldred, *Community Civics*, 53.

50. Edwin W. Adams, *A Community Civics: A Textbook in Loyal Citizenship* (Chicago: C. Scribner's Sons, 1920), 55.

51. Ames and Eldred, *Community Civics,* 26.

52. Roberts, *Civics for Coming Americans*, 51–52.

53. Ibid., 52.

54. Ashley, *The New Civics*, 13.

55. Ames and Eldred, *Community Civics,* 96.

56. Reuben, "Beyond Politics," 416.

57. Charles McCarthy, Flora Swan, and Jennie W. McMullin, *Elementary Civics: The New Civics* (New York: Thompson, 1918), 22–24.

58. Ames and Eldred, *Community Civics,* 61.

59. Roberts, *Civics for Coming Americans*, 54.

60. Hill and Davis, *Civics for New Americans,* 49.

61. Maria Kaika and Erik Swyngedouw, "Fetishizing the Modern City: The Phantasmagoria of Urban Technological Networks," *International Journal of Urban and Regional Research* 24, no. 1 (March 2000): 130.

62. Ibid., 129.

63. Ibid., 131–132.

64. Jon C. Teaford, *The Unheralded Triumph: City Government in America, 1870–1900* (Baltimore: Johns Hopkins University Press, 1984).

65. Ibid., 134.

66. William B. Munro, *Principles and Methods of Municipal Administration* (New York: Macmillan 1916), 4.

67. Education for Citizenship, *A report prepared by the Committee on Civic Education of the Superintendent's Advisory Council of the Chicago Public Schools* (March, 1933), 29–30.

68. *Suggestions to Instructors on a course in citizenship and language adapted to adults having little command of England who are applicants for citizenship—based on naturalization forms, student's textbooks, with lessons adapted to the Chicago standpoint* (Chicago, 1921).

69. Ibid., 5.

70. Ibid., 8.

71. Ibid., 27.

72. Ibid., 28.

73. Ibid., 30.

74. Ibid., 30.

75. Ibid., 27.

76. Ibid., 28.

77. Peter N. Stearns, *Battleground of Desire: The Struggle for Self-Control in Modern America* (New York: New York University Press, 1999), 20.

78. Chicago Commission on Citizenship Education, *Local Government in Chicago* [tentative draft of an outline] (1932).

79. While municipal government had notable success with municipal aviation in the interwar period, and Chicago was the headquarters of the Public Ownership League of America, there was constant distrust of municipal government because of its infamous corruption. Consequently, any municipal failure was jumped on as an indication of its winder unsuitability for ownership. The local press is the best medium to trace these attitudes—so far as I am aware, there is no recent study of municipal ownership in the city. For aviation, see "Chicago Gets Public Airport on School Land," *Chicago Tribune* [henceforth *CT*] (April 4, 1925) and "Chicago Puts Air Mastery Next on List," *CT* (December 14, 1927). For the negative attitudes displayed toward municipal ownership, see "A Sidelight on Municipal Ownership," *CT* (August 9, 1924); "Public Ownership," *CT* (March 24, 1924); "Give Black Eye to Municipal Ownership Idea," *CT* (November, 1933); "$1,500,000 City Garbage Plant Being Wrecked," *CT* (January 3, 1936); and "City Ownership Project to Fall Under Wreckers," *CT* (February 26, 1934).

80. Chicago Commission, *Local Government in Chicago*, 89.

81. Ibid., 90.

82. Ibid., 33.

83. Ibid., 2

84. *Adult Education Annual Report for 1937 Conducted by the Chicago Board of Education with cooperation of the Works Progress Administration* (1938), 3.

85. *Adult Education Annual Report*, 13.

86. Vernon Bowyer, "Some New Tendencies in Adult Education" (Talk given at Roseland Kiwanis Club, October 1, 1940), *Chicago History Museum*, Vernon Bowyer Papers, M1970, Box 2, Folder 14, page 2. See "Report: Special Committee appointed to study the authority, responsibilities and duties of the persons employed on the Adult Education Project of the Chicago Board of Education," January 1939 [Miscellaneous pamphlets on the Adult Education Program of the Work Projects Administration sponsored by the Chicago Board of Education], 1940, *Chicago History Museum*. "Introducing Association House" (1935), *Chicago History Museum*, Association House of Chicago Records, 1899–1972, MSS Lot A, Box 1.

87. "Have You Leisure Time? Why Not Make It Count?" (undated—late 1930s, early 1940s), *Chicago History Museum*, Vernon Bowyer Papers, M1970, Box 2, Folder 17.

88. [Miscellaneous pamphlets on the Adult Education Program of the Work Projects Administration sponsored by the Chicago Board of Education], 1940, You Are Invited to Visit Projects of the Professional and Service Division of the Work Projects Administration. Sponsored by the Education Department of the Chicago Board of Education During the Week of May 20–25, 1940, 2, *Chicago History Museum*.

89. Chicago Board of Education, Adult Education Program, A Guide for New Teachers, Prepared by Reuel G. Hemdahl, section 2 in Adult Education Council of Greater Chicago, [miscellaneous pamphlets), *Chicago History Museum*.

90. Reproduced by Work Projects Administration (IL) (March 11, 1937), page 1, *Chicago History Museum*, Vernon Bowyer Papers, M1970, Box 2, Folder 17.

91. It has not been possible to locate much teaching material used in this period of adult education. What lessons and lesson plans that can be found are in the Vernon Bowyer Papers held at the Chicago History Museum, though often material is undated or incomplete. Vernon Bowyer Papers, M1970 (Boxes 1–4), *Chicago History Museum*.

92. *Chicago History Museum*, "Social Studies Conference December 20 and 22, 1937 Central Y.M.C.A 19 South LaSalle St. Chicago, Illinois. Adult Education Program conducted by the Chicago Board of Education with the Cooperation of the Works Progress Administration" [Miscellaneous pamphlets on the Adult Education Program of the Work Projects Administration sponsored by the Chicago Board of Education], 1940, *Chicago History Museum*.

93. *Chicago History Museum*, M1970: Vernon Bowyer Papers Box 2, Folder 15, *Lesson 52* (Undated, likely late 1930s).

94. Ibid., *Lesson 53*

95. Ibid.

96. *Adult Education Annual Report for 1937,* 17.

97. Tryon, *The Social Sciences,* 282.

98. Armand J. Gerson, "The Social Studies in the Grades—1909–1929, *Historical Outlook, xx* (1929), 272.

99. See Bachin, "At the Nexus"; L. Cohen, *Making a New Deal: Industrial Workers in Chicago, 1919–1939* (Cambridge: Cambridge University Press, 1990), 28; W. Tuttle, *Race Riot: Chicago in the Red Summer of 1919* (New York: Athenaeum, 1970); T. L. Philpott, *The Slum and the Ghetto: Immigrants, Blacks, and Reformers in Chicago, 1890–1930* (New York: Oxford University Press, 1978), 162–180.

100. See the Municipal Voter's League, *Annual Preliminary Report* (Chicago, 1929); J. C. Teaford, *The Twentieth-Century American City: Problem, Promise and Reality* (Baltimore: The John Hopkins University Press, 1986), 49; H.F. Gosnell, *Machine Politics: Chicago Model* (Chicago: University of Chicago Press, 1937).

101. Marsden, *The School Textbook,* 130. The case of educationalist Harold Rugg is particularly illuminating in this respect. A leader of "the American social reconstructionist group of educators . . . deeply affected the social and economic downturns during the Great Depression," his textbooks introduced controversial themes relating to criticism of capitalism, the government and the military. Between 1938 and 1942, a vociferous censorship campaign was waged against him, as he was lambasted as "un-American," and accused of receiving funding from the Russian government. Marsden, *The School Textbook,* 175.

102. Ibid.

103. "Text Books in Mississippi," *Opportunity* 18 (1940), 99–100.

104. Pierce, *Citizens' Organizations and the Civic Training of Youth,* 251.

105. Ibid., 251.

106. Ernest Gruening, *The Public Pays: A Study of Power Propaganda* (New York: Vanguard Press, 1931), 18. This illuminating document was published by the Vanguard Press, a publishing house funded until the late 1930s by the left wing American Fund for Public Service. In it, Gruening details the investigation by the Federal trade commission into the propaganda of the public utilities.

107. For the Chicago Boosters' Publicity Club, by the Illinois Committee on Public Utility Information, *Chicago's Genii, The Public Utilities* (Chicago: Illinois Committee on Public Utility Information, 1921).

108. Ibid., 1.

109. Pierce, *Citizens' Organizations and the Civic Training of Youth,* 272.

110. Bukowski describes the official mouthpiece of the Club, *Greater Chicago,* as "a primer on modern propaganda technique." Douglas Bukowski, *Big Bill Thompson, Chicago and the Politics of Image* (Urbana: University of Illinois Press, 1998) 109. For examples of Thompson's municipal hypocrisy, see the report of the Public Ownership Conference held in Chicago in 1919, where Thompson sent a delegate to show he was "in favor of municipal ownership of the street rail-

ways." F. B. Ayers, representing Hon. William Hale Thompson, mayor of Chicago, "Plan for People's Ownership and Operation of Chicago Street Railway System," *Proceedings of Public Ownership Conference*, Bulletin No. 14, held in Chicago on November 15, 16, 17 (1919), 51.

111. James T. Sparrow, *Warfare State: World War II Americans and the Age of Big Government* (Oxford: University of Oxford Press, 2011), 3–5.

112. A. H. Spear, *Chicago: The Making of a Negro Ghetto* (Chicago: University of Chicago Press, 1967); M. W. Homel, *Down From Equality: Chicagoans and the Public Schools, 1920–1941* (Chicago: University of Illinois Press 1984); R. Biles, "Race and Housing in Chicago," *Journal of the Illinois State Historical Society* 94, no. 1 (2001): 32.

113. "Monthly Report, February 1939," Association House of Chicago Records, 1899–1972, MSS Lot A, Box 3, Folder 5. This report stated that "whites and blacks must be kept separate."

114. C. R. Reed, *The Chicago NAACP and the Rise of Black Professional Leadership, 1910–1966* (Bloomington: Indiana University Press, 1997); S. Nance, "Respectability and Representation: the Moorish Science Temple, Morocco, and Black Public Culture in 1920s Chicago," *American Quarterly* 54, no. 4 (2002); H. Sitkoff, *A New Deal for Blacks: The Emergence of Civil Rights as a National Issue* (New York: Oxford University Press, 1978).

115. C. R. Reed, *The Depression Comes to the South Side: Protest and Politics in the Black Metropolis, 1930–1933* (Bloomington: Indiana University Press, 2011), 67, 96; A. Meier and E. M. Rudwick, *CORE: A Study in the Civil Rights Movement, 1942–1968* (New York: Oxford University Press, 1973); M. T. Shockley, "Working for Democracy: Working-Class African Women, Citizenship, and Civil Rights in Detroit, 1940–1954," *Michigan Historical Review* 29, no. 2 (2003).

116. Michael Schudson, *The Good Citizen: A History of American Civic Life* (New York: Martin Kessler Books, 1998), 231–232, 250.

3

Latino Public School Engagement and Political Socialization

Marion Orr, Kenneth K. Wong, Emily M. Farris, and Domingo Morel

Public schools have long played a central role in the lives of new immigrants and other new arrivals to the city. Throughout much of the late 1800s and the early decades of the twentieth century, the urban public school system played a key role in acculturating immigrant children from Europe into American social and civic life. Although immigrant children created challenges for school leaders, urban school systems were credited for designing innovative programs to help the growing number of foreign students flowing into the schools. For example, in the late nineteenth century, Chicago and San Francisco officials implemented foreign language (German and French) instruction into the public schools.[1] In New York City, school Superintendent William Maxwell reorganized many of the city's schools to target assistance to the thousands of immigrant children entering the public schools. "He created a whole new range of services: special classes for the handicapped, school lunch programs, medical inspections, vocational training, vacation schools, and rooftop playgrounds for children."[2] In early 1900s, Newark, New Jersey, stood out as a national example of an urban school district that developed "innovative" programs to address the needs of immigrant children.[3] "As the number of foreign children swelled the schools, the school system received plaudits for a series of innovative programs designed to attract and hold the children of immigrants."[4]

Just as education was important to the immigrant communities of the early twentieth century, today public education is playing a significant role in the nation's growing Latino community. What is different today, however, is that a century ago a major reform was to take the public out of education. In those days, "progressive" reformers held that the professional educator could or should operate in isolation from the community.[5] Today, however, school reformers now look to members of the public to energize students and educators, secure additional resources, and improve school conditions. For example, while researchers acknowledge the complexity of the concept of "parental engagement," few educators would argue about the benefits of parental engagement in schooling.[6] In fact, schools have put in place structures and activities intended to support parental engagement. Examples of these activities include, but are not limited to, Parent Teacher Associations committees, scheduled teacher/parent conferences, school festivals, classroom or office volunteer activities for parents, and field trips. Parental engagement socializes children by sending a message to their children that education is important, and these children are more likely to value education themselves. Parental engagement, however, also provides parents with a means of social control; involved parents get to know other parents, teachers, and administrators.

In this chapter, we explore how urban school systems are playing an important political socialization role in the Latino community. We maintain that Latinos are important stakeholders in America's local public schools. Latino parents in particular are key constituents to the public schools. The old argument that Latino parents do not value education is simply not true. National polls consistently show that Latinos consider education an important aspect of their lives and believe in its ability to provide opportunities for upward mobility. According to a 2004 Pew Hispanic Center poll of Latino registered voters, education was ranked the number-one issue in determining Latino presidential voting preference.[7] In the 2006 Latino National Survey (LNS), the most recent comprehensive survey of Latino public opinion in the United States, when respondents were asked to choose "the most important problem facing the Latino community today," education ranked third, chosen by 9 percent of respondents, behind illegal immigration (30 percent) and unemployment/jobs (12 percent).[8] Findings from the LNS also show that large majorities of Latinos are actively engaged in their public schools.

In this chapter, we examine two related issues concerning Latinos: public schools and civic engagement. First, we probe deeper into the issue of Latino involvement in their local schools. The high percentage of Latinos who report that they are engaged in public schools goes against the grain of what we know about political and civic engagement. The standard model of political participation associates increased levels of education, income, and other resources with higher levels of public engagement. We are interested in determining the individual and contextual factors that predict whether Latinos are more likely to be actively engaged in their local schools. Second, we look more closely at Latino participation in political and civic life more generally and its relationship to public schools. Drawing on the policy feedback literature, we ask if involvement in one's local school has an impact on a person's level of political activity. We consider the institutional role public schools are playing in Latino politics and show how the nation's public schools are increasingly becoming the arena in which Latinos are becoming politically socialized.

To address these issues, we apply regression analysis to the 2006 Latino National Survey (LNS), which includes a randomly selected sample of 8,634 individual Latino respondents from fifteen states and Washington, DC. In the next section, we briefly describe the relationship between Latinos, political participation, and America's public schools. Next, we use results from the LNS to examine Latino perceptions of their local school. This is followed by a discussion of Latino participation in their local schools. We then explore Latino civic engagement more generally. In the final section, we offer some concluding comments.

Latino Political and Civic Engagement

The standard literature on civic and political participation shows that there are individual-level socioeconomic characteristics, such as education and income, that are highly correlated with levels of political participation.[9] Looking at the typical SES variables, education and income, Latinos lack the same resources as other racial or ethnic groups in the United States. Although at least 80 percent or more of the white, black, and Asian population complete high school before the age of twenty-five, only about 60 percent of Latinos graduate from high school before the age of twenty-five.[10] Also, Latinos have lower median household incomes ($37,913) than whites ($52,312), and, similarly, the poverty rate for Latinos (23.2 percent) is much higher than for whites (11.2 percent).[11] Given the limited income and educational attainment among Latinos, it is consistent with the resource model that most studies of Latino political participation find low levels participation among Latinos relative to other groups.[12] For example, the turnout rate of eligible Latino voters has historically lagged behind those of whites and blacks by substantial margins. In 2004, only

45 percent of eligible Latinos voted in the 2004 presidential election, a comparatively low rate when compared with those of blacks and whites.[13] According to the Pew Research Service, in 2008, 50 percent of eligible Latino voters cast ballots, compared with 65 percent of blacks and 66 percent of whites. Overall, 48 percent of Hispanic eligible voters turned out to vote in the 2012 presidential election. By comparison, voter turnout rate was 66.6 percent among blacks and 64.1 percent among whites, both significantly higher than the turnout rate among Hispanics.

A number of hypotheses have been offered to explain the low electoral participation of Latinos. A growing part of the literature looks beyond the traditional SES model to explain Latino political participation, bringing greater focus to group and contextual variables: linguistic and citizenship barriers, immigrant Latinos' ties to the politics of their home country, weak efforts of political parties in their recruitment and mobilization, and unfavorable districting and electoral rules.[14] Research on Latinos illustrates the number of factors beyond socioeconomic traits that help explain Latino political participation.

An alternative way to explain political participation looks at social networks and organizational participation. Verba, Schlozman, and Brady extend the traditional SES model to focus on how resources, engagement, and recruitment impact political participation.[15] They emphasize the ways in which "institutions—the families into which individuals are born, the schools they attend, the families they form as adults, the jobs they take, and the nonpolitical organizations and religious institutions with which they become affiliated—produce the factors that foster participation."[16] Verba and colleagues particularly note the church as an important institution in the development of black or African American civic skills.[17] The low participation rates of Latinos, a primarily Catholic group, can be explained in part by the fact that Catholics, unlike some Protestants, do not devote significant attention to developing their members' civic skills.[18] In recent years, churches in urban communities have become more responsive to their growingly diverse constituencies, including Latino immigrants. With declining enrollment, traditional Catholic schools are serving a larger percentage of urban minority students.

If the role of churches is mixed, what other social networks might Latinos develop as resources for political and civic engagement? Throughout American political history, immigrant groups have relied on organizational venues to gain access to the broader political and civic community. During the late nineteenth and early twentieth centuries, Irish and Italian immigrants were mobilized by local party machinery, or often referred to as political machines, to first gain citizenship and then turn out on election days.[19] In return for their electoral loyalty, local machine bosses rewarded the immigrant precincts with social services, jobs, and public work contracts. Today, however, political parties no longer commit the same resources to cultivate immigrant political incorporation.[20] Instead, other community organizations play an important in immigrant political development.[21]

Public Schools in Latino Political Life

Today, schools are one of the first community institutions immigrants come in contact with. Since 1990, Latinos' enrollment in public education has nearly doubled; now one of every five students is Latino.[22] This increase in enrollment accounts "for 60% of the total growth of public school enrollments" between 1990 and 2006.[23] While Latino enrollment has increased, white student enrollment has declined. From 2000 to 2008, white student enrollment in public schools decreased from 61 to 56 percent. At the same time, Latino student enrollment increased from 17 to 21 percent. All regions of the United States have seen Latino students' numbers increase. For example, the percentage of Latinos students in the South increased from 15 to 20 percent during that same time period. According to National Center for Education Statistics, in the 2007–2008 school year, a total of 10,237,009 Latinos were enrolled in public schools.[24] Nationally, Latino students are enrolling at unprecedented rates. As Latino enrollment increases, local public schools become an important place for Latino engagement.

For many people, public engagement starts at the local level around immediate concerns. As more and more Latino children enter the public schools, local education systems are increasingly providing many immigrants with their most direct exposure to a government institution. However, the political science literature on Latinos, politics, and schools has given much less attention to this micro-level, less formal mode of political engagement for Latinos. Instead, it has primarily focused on formal electoral process, primarily on the issue of Latino representation in school board elections.[25] Collectively, research shows the importance of the Latino presence in the educational system.

For Latino parents, particularly those who are immigrants, their first contact with the educational system is not with the school board but with the local schools their children attend. Michael Jones-Correa points out that schools "play a key role in the lives" of immigrant families, especially women.[26] John Ogbu's work details the different responses of minority and immigrant groups to the American educational system.[27] Faced with cultural and societal barriers such as discrimination, immigrant groups who migrated involuntarily have lower expectations for their children's success through education. Latinos today seem to relate more with voluntary immigrants, according to Ogbu's dichotomy, with higher expectations of schools.[28] Findings from the LNS also show that Latino parents are active in their schools and have high expectations for their children. One hundred percent of Latinos with children in schools reported in the LNS that they would like to see their child graduate from high school or attain a higher degree. Kasinitz and colleagues find that immigrant parents expect education to be "the only route out of poverty."[29]

Latino parental expectations and engagement are shown to be an important component of Latino students' success. Mounting scholarship demonstrates the important role of parents in supporting student learning outcomes.[30] However, as Noguera notes, parental engagement in schools can be limited by time constraints from work and limited English skills.[31] Carreón and colleagues describe the complexity of parental engagement in school affairs by exploring the different ways of understanding parental engagement or participation in schools.[32] Given the benefits of parental involvement for students, it is important to understand why parents are or are not involved. Moreover, we expect there is a benefit of parental engagement for the parents themselves, as schools become an important place for their own political learning and socialization.

Policy Feedback and Latino School Engagement

We are interested in the empirical question of whether, in the end, Latino parental engagement with local public schools "promotes or discourages . . . involvement in the day-to-day activities of American democracy."[33] The wide literature on policy feedback illustrates how policies and institutional design "can influence beliefs about what is possible, desirable, and normal."[34] Paul Pierson writes about political learning as a policy feedback.[35] Mettler observes that "[t]hrough features of their design, policies may shape beneficiaries' subjective experience of what it means to be a citizen, giving them a sense of their role, place, and value within the polity."[36] Much of the policy feedback literature focuses on national institutions and/or national policies. The G.I. Bill, for example, has been found to promote civic engagement and participation among veterans from less privileged backgrounds.[37] Andrea Campbell shows how another national program, Social Security, positively affected civic involvement of low- and moderate-income seniors.[38] On the other hand, while recipients of the G.I. Bill and social security show increased levels of participation, beneficiaries of means-tested social/welfare programs rarely participate in politics.[39]

Policy and institutional design may have either a positive or a negative feedback loop. Institutional arrangements can leave an imprint on those who interface with them and ultimately influence political learning and participation. Schools differ in that they have distinct cultures and unique histories. Some schools are more welcoming to parents than others. We know that the strongest and most consistent predictors of parent involvement in schools are specific programs and teacher practices that encourage parent engagement.[40] For example, schools in which teachers and administrators understand the cultural differences of immigrant children and incorporate multicultural strategies to enhance the growth of students are more likely to have a positive impact on Latino parental engagement.[41] Schools with Latino teachers and administrators "have a positive effect on the psychological orientations of Latino parents that lead to an increase in their involvement in both everyday school activities, such as PTA meetings and volunteering within the schools, and school governance structures."[42]

Political learning is a dynamic process that can produce positive learning conclusions and at other times engender lessons that generate negative conclusions. Annette Lareau examined how teachers and administrators interacted with parents at an inner-city high school. She found that parents felt rejected and looked down on.[43] One working-class mother in Lareau's study said she "felt bullied and powerless" when she visited teachers and principals.[44] When Latino and African-American parents in the Bronx complained that their children's schools lacked basic supplies and that students could not bring textbooks home, school officials were not only unresponsive, but they "also blamed parents for the school's poor performance." As one parent stated, "They treated us like we were kids—like we were uneducated and knew nothing about anything."[45] How might these parents consider their future role in the polity?

Hypotheses

This paper seeks to examine Latino parents' school participation and political engagement. From the extant literature, we generate the following hypotheses.

1. Latino parents who experience a welcoming school environment are more likely to be engaged in school activities.

Research has shown that teachers and administrators have a significant impact in setting the scope and nature of the relationship between schools and parents.[46] As a result, there is variation across schools in the kinds of experience parents encounter when interacting with their children's schools. Research shows, for example, that when teachers and administrators willingly identify and celebrate ethnic, language, and cultural differences, immigrant parents become more involved in school activities and are supportive of the schools. When parents sense that they are welcome and can contribute something of value, they become more involved in the work of the school and in the education of their children.[47]

2. Latino parents who have children who attend schools that have implemented specialized programs for English language learners are more likely to be engaged in school activities.

The research on policy feedback in political science offers strong empirical evidence that certain policies and institutional designs have measurable effects on outcomes such as political participation, a sense of civic belonging, and self-worth.[48] We assume that the presence of a specialized language program for Latino children will have the cognitive effect of signaling to Latino parents a level of linguistic and ethnic tolerance. In the context of a political environment in which many immigrants are experiencing linguistic chauvinism and anti-immigrant hostilities (Chavez 2008), the presence of a specialized language program for Latino children can have a positive effect on parental participation.[49]

3. As parental involvement in the schools increases, parents' political knowledge and political participation is more likely to increase.

Schools provide many Latino parents with their most direct exposure to a government institution. We assume that as Latino parents become more involved with their schools, they learn more about the structure and function of American political institutions. They learn, for example, that teachers report to principals, and principals are accountable to district-level officials. They learn about the role and function of local elected officials, like those on their local school board. We also assume that as Latino parental involvement increases, parents' sense of political efficacy increases. Research in political psychology shows that political efficacy is positively related to political knowledge and political participation.[50]

Data, Methods, and Findings

To examine Latino political and civic engagement, we use the 2006 Latino National Survey (LNS), which contains 8,634 completed interviews of self-identified Latino residents of the United States. Survey respondents were randomly selected from a sample of Latino households in fifteen states and Washington, DC. The survey was conducted in English and Spanish and included questions about political attitudes and experiences, policy preferences, and, of particular importance to our study, school-related questions. The range of questions in the survey allows us to link and explore variables that examine various aspects of political and civic participation.

The Latino National Survey primarily has been used by researchers to examine more traditional forms of political attitudes, identity, and behavior.[51] Embedded in the survey are interesting components of local politics linked to education that have not yet been explored. Our study proposes examining two sections of the LNS data that have not been previously linked: education data and data on the various forms of political behavior. The use of the data in this way has some limitations, however. The data are cross-sectional, not longitudinal. This only allows us to see if there is an association between our variables of interest instead of establishing any sort of causal relationship. Furthermore, as with any survey instrument, not all questions or variables are captured—as evidenced by the LNS principal investigators' follow-up work in focus groups.[52] We encourage other scholars to collect new data to explore our findings further. Although the data may have some limitations for our research questions, we view our project as an important exploratory study in assessing the relationship between Latinos' political behavior and school engagement.

We divide our analysis into three sections. First, we explore the factors behind the high level of parental engagement in schools, as reported in the LNS. Next, we test whether increased parental engagement by Latino parents in their children's school translates into a rise in political knowledge and increased participation in other areas of political and civic affairs. We provide an in-depth examination of each respective area and contribute to the expanding knowledge of Latino political and civic participation in the United States. We turn first to the factors that help predict Latino involvement in local schools.

Latino Parent Engagement in Schools

Schools are traditionally connected to the community and are a frequent place of contact for parents with public sector officials. Schools have been shown to be a place where people develop citizenship skills through their contact with principals, teachers, and other school officials.[53] Figure 3.1 shows that a majority of LNS respondents have participated in several school-related activities: meeting with their child's teacher, attending a PTA meeting, and volunteering in their child's school. In fact, 90 percent of all parents reported that they met with their child's teacher; 74 percent of the LNS respondents said they attended a PTA meeting; and more than half (52.4 percent) reported volunteering in their child's school.

We constructed a series of logit regression models to gain a better understanding of the factors that may influence school-related participation among Latinos. Specifically, we wanted to know what factors predict that a Latino parent reported that he or she 1) met with a teacher; 2) attended a PTA meeting; and 3) volunteered in the school. We included in the models several independent variables that might predict if a Latino parent would be involved in the three school activities: 1) English proficiency, 2) years in the United States (for Latinos born outside the mainland United States), 3) age, 4) gender, 5) income, 6) education, 7) US citizenship, and 8) gateway state. We include "gateway state" as an independent variable to examine whether Latinos in "traditional" destination states have a different experience than Latinos in "nontraditional" destination states. Karen Kaufman and Antonio Rodriguez (2011) argue that nontraditional destination states "currently present obstacles to the full political incorporation

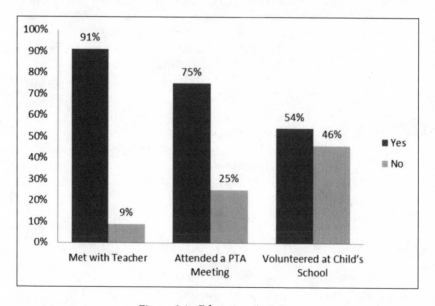

Figure 3.1. Education Activity.

of Latinos into the U.S. political system" (see Appendix A for the list of traditional and nontraditional destination states, wording of the questions in the survey, and descriptive statistics for each question).

Given the findings in the policy feedback literature that institutional design and contextual factors influence and structure the political behavior of those who interface with public programs, we included three school-related contextual variables to evaluate how these institutional factors might influence Latino parents' involvement in school activities. First, we included whether the school had a "specialized program for teaching English to Spanish-speaking" students (0 = No/1 = Yes). These are programs designed to address the specific linguistic and cultural needs of students whose first language is not English. Next, we included a variable that captures the nature of the experience parents had when they had contact with a school official ("Contact with school official" 0 = Not good/1 = Good). We also included "School Grade"—the grade that respondents gave to their community's public schools (A, B, C, D, or F). In addition to constructing the logit regression model, we also calculated odds ratios for each of the independent variables.

As shown in Table 3.1, various factors were important in the different school engagement activities. For example, age, being female, and the presence of ESL/ELL program were significant in explaining meetings

Table 3.1. Education Activity

	Odds Ratio (Standard Error)		
Independent Variable	Met with Teacher	Attended a PTA Meeting	Volunteered in Child's School
English Proficiency	1.37 (.247)	1.13 (.133)	**1.38 (.120)*****
Years in United States	1.05 (.149)	.976 (.094)	1.06 (.083)
Age	**.737 (.104)***	1.05 (.098)	.928 (.069)
Female	**2.86 (.658)*****	**1.62 (.253)****	**1.54 (.191)*****
Household Income	1.04 (.081)	1.01 (.055)	.957 (.039)
Education	1.12 (.076)	1.00 (.046)	**1.08 (.038)***
US Citizenship	1.10 (.317)	1.18 (.230)	**1.37 (.207)***
ESL/ELL Programs	**2.00 (.461)***	**1.45 (.248)***	1.10 (.158)
Contact with School Officials	1.15 (.535)	1.65 (.508)	1.60 (.450)
School Grade	1.03 (.114)	.997 (.073)	.968 (.058)
Gateway State	1.02 (.224)	1.13 (.168)	.942 (.110)

N=1,306
*p<.05, **p<.01, ***p<.001
Reported estimates with robust standard errors.

with teachers. Not all of these factors, however, were important in determining if a Latino parent attended a PTA meeting or volunteered in the
child's schools. In each of the three models, odds are that women are more
likely than men to be engaged in education activities. Women are nearly
three times more likely than men to have met with their child's teacher,
1.62 times more likely to have attended a PTA meeting, and 1.54 times
more likely to have volunteered at their child's school. The findings from
the education activity models demonstrate that Latinas are more likely to
be involved in their children's schools. These findings on Latina involvement in the schools are supported by the growing literature on political
participation that emphasize the importance of personal connections and
interests as the motivating factors for civic and political engagement, particularly for underrepresented and marginalized groups.[54]

In addition to the findings on gender, we also found that schools
with specialized programs for teaching English to Spanish-speaking children (ESL/ELL) increased the likelihood of parents meeting with their
child's teachers and attending a PTA meeting. This finding partly confirms
our second hypothesis: Latino parents with children who attend schools
that have implemented specialized programs for English language learners are more likely to be engaged in school activities. A parent is twice
as likely to attend a meeting with a teacher when the school has an ESL/
ELL programs than when it doesn't and 1.45 times more likely to attend
a PTA meeting. This is an important finding because the existing literature on Latino parental involvement in the schools often points to the
lack of Spanish-speaking and culturally sensitive programs as obstacles to
parental engagement.[55] These findings suggest that schools with specialized programs for Spanish-speaking populations are more likely to have
Latino parents involved. However, we did not find that the nature of
the contact with school officials, as we hypothesized, had any impact on
Latino parental engagement in the schools.

Latino Parent Involvement and Political Knowledge

Research has shown that the amount of information one possesses about
government and politics helps to explain a wide range of political behaviors, including turnout and voting.[56] "Politically knowledgeable individuals behave differently from those who are less knowledgeable, because they
possess a more tightly connected cognitive structure that allows them to
organize their political beliefs and ideology."[57] We are interested in the
connection between Latino parental involvement in public schools and
political knowledge.

To measure political knowledge, we use the question in the LNS that asked respondents about their knowledge of political parties and the US Congress. Respondents were asked: "Which political party, Democrat or Republican, has a majority in the U.S. House of Representatives?" To test the predictors of political knowledge, we included the same independent variables (English proficiency, years in the United States, age, gender, income, education, citizenship, and gateway state) as the previous model and add two new variables ("education activity" and "Latino linked fate"). In addition, we use an interaction term (education activity* female) because of our findings in the last model regarding Latina involvement in schools.

Education activity is a composite variable consisting of the three school-related dependent variables in the previous model (met with teacher, attended a PTA meeting, and volunteered in school). The variable has four values: have a child in school but did not participate in school activities = 0; child in school and participated in one activity = 1; child in school and participated in two activities = 2; child in school and participated in all three activities = 3. The other variable, "Latino linked fate," asks respondents: "How much does 'doing well' depend on how other Latinos are also doing well?"

Results from our political knowledge model (see Table 3.2) show that an increase in education activities is associated with an increase in the likelihood of answering the knowledge question correctly. In other words,

Table 3.2. Political Knowledge

Independent Variable	Coefficient (Standard Error)	Odds Ratio
Education Activities	**.233 (.107)***	**1.27**
English Proficiency	**.217 (.092)***	**1.24**
Years in United States	.080 (.081)	1.10
Age	.115 (.082)	1.12
Female	−.491 (.370)	.616
Household Income	.062 (.043)	1.06
Education	**.113 (.038)****	**1.12**
US Citizenship	.260 (.153)	1.30
Latino Linked Fate	**.283 (.076)*****	**1.33**
Education Activity* Female	−.093 (.156)	.911
Gateway State	.201 (.131)	1.22

N=1347
*p<.05, **p<.01, ***p<.001
Reported estimates with robust standard errors.

the more school activities LNS respondents were involved in, the more likely they were to know which political party controlled the US House of Representatives. Likewise, increases in level of English proficiency and education are also associated with an increase in the likelihood of answering the knowledge question correctly. Further, as feelings of "linked fate" increase, so do the odds of answering the question correctly. Latinos who believe that their "doing well" depends on how other Latinos are "doing well" are 1.33 more likely to answer the question correctly. Finally, we ran an interaction term to examine the relation between education activity and gender. The results of the interaction term are not statistically significant.

Latino Parental Involvement and Political/Civic Activity

To test for political activity, we ran three separate binary logit models that examine a continuum of political engagement measures. First, we examined if school engagement is related to a general interest in politics. A general interest in politics and political events is considered "a more passive form" of activity on a political participation continuum.[58] As a measurement of "passive" participation, we used the LNS question that examined the respondents' general interest in politics and public affairs. Respondents were asked, "How interested are you in politics and public affairs?" Next, we examined if school engagement is related to contacting a government official. Contacting a public official is considered by researchers to be "more instrumental or goal oriented" and hence more proactive, costly, and difficult than "passive" participation.[59] In the LNS, respondents were asked: "Have you ever tried to get government officials to pay attention to something that concerned you, either by calling, writing a letter, or going to a meeting?" We used this question in the model.

Finally, to help capture the unique nature and complexity of Latino political and civic participation, we included a model with a dependent variable that examined areas of political or civic participation *outside* government-related political engagement. It may be that Latino immigrants choose to participate by working with others to obtain a particular outcome rather than appealing directly to elected officials. Especially if they are undocumented, immigrants may choose to participate through protest or community organizing—not interfacing directly with government officials. The LNS asked respondents: "When an issue or problem needs to be addressed, would you work through existing groups or organizations to bring people together, would you get together informally, or would you do nothing to deal with this matter?" We constructed a regression model to measure the more "unconventional" mode of political participation.[60] In Tables 3.3 to 3.5, we present the results of the models designed to measure the impact of Latino parental involvement in schools on these areas of political behavior.

Interest in Politics and Public Affairs

Table 3.3 shows the results from the "passive" form of participation on general interest in politics and public affairs. The model shows that parents who engage in multiple education activities are 1.22 times more likely than a parent who does not engage in education activities to have an interest in politics and public affairs. This association is statistically significant. Increases in the level of English proficiency and education are also positively and significantly associated with an increase in the likelihood of having an interest in politics and public affairs as well. Feelings of Latino linked fate are also positively correlated.

Table 3.3. Interest in Politics and Public Affairs

Independent Variable	Coefficient (Standard Error)	Odds Ratio
Education Activities	**.202 (.073)****	**1.22**
English Proficiency	.366 (.092)***	1.44
Years in US	.043 (.079)	1.04
Age	−.036 (.075)	.965
Female	−.150 (.129)	.860
Household Income	−.020 (.042)	.980
Education	**.155 (.037)*****	**1.17**
U.S. Citizenship	−.003(.155)	.998
Latino Linked Fate	**.153 (.066)***	**1.16**
Gateway State	.071 (.120)	1.07

N=1347
*p<.05, **p<.01, ***p<.001
Reported estimates with robust standard errors

Contacting Public Officials

Table 3.4 shows the results of the model predicting the factors related to Latinos contacting government officials. Our findings from this model are consistent with much of the literature on political participation. We find that increases in level of English proficiency, income, education and years in the United States (for Latinos born outside the mainland United States) are all associated with an increase in likelihood of contacting a government official. In addition, being a US citizen and having feelings of linked fate with other Latinos is associated with an increase in the likelihood of contacting a government official. However, we also find that participating in education activities increases the likelihood of contacting a government official. The only negative correlation we find in this model is associated with gender. Our findings suggest that women are less likely than men to have contacted a government official. While our research demonstrates that women are more likely than men to participate in education activities, they are less likely than men to engage in this government-related political activity. This finding is not surprising. In a study of gender differences among Latinos, Hardy-Fanta found that Latinas were more likely to be involved in political activities that involved "affiliation, connection, and community" and were less likely to be involved in the more "traditional"

Table 3.4. Contact Government Official

Independent Variable	Coefficient (Standard Error)	Odds Ratio
Education Activities	.498 (.098)***	**1.65**
English Proficiency	.330 (.100)**	**1.40**
Years in United States	.180 (.090)*	**1.20**
Age	.045 (.088)	1.05
Female	−.312 (.144)*	**.732**
Household Income	.106 (.047)*	**1.11**
Education	.090 (.041)*	**1.10**
US Citizenship	.416 (.161)**	**1.52**
Latino Linked Fate	.170 (.085)*	**1.20**
Gateway State	.433 (.530)**	**1.54**

N=1,347
*p<.05, **p<.01, ***p<.001
Reported estimates with robust standard errors.

forms of political participation.[61] According to Hardy-Fanta, the impersonal elements of the traditional forms of political participation, combined with structural constraints that prevent full political participation, help create an environment where Latinas are more likely to participate in community-related political activities and less likely to participate in more formal modes of political involvement, like contacting a government official.

Finally, we find that Latinos who reside in a traditional destination state are more likely than Latinos in nontraditional destination states to have contacted a government official. This is the only model where we find a statistically significant difference between Latinos in traditional and nontraditional destination states.

Organizing With Others outside Government

Table 3.5 presents the results from the model designed to examine the potential for political and civic engagement outside the realm of government. Our dependent variable is whether or not the respondent organized through existing organizations or informally to address issues. Again, we find that participating in education activities is positively and significantly associated with political and civic engagement. Latino parents who engage

Table 3.5. Organize to Solve Problems

Independent Variable	Coefficient (Standard Error)	Odds Ratio
Education Activities	**.353 (.103)****	**1.42**
English Proficiency	.026 (.146)	1.03
Years in United States	.130 (.124)	1.14
Age	−.036 (.119)	.965
Female	−.057 (.203)	.944
Household Income	.042 (.071)	1.04
Education	**.122 (.055)***	**1.13**
US Citizenship	−.344 (.225)	.709
Latino Linked Fate	.077 (.098)	1.08
Gateway State	−.016 (.188)	.984

N=1,183
*p<.05, **p<.01, ***p<.001
Reported estimates with robust standard errors.

in multiple education activities are 1.42 times more likely than parents who do not participate in any activities to organize, formally or informally, to solve problems. In addition to education activities, we find that increases in level of education are also positively associated with organizing to solve problems.

Conclusion

In *Democracy in America*, Tocqueville emphasized the key role of states and local communities. This chapter started with the observation that urban schools have long been important local institutions. With a long history of local autonomy, America's public schools represent the purest of Tocquevillian impulses. Our chapter calls attention to the important role schools play as a political socializing mechanism for the nation's growing Latino community. We have shown that the presence of programs that address the cultural and linguistic needs of Latino children was significantly associated with their parents being involved in two of the three school activities reported in the LNS. Research supports the importance of parental involvement for improved student achievement, better school attendance, and reduced dropout rates regardless of socioeconomic background or ethnicity. Thus it is important to identify institutional designs that may improve parental involvement. Our findings are also part of a story about—and consistent with some of the literature on—policy feedback. Our findings demonstrate considerable feedback between policies in local schools and Latino political participation. Much of the literature on policy feedback, however, tends to focus on federal institutions and their federal-level programs. This chapter highlights that institutional design and contextual factors within a local school can have an effect on Latino parental engagement.

This chapter also considered how Latino parental engagement in schools impacts other political activities. The LNS allowed us to consider different dimensions of political participation. Using multiple regression analysis, we demonstrated a positive and significant connection between Latino parental involvement in schools and other political activities. It appears that Latino parental engagement is a strong predictor of whether or not a Latino parent shows an interest in politics and public affairs, organizes with others to address a civic problem, contacts a government official, and demonstrates some level of political knowledge.

Our findings have implications for the ongoing search for workable strategies to build "civic capacity" to address collective policy priorities. Civic capacity is about various sectors of the community coming together to solve major problems. Civic capacity is often viewed as out of the ordinary and that maintaining sustained civic engagement remains a challenge.[62] Our findings sharpen the role of local schools as the institutional mechanisms that form the basis for sustaining civic engagement. For example, as our study shows, Latino parents are twice as likely to meet with teachers and almost one and a half times more likely to attend PTA activities when schools implement specialized programs that address English language learners. Clearly an investment in these and other school-based initiatives will facilitate Latino engagement, thereby moving our democratic process in a productive direction.

Appendix A

Description of the Dependent Variables

Met with Teacher: Here is a list of things that some parents have done and others have not regarding their children's school. Which of these things have you done? Have you met with my child's teacher?

Values	Frequency	Percentage
0. No	245	8.7%
1. Yes	2,570	91.3%

Observations	Mean	Std. Dev.	Min.	Max.
2,815	.912	.281	0	1

Attended a PTA Meeting: Here is a list of things that some parents have done and others have not regarding their children's school. Which of these things have you done? Have you attended a PTA meeting?

Values	Frequency	Percentage
0. No	706	25.1%
1. Yes	2,109	74.9%

Observations	Mean	Std. Dev.	Min.	Max.
2,815	.749	.434	0	1

Volunteered in child's school: Here is a list of things that some parents have done and others have not regarding their children's school. Which of these things have you done? Have you acted as a school volunteer for your child's school?

Values	Frequency	Percentage
0. No	1,303	46.2%
1. Yes	1,512	53.7%

Observations	Mean	Std. Dev.	Min.	Max.
2,815	.537	.499	0	1

"Majority Party in US House": Which political party, Democrat or Republican, has a majority in the United States House of Representatives?

Values	Frequency	Percentage
0. Democrats/ Don't Know	5,123	59.3%
1. Republicans	3,511	41.0%

Observations	Mean	Std. Dev.	Min.	Max.
8,634	.407	.491	0	1

Variable was rescaled to a dichotomous variable. Original values were Democrat, Republican, and Don't Know. Because the correct answer was "Republicans," we combined "Democrats" and "Don't Know" into one value.

Interest in Politics and Public affairs: How interested are you in politics and public affairs?

Values	Frequency	Percentage
0. Not Interested	2,967	34.3%
1. Interested	5,667	65.6%

Observations	Mean	Std. Dev.	Min.	Max.
8,634	.656	.475	0	1

Variable was rescaled to a dichotomous variable. Original values were not interested, somewhat interested, and very interested.

Organize to Solve Problems: When an issue or problem needs to be addressed, would you work through existing groups or organizations to bring people together, would you get together informally, or would you do nothing to deal with this matter?

Values	Frequency	Percentage
0. Do nothing	1,630	21.84%
1. Use existing	5,834	78.2%

Variable was rescaled to a dichotomous variable (collapsed use existing organizations, get together informally, or both into one value).

Observations	Mean	Std. Dev.	Min.	Max.
7,464	.782	.413	0	1

Contacted Government Official: Have you ever tried to get government officials to pay attention to something that concerned you, either by calling, writing a letter, or going to a meeting?

Values	Frequency	Percentage
0. No	5,887	68.2%
1. Yes	2,747	32.0%

Observations	Mean	Std. Dev.	Min.	Max.
8,634	.318	.466	0	1

Appendix B

Description of the Independent Variables

English Proficiency: How good is your spoken English? Would you say you could carry on a conversation in English (both understanding and speaking) very well, pretty well, just a little, or not at all?

Values	Frequency	Percentage
1. Not at all	1,041	19.53%
2. Just a little	2,735	51.31%
3. Pretty well	860	16.14%
4. Very well	694	13.02%

Observations	Mean	Std. Dev.	Min.	Max.
5,330	2.23	.909	1	4

Years in US: The variable YEARS IN US is a recoded and rescaled variable from the original ARRIVEUS variable, which asks respondents: "When did you first arrive to live in the US [mainland]?"

Values	Frequency	Percentage
1. 0–10 Years	1,879	32.68%
2. 11–20 Years	1,687	29.34%
3. 21–30 Years	1,061	18.45%
4. 31–40 Years	593	10.31%
5. 41–50 Years	333	5.79%
6. 51–60 Years	152	2.64%
7. 61–85 Years	45	.78%

Observations	Mean	Std. Dev.	Min.	Max.
5,750	2.38	1.38	1	7

Age

Values	Frequency	Percentage
1. 18–25	1,483	18.22%
2. 26–35	2,092	25.70%
3. 36–45	1,828	22.45%
4. 46–55	1,268	15.58%
5. 56–65	831	10.21%
6. 66–75	439	5.39%
7. 75–85	182	2.24%
8. 86–97	18	.22%

Observations	Mean	Std. Dev.	Min.	Max.
8141	3.00	1.56	1	8

Gender (Female)

Values	Frequency	Percentage
0. Male	3,896	45.12%
1. Female	4,738	54.88%

Observations	Mean	Std. Dev.	Min.	Max.
8,634	.549	.498	0	1

Household Income: Which of the following best describes the total income earned by all members of your household during 2004?

Values	Frequency	Percentage
1. BELOW $15,000K	1,277	14.79%
2. $15,000–$24,999	1,529	17.71%
3. $25,000–$34,999	1,483	17.18%
4. $35,000–$44,999	1,680	19.46%
5. $45,000–$54,999	1,125	13.03%
6. $55,000–$64,999	529	6.13%
7. ABOVE $65,000	1,011	11.71%

Household income variable was recoded and rescaled.

Observations	Mean	Std. Dev.	Min.	Max.
8,634	3.63	1.87	1	7

Education: What is your highest level of formal education completed?

Values	Frequency	Percentage
1. Eight grade or below	1,936	22.42%
2. Some High School	1,256	14.55%
3. GED	286	3.31%
4. High School Graduate	2,110	24.44%
5. Some College	1,646	19.06%
6. Four-Year College Degree	818	9.47%
7. Graduate or Professional Degree	582	6.74%

Observations	Mean	Std. Dev.	Min.	Max.
8,634	3.59	1.91	1	7

ESL/ELL Program: Was there a specialized program for teaching English to Spanish-speaking children in your child's school?

Values	Frequency	Percentage
0. No	383	21.54%
1. Yes	1,395	78.46%

Observations	Mean	Std. Dev.	Min.	Max.
1,778	.785	.411	0	1

Contact with School Officials: When you have had contact with school officials, would you say your experience has been good or not good?

Values	Frequency	Percentage
0. Not Good	155	5.84%
1. Good	2,499	94.16%

Variable was rescaled to a dichotomous variable. Original values were very good, somewhat good, not too good, and not good at all.

Observations	Mean	Std. Dev.	Min.	Max.
2,654	.942	.235	0	1

Citizenship: Are you a naturalized American citizen?

Values	Frequency	Percentage
0. No	,3778	66.83%
1. Yes	1,875	33.17%

Observations	Mean	Std. Dev.	Min.	Max.
5,653	.332	.471	0	1

School Grade: What grade would you give your community's public schools: A, B, C, D, or FAIL?

Values	Frequency	Percentage
1. F	474	5.49%
2. D	470	5.44%
3. C	1,620	18.76%
4. B	3,257	37.72%
5. A	2,813	32.58%

Observations	Mean	Std. Dev.	Min.	Max.
8,634	3.86	1.10	1	5

Education Activity: "Education Activity" is a composite variable consisting of the three school-related dependent variables (met with teacher, attended a PTA meeting, and volunteered in School).

Values	Frequency	Percentage
0. Child in School and participated in 0 activities	136	4.8%
1. Child in School and participated in 1 activity	366	13.0%
2. Child in School and participated in 2 activities	1,114	39.6%
3. Child in School and participated in 3 activities	1,199	42.6%

Observations	Mean	Std. Dev.	Min.	Max.
2,815	2.20	8.42	0	3

Latino Linked Fate: "How much does 'doing well' depend on how other Latinos are also doing well?"

Values	Frequency	Percentage
1. Nothing	692	8.7%
2. Little	1,121	14.1%
3. Some	2,161	27.1%
4. Lot	3,998	50.1%

Observations	Mean	Std. Dev.	Min.	Max.
7,962	3.19	.977	1	4

Gateway State: State of residence.

Values	Frequency	Percentage
0. Nontraditional Destination State	3,216	37.25%
1. Traditional Destination State	5,418	62.75 %

Variable was rescaled to a dichotomous variable. **Nontraditional Destination States** (frequency in parentheses): Arkansas (401); Colorado (404); Georgia (400); Iowa (400); Maryland (166); Nevada (403); North Carolina (401); Virginia (176); Washington (403); and District of Columbia (62). **Traditional Destination States:** Arizona (400); California (1204); Florida (800); Illinois (600); New Mexico (400); New Jersey (403); New York (800); and Texas (811).

Observations	Mean	Std. Dev.	Min.	Max.
8,634	.628	.483	0	1

Notes

1. Paul E. Peterson, *The Politics of School Reform, 1870–1940* (Chicago: University of Chicago Press, 1985).

2. David B. Tyack, *Managers of Virtue: Public School Leadership in America, 1820–1980* (New York: Basic Books, 1982).

3. Jean Anyon, *Ghetto Schooling: A Political Economy of Urban Educational Reform* (New York: Teachers College Press, 1997).

4. Ibid., 47.

5. David B. Tyack, *The One Best System: A History of American Urban Education* (Cambridge: Harvard University Press, 1974).

6. Gustavos P. Carreón, Corey Drake, and Angela C. Barton, "The Importance of Presence: Immigrant Parents' School Engagement Experiences," *American Education Research Journal* 42 (2005): 465–498.

7. Pew Hispanic Center/Kaiser Family Foundation (2004), "2004 National Survey of Latinos: Politics and Civic Engagement," www.pewhispanic.org/files/reports/33.pdf.

8. Luis Fraga, John A. Garcia, Rodney Hero, Michael Jones-Correa, Valerie Martinez-Ebers, and Gary M. Segura (2006), Latino National Survey.

9. Angus Campbell, Philip Converse, Warren Miller, and Donald Stokes, *The American Voter* (New York: John Wiley & Sons, Inc., 1960); Sidney Verba and Norman Nie, *Participation in America: Political Democracy and Social Equality* (New York: Harper and Row, 1972); Raymond Wolfinger and Steven Rosenstone, *Who Votes?* (New Haven: Yale University Press, 1980).

10. US Census Bureau, Current Population reports (2009).

11. US Census Bureau, Current Population reports (2009).

12. Marisa A. Abrajano and R. Michael Alvarez, *New Faces, New Voices: The Hispanic Electorate in America* (Princeton: Princeton University Press, 2010).

13. Rodolfo O. de la Garza and Louis DeSipio, "Save the Baby, Change the Bathwater, and Scrub the Tub: Latino Electoral Participation after Seventeen Years of Voting Rights Act Coverage," *Texas Law Review* 71, no. 7 (1993): 1479–1539.

14. Rodolfo O. de la Garza, "Latino Politics," *Annual Review of Political Science* 7, no. 1 (2004): 91–123; Michael Jones-Correa, *Between Two Nations: The Political Predicament of Latinos in New York City* (Ithaca, NY: Cornell University Press, 1998); Daron Shaw, Rodolfo O. de la Garza, and Jongho Lee, "Examining Latino Turnout in 1996: A Three-State, Validated Survey Approach," *American Journal of Political Science* 44, no. 2 (2000): 338–346; Adrian D. Pantoja, Ricardo Ramirez, and Gary M. Segura, "Citizens by Choice, Voters by Necessity: Patterns in Political Mobilization by Naturalized Latinos," *Political Research Quarterly* 54, no. 4 (2001): 729–750; David Lublin, *The Paradox of Representation: Racial Gerrymandering and Minority Interests in Congress* (Princeton: Princeton University Press, 1997); Harry Pachon and Louis Desipio, "Latino Elected Officials in the 1990s," *PS: Political Science and Politics* 25, no. 2 (1992): 212–217; Rodolfo O. de la Garza and Louis DeSipio, *Muted Voices: Latino Politics in the 2000 Elections* (Lanham, MD: Rowman and Littlefield, 2005); Rodolfo O. de la Garza, Martha Menchaca, and Louis DeSipio, eds., *Barrio Ballots: Latino Politics in the 1990 Election* (Boulder, CO: Westview Press; 1994); Jane E. Leighley, *Strength in Numbers? The Political Mobilization of Racial and Ethnic Minorities* (Princeton: Princeton University Press, 2001).

15. Sidney Verba, Kay L. Schlozman, and Henry Brady, *Voice and Equality: Civic Voluntarism in American Politics* (Cambridge: Harvard University Press, 1995).

16. Verba, Schlozman, and Brady, *Voice and Equality*, 17.

17. Verba, Schlozman, and Brady, *Voice and Equality*; Fredrick C. Harris, *Something Within: Religion in African American Political Activism* (Oxford: Oxford University Press, 1999).

18. Verba, Schlozman, and Brady, *Voice and Equality*; Michael Jones-Correa and David L. Leal, "Political Participation: Does Religion Matter?," *Political Research Quarterly* 54 (2001): 751–770.

19. Steve Erie, *Rainbow's End: Irish Americans and the Dilemmas of Urban Machine Politics, 1840–1985* (Berkeley: University of California Press, 1988).

20. Kristi Andersen, "In Whose Interest? Political Parties, Context and Incorporation of Immigrants," in *New Race Politics in America: Understanding Minority and Immigrant Politics*, ed. Jane Junn and Kerry L. Haynie (New York: Cambridge University Press, 2008).

21. Janelle S. Wong, *Democracy's Promise: Immigrants and American Civic Institutions* (Ann Arbor: University of Michigan Press, 2006).

22. Richard Fry and Felisa Gonzales, "One-in-Five and Growing Fast: A Profile of Hispanic Public School Students" (Washington, DC: Pew Hispanic Center, 2008).

23. Fry and Gonzales, "One-in-Five and Growing Fast."

24. Susan Aud, Mary Ann Fox, and Angelina Kewal Ramani, "Status and Trends in the Education of Racial and Ethnic Groups" (NCES 2010-015), US Department of Education, National Center for Education Statistics (Washington, DC: US Government Printing Office, 2010).

25. Melissa Marschall, "Minority Incorporation and Local School Boards," in *Besieged: School Boards and the Future of Education Politics*, ed. William Howell (Washington, DC: Brookings Institution Press, 2005), 173–198; Rene R. Rocha, "Black-Brown Coalitions in Local School Board Elections," *Political Research Quarterly* 60 (2007): 315–328; Frederick M. Hess and David L. Leal, "School House Politics: Expenditures, Interests, and Competition in School Board Elections," in *Besieged: School Boards and the Future of Education Politics*, ed. Howell, 228–253; Kenneth J. Meier and Joseph Stewart, *The Politics of Hispanic Education: Un Paso Pa'Lante Y Dos Pa'tras* (Albany: State University of New York Press, 1991).

26. Jones-Correa, *Between Two Nations*, 176.

27. John U. Ogbu, *Black American Students in an Affluent Suburb: A Study of Academic Disengagement* (Mahwah, NJ: Lawrence Erlbaum Associates, Inc., 2003).

28. Ogbu, *Black American Students in an Affluent Suburb*.

29. Philip Kasinitz, John H. Mollenkopf, Mary C. Waters, and Jennifer Holdaway, *Inheriting the City: The Children of Immigrants Come of Age* (Cambridge: Harvard University Press, 2008).

30. Joyce L. Epstein and Susan Dauber, "School Programs and Teacher Practices of Parent Involvement in Inner-City Elementary and Middle Schools," *Elementary School Journal* 91 (1991): 289–305; Kathleen V. Hoover-Dempsey and Howard M. Sandler, "Parent Involvement in Children's Education: Why Does It Make a Difference?," *Teachers College Record* 97 (1995): 310–331; Gail Zellman and Jill Waterman, "Understanding the Impact of Parent School Involvement on Children's Educational Outcomes," *Journal of Educational Research* 91 (1998): 370–380; Mavis Sanders, "The Role of 'Community' in Comprehensive School, Family, and Community Partnerships," *Elementary School Journal* 102 (2001):19–34; Xitao Fan and Michael Chen, "Parental Involvement and Students' Academic Achievement: A Meta-Analysis," *Educational Psychology Review* 13 (2001):1–22; William H. Jeynes, "A Meta-Analysis: The Effects of Parental Involvement on Minority Children's Academic Achievement," *Education and Urban Society* 25 (2003): 202–218; William H. Jeynes, "A Meta-Analysis on the Relation of Parental Involvement to Urban Elementary School Student Academic Achievement," *Urban Education* 40 (2005): 237–269.

31. Pedro Noguera, "Latino Youth: Immigration, Education, and the Future," *Latino Studies* 4 (2006): 313–320.

32. Gustavo P. Carreón, Corey Drake, and Angela C. Barton, "The Importance of Presence: Immigrant Parents' School Engagement Experiences," *American Educational Research Journal* 42 (2005): 465–498.

33. Suzanne S. Mettler, "Bringing the State Back in to Civic Engagement: Policy Feedback Effects of the G.I. Bill for World War II Veterans," *American Political Science Review* 96 (2002): 351–365.

34. Joe Soss and Sanford F. Schram, "A Public Transformed? Welfare Reform as Policy Feedback," *American Political Science Review* 101 (2007): 111–127.

35. Paul Pierson, "When Effect Becomes Cause: Policy Feedback and Political Change," *World Politics* 45 (1993): 595–628.

36. Mettler, "Bringing the State Back in to Civic Engagement," 351–385.

37. Mettler, "Bringing the State Back in to Civic Engagement," 351–385.

38. Andrea L. Campbell, *How Policies Make Citizens: Senior Citizen Activism and the American Welfare State* (Princeton: Princeton University Press, 2003).

39. Joe Soss, "Lessons of Welfare: Policy Design, Political Learning, and Political Action," *American Political Science Review* 93 (1999): 363–380.

40. Joyce L. Epstein, *Schools, Families and Community Partnerships* (Boulder, CO: Westview Press, 2001).

41. A. Y. Fred Ramirez, "Dismay and Disappointment: Parental Involvement for Immigrant Parents," *Urban Review* 35 (2003): 93–110.

42. Paru Shah, "Motivating Participation: Estimating the Impact of Symbolic Representation on Latino Parent Involvement," *Social Science Quarterly* 90 (2009): 212–230.

43. Annette Lareau, *Unequal Childhoods: Class, Race, and Family Life* (Berkeley: University of California Press, 2003).

44. Lareau, *Unequal Childhoods*.

45. Kavitha Mediratta and Jessica Karp, *Parent Power and Urban School Reform: The Story of Mothers on the Move* (New York: Institute for Education and Social Policy, New York University, 2003).

46. Epstein, *Schools, Families and Community Partnerships*.

47. Ramirez, "Dismay and Disappointment," 93–110.

48. Soss, "Lessons of Welfare," 363–380; Mettler, "Bringing the State Back in to Civic Engagement," 351–385; Leo R. Chavez, *The Latino Threat: Constructing Immigrants, Citizens, and the Nation* (Stanford, CA: Stanford University Press, 2008).

49. Campbell, *How Policies Make Citizens*.

50. M. Margaret Conway, *Political Participation in the United States*, 3rd ed. (Washington, DC: Congressional Quarterly Press, 2000).

51. For a survey of some of the latest research using the LNS, see the collection of essays in Tony Affigne, Evelyn Hu-DeHart, and Marion Orr, eds., *Latino Politics en Ciencia Politica: The Search for Latino Identity and Racial Consciousness* (New York: New York University Press, forthcoming).

52. Luis Fraga, John A. Garcia, Rodney Hero, Michael Jones-Correa, Valerie Martinez-Ebers, and Gary M. Segura, *Latino Lives in America: Making It Home* (Philadelphia: Temple University Press, 2010).

53. Verba, Schlozman, and Brady, *Voice and Equality*, 411–413; Marion Orr and John Rogers, "Unequal Schools, Unequal Voice: The Need for Public Engagement for Public Engagement for Public Education," in *Public Engagement for Public Education: Joining Forces to Revitalize Democracy and Equalize Schools*, ed. Marion Orr and John Rogers (Stanford, CA: Stanford University Press, 2011).

54. Hahrie Han, *Moved to Action: Motivation, Participation and Inequality in American Politics* (Stanford, CA: Stanford University Press, 2009).

55. Luis Ricardo Farga and Ann Frost, "Democratic Institutions, Public Engagement, and Latinos in American Public Schools," in *Public Engagement for Public Education*, ed. Orr and Rogers, pp. 117–138.

56. Michael X. Delli Carpini and Scott Keeter, *What Americans Know about Politics and Why It Matters* (New Haven: Yale University Press, 1996).

57. Abrajano and Alvarez, *New Faces, New Voices: The Hispanic Electorate in America*, 102.

58. M. Margaret Conway, *Political Participation in the United States* (Washington, DC: Congressional Quarterly Press, 2000), 9.

59. Conway, *Political Participation in the United States*, 3.

60. Conway, *Political Participation in the United States*, 4.

61. Carol Hardy-Fanta, *Latina Politics, Latino Politics: Gender, Culture, and Political Participation in Boston* (Philadelphia: Temple University Press, 1993).

62. Clarence N. Stone, Jeffrey R. Henig, Bryan D. Jones, and Carol Pierannunzi, *Building Civic Capacity The Politics of Reforming Urban Schools* (Lawrence: University of Kansas Press, 2001).

4

Farewell to the Urban Growth Machine

Community Development Regimes in Smaller, Distressed Cities

Richard A. Harris

The New Jersey Partnership for Healthy Kids-Camden would like to thank the members of the Core Planning Team for their direction, assistance and support during the planning phase. Members of the Core Planning Team represent the following institutions and organizations: the Co-Director Institutions, YMCA of Burlington and Camden Counties and United Way of Camden County, Campbell Soup Company, Camden Coalition of Healthcare Providers, Cooper University Hospital, Rutgers Cooperative Extension of Camden County, University of Medicine and Dentistry of New Jersey and Woodland CDC.

We also wish to thank our consultants at Rutgers University-Camden, The Walter Rand Institute for Public Affairs for their guidance and development of the Community Strategic Plan and CAMConnect for their support on data and mapping. Special thanks to The New Jersey YMCA State Alliance-State Program Office for their technical assistance and support throughout the planning phase and guidance in preparation for the implementation phase. We also wish to thank Campbell Soup Company for their investment to The New Jersey Partnership Healthy Kids-Camden and the City of Camden.

Finally, we thank our pilot sites for their participation and dedica-
tion to this initiative. Our sites include Cooper's Poynt School, Early
Childhood Development Center, Forest Hill Elementary School, Holy
Name School, Parkside United Methodist Church and Respond, Inc.
[From New Jersey Partnership for Healthy Kids-Camden Strategic
Plan].

The long epigram above is quoted from a strategic plan for improving
the health of youth in Camden, New Jersey, and the set of participants
named throughout provides some powerful clues as to the contours of a
new kind of "urban regime" operating in that city.[1] One other critically
important institutional actor in the New Jersey Partnership for Healthy
Kids-Camden (NJPHK–C), not mentioned in the excerpt, is the Robert
Wood Johnson Foundation, which has funded this effort as well as similar
ones in several other New Jersey localities. Remarkably, this broad-based
initiative marshaling the resources of a major philanthropic organization, higher education, health care providers, community and faith-based
nonprofits, public schools, county-level social service organizations, and
the Campbell Soup Company included neither the mayor nor the City
Council of Camden in its process of setting a sweeping quality-of-life
agenda for the city. To be sure, the mayor and council members were kept
informed of the planning activities as they unfolded. No elected leaders,
however, or their representatives served on the core planning team that
framed and organized the program.

This scenario contrasts sharply with decades of urban governance
scholarship that documented the widespread existence of a tight mutual
dependence between business and municipal government, constituting
a regime and controlling city agendas and policy making.[2] Social science theorists have characterized this relationship as an "urban growth
machine," a variant of the business dominance model of politics, in which
urban economic elites, especially those tied to real estate development,
partner with elected leaders to assure a policy agenda dedicated to the
physical development of the city.[3] As urban sociologist Harvey Molotch
points out, this policy model elevates the "exchange value" of land over
the "use value" of land. Exchange value, he explains, is central to the
profit motive of private capital and to municipal leaders' need to attract
external investment, while use value refers to the assessment neighborhoods and citizens apply their physical environment and quality of life.[4]
Urban regimes, based on a framework of exchange valuation, were seen as

typifying an elite-based, non-decisions model of policy making in which influence is exercised privately by a business-government bloc that funnels city resources and external investment to a growth agenda and suppresses issues rooted in use valuation.[5] In the post–World War II world, this model fit Camden quite well. As the commercial, retail, political, and cultural hub of southern New Jersey, boasting a manufacturing sector that employed tens of thousands in a city of just over 100,000, Camden displayed the classic elements and behaviors of an urban growth machine. In Camden, though, as in many cities in the Northeast and Midwestern rust belt, familiar patterns of deindustrialization and suburban sprawl moved into high gear by the 1970s and undermined the city's economic and political institutions.

By the end of the 1980s, the private sector in Camden had been decimated. Major manufacturers such as RCA Victor, the New York Shipbuilding Corporation, and Esterbrook Pen Corporation shuttered their Camden facilities.[6] Smaller businesses as well as retailers moved to newer suburbs following the exodus of largely white, middle and upper-middle class homeowners who provided their customer base. Campbell Soup Company maintains its world headquarters in Camden but closed its huge waterfront processing facility. Not surprisingly, business associations such as the Camden Chamber of Commerce and Rotary Club, which provided an important organizational base of the growth machine, withered in membership and influence. The Camden Chamber of Commerce reconstituted itself in 1999 as a local chapter of the Greater Cherry Hill Chamber of Commerce, an eloquent testament to the effects of sprawl and deindustrialization on Camden's former economic preeminence. While this history of manufacturing and commercial decline manifested itself across America's urban landscape in the late twentieth century, smaller manufacturing-centered economies like Camden were particularly hard hit. More importantly for our purposes, without a robust and well-organized private sector to function as the ideological and policy driver of the urban regime, the concept of an urban growth machine lost a good deal of its descriptive and explanatory traction.

Paralleling the economic decline of Camden and the attendant erosion of its tax base, the city government lost not only clout in state and regional politics but also a good deal of its capacity to effectively deliver municipal services.[7] Camden, of course, represents an extreme case of political and administrative deterioration, which resulted in and was exacerbated by voter disengagement.[8] Following years of mounting structural deficits, the state of New Jersey installed a chief operating officer (COO) for the city and conferred extraordinary powers on the individual holding that office, including the authority to veto minutes of the planning and zoning boards, to eliminate municipal departments, to appoint new department directors, and to override actions of the mayor or City Council.[9] In the period from 2001 to 2008, under the Municipal Rehabilitation and Economic Recovery Act (MRERA), Camden's government was subordinated to the COO, who was charged with rebuilding both the governmental and economic bases in Camden. Backed with a $175,000,000 infrastructure fund and given direct control of the Camden Redevelopment Authority, the COO could act as a state-appointed czar, supplanting local political leadership, reorganizing municipal government functions, and negotiating deals with potential private investors. The intent of the legislation was to give the COO up to five years to put the city government on a sound footing and set the private sector on a course to recovery.[10] At the end of five years, the state was to assess progress and decide whether to cede authority back to local officials or retain its COO for another five-year stint.

In retrospect, however, the MRERA may be viewed as a quixotic attempt to reconstitute Camden's growth machine. The COO, with state support, in fact merged the City Department of Planning with the Redevelopment Authority, thereby centralizing control of economic and land development under his direct control in an effort to reassure potential investors of a sympathetic hearing and timely responses. Unfortunately for the COO, given his enormous responsibilities and no regular budget beyond basic operational expenses plus salary for himself and an assistant, MRERA amounted to an unfunded mandate to remake Camden. While the COO's office was able to garner additional state funds for projects, each ask required the specific approval of the state treasurer, which became harder and harder as New Jersey's fiscal situation deteriorated. In addition, beyond the historical reality that urban regimes developed organically from below rather than artificially from above, reestablishing a growth machine in Camden (or similarly situated cities) would prove chimerical in part because a new kind of urban regime, a regime without the business-government nexus that defined the old urban growth machine, was emerging in Camden (and elsewhere). Even before the enactment of the MRERA, institutional and nonprofit actors in Camden as well as other levels of government had become accustomed to working around rather than through City Hall. Indeed, a coalition of hospitals, universities, regional actors, and faith-based and community organizations worked with Trenton to craft the MRERA in opposition to the sitting mayor and

City Council. And it must be noted that a significant percentage of the $175 million infrastructure fund went to construction projects earmarked for large nonprofit institutions in that coalition. Given its members' level of concern about the local government's capacity to provide municipal services or respond effectively to private investors with an interest in Camden, this coalition saw in the MRERA an opportunity to establish a more effective and responsive local administration while simultaneously engaging the state directly in funding the development needs of hospitals, universities, and waterfront opportunities on the Delaware River. The state saw the MRERA as an opportunity to fix Camden's structural deficit and thereby sharply reduce the transfer of public funds from suburban voters to the urban core. In effect, the MRERA recognized and legitimated a new urban regime that was already taking root in Camden, one that included, at its core, neither the local government because it was deemed nonresponsive nor the private sector that was essentially nonexistent.

The hypothesis or, perhaps more appropriately at this early exploratory phase, the claim, advanced in this chapter is that the late twentieth-century political-economic decline in the United States has affected smaller distressed cities especially acutely, fostering the emergence of a "community development regime," a governing arrangement based more on the concept of use value than exchange value. Urban scholars have long noted that we live in an urban-centric society. At the time of the 2000 census, 60 percent of the US population resided in cities of 200,000 or more. However, this 60 percent lived in only 153 municipalities. On the other hand, 20 percent of the population resided in urban jurisdictions ranging between 5,000 and 199,000 people, covering 2,148 municipalities.[11] While the media are drawn to the economic and fiscal deterioration of major cities, state governments and astute observers of urban affairs recognize that the plight of more than 2,000 local governments, without the human, financial, or physical capital of larger units, creates "wicked" policy problems and at times a political imperative to intervene. If the continued socioeconomic pressure on these smaller cities generated by decades of suburban sprawl and technological innovation created their distress, the 2008 housing bubble and ensuing financial meltdown intensified it, wreaking havoc on municipal revenue and causing alarming layoffs and service reductions, especially in police and fire departments in smaller cities. In the wake of these historical trends and recent phenomena, municipalities such as East St. Louis, Benton Harbor, and Camden found themselves bereft of a vital private sector, while their place-bound institutions and community organizations that remained could not supply local government with the same level of revenue or electoral support as private business. In addition, the transaction costs (for both sides) of building and sustaining a strategic partnership between local government and nonprofit actors are much higher than those faced by elected leaders and a healthy, well-organized business community.[12] Thus, the mutual dependence between business and government that defines a classic urban regime is no longer in play for these smaller distressed cities, at least not at the same level of efficacy.

Camden, of course, is not unique. Rather, like other smaller distressed cities, it is characterized by a new urban regime typified by the NJPHK-C or the coalition that supported the MRERA, and markedly different from the concept as delineated in common academic usage of the term. In fact, the institutional membership of NJPHK-C and the MRERA coalition overlapped, indicating that the same set of actors was engaged in social as well as economic policy arenas. Unlike the urban growth machine, managed by an insular business-government partnership that sacrifices community or citizen preferences on the altar of economic development, the new regime does focus on the use value of land and is defined by wider partnerships that tackle a range of common problems. Stated baldly, in smaller distressed cities stripped of a healthy private sector, municipal government is reduced to a situational variable for an emergent community development regime, defined by alliances between higher-capacity nonprofits, including faith-based organizations, and some combination of state government, federal agencies, and major philanthropic organizations with technical assistance from universities or think tanks. This new regime type, despite its attention to use value and civic engagement, excludes not only elected officialdom but also the electorate itself from meaningful roles in agenda setting or policy design.

From a normative standpoint, then, the fundamental political science issue posed by the new community development regime mirrors the classic complaint leveled against the old urban growth machine, namely that democratic accountability and popular sovereignty are at best fig leaves when it comes to core matters of governance. Given the decline in voter participation in cities like Camden, community development regimes redefined principles of accountability from a traditional electoral politics foundation to a new basis rooted in civic engagement,[13] but the general citizenry's voice remains a muted one in agenda setting and policy design. Indeed, the community development regime may be more insidious than its predecessor because civic engagement requires sustained involvement without the ready incentives of patronage and side payments or the regularity of scheduled opportunities for voting available in electoral politics. Thus, citizens in practice are engaged sporadically and instrumentally, ordinarily in the stages of an initiative to garner their input—a model of democracy that offers thin gruel indeed for accountability or legitimacy. The original impetus for political scientists' interest in urban regime theory was, of course, the concern that, despite elections, citizens were essentially cut out of agenda setting and policy decisions, which were monopolized by government and business leaders. In the new regime, citizens may also be frozen out, albeit by a different and more overtly civic-minded set of relationships.

This exploration of a new urban regime type proceeds in four steps. It begins with a brief review of traditional urban regime theory, pointing out its essential characteristics and explaining its limited continuing applicability in the case of smaller distressed cities. Second, it elaborates the character and implications of the new variant I believe is taking hold and describes the national network and conversation that is shaping community development policy. Third, it presents an overview of the community development regime's operational character by expounding specific initiatives in Camden across three policy domains: public health, public safety, and physical development. As noted above, Camden presents an extreme case, given the degree of its political-economic decline. Camden, therefore, approximates an ideal typical community development regime. Urban regimes may vary in composition from city to city, some exhibiting alliances and behaviors that bear a resemblance to classical urban growth machines, while others closely approximate Camden, and still others exhibit a mixed-regime model with strong elements of both community development and growth. The appearance and vigor of a community development regime correlates inversely with the size and economic health of a city; those cities are the most fertile ground for community development regimes to blossom precisely because they are the least fertile ground for effective government and private investment to take root. Moreover, state governments are more likely to intervene and encourage such regimes in smaller distressed cities as a strategy to reduce or at least increase the efficiency of state aid. The analysis concludes with some observations and speculation about the political, policy, and theoretical challenges posed by urban regimes in small, distressed cities.

Urban Regimes Revisited

Urban regimes, of course, are distinguished from urban politics in that the former set strategy, agendas and rules of the game rather than merely resolve competing demands for programs, projects, or patronage.[14] These regimes are defined by systems of governance rather than government activity per se and, in the classic formulation, are characterized by mutual dependence between local government and business interests. Government, directed by elected politicians, relies on the private sector for a level of business performance to satisfy residents and voters, to husband resources necessary for growth and development, and to assure a healthy tax base. Business, in turn, depends on government to provide municipal services, to assist in policy and regulatory compliance, and to address specific needs in support of the urban growth machine. Most importantly, though, business and government leaders together set the policy agenda, deciding on what is legitimate for political discourse and what is not. While the nexus of local government and business elites provides the growth machine's core, its real-world efficacy depends, albeit to a lesser extent, on buy-in from: 1) state and federal authorities that provide judicial, regulatory, and statutory support for growth policy as well as direct infrastructure investment; 2) print, television, and radio outlets that provide positive coverage of physical development both as a source of local or regional pride and as an antidote to urban decay; and 3) private capital with the mobility and reserves to support major land development projects. As Clarence Stone explains, under an urban regime "[t]he capacity to build, modify or reinforce governing arrangements requires resources and skills that are not widely available. Inequalities in that capacity are substantial, systemic and persistent, qualities that run counter to classic pluralism's idea of an open and penetrable system."[15] In general, elected urban leaders depend on business because government alone does not control resources necessary to achieve their policy or political goals. Stone is not a dogmatic economic determinist and cautions that business dominance or even prominence depends on the issues in play as well as the level of community mobilization. Nevertheless, he concludes that,

> [i]n U.S. localities, for many structural reasons, business typically has a heavy presence in local civic life. The character of land ownership and of land-use planning, the nature of the system of taxation and revenue distribution, the pattern of city-suburb relations, and the importance of private credit to public borrowing are among the contributors to this pattern. . . .[16]

Urban regime theory rests ultimately on a mutually dependent business-government relationship defining the core of urban governing arrangements.

Stephen Elkin portrays this mutual dependence as characteristic of a "commercial republic" in which business enjoys a "privileged position" in politics. At the national level in 2008–2009, this commercial republic and business privilege were paraded before our eyes in the form of the Troubled Asset Relief Program (TARP) bailouts, the rescue of the American auto industry, and the influence of banks and insurance firms on financial and health care reform, all against a backdrop of unemployment, declining real wages, concerted attacks on public employee benefits and bargaining at the state level, and proposed draconian cuts in federal spending on programs that serve the working poor and middle class. Elkin suggests, however, that the commercial republic is best observed and may have its most pernicious impact in urban government. It is at this level where the threat of capital mobility and the fierce competition for tax-ratable property puts business in a truly privileged position and effectively deals the residents and neighborhood leadership out of agenda setting and policy design. The practical problem this situation presents for Elkin is how to construct political institutions, indeed a regime, that meaningfully engages the voting public in policy deliberation, thereby limiting the extent of business hegemony and preserving popular sovereignty. He sees the local urban setting as the prime venue for such deliberative engagement, with the important caveat that urban political systems should have the capacity to serve this function, "except in the unlikely case that localities are counted as financial wards of the central government, thus making the question of economic vitality moot, at least for the locals."[17] At the time Elkin was writing, 1994, this case may have seemed a rarity; it is not so now.

Camden is but one example that qualifies as a "financial ward," of the state government, a fact amplified by the enactment of the MRERA. Even disregarding its recent period of direct state supervision, which ended in 2010, the fact that the vast majority of its revenues still come from external federal and state aid amply demonstrates the structural character of its fiscal dependence. Currently, Benton Harbor, Michigan, is subject to its own state intervention that effectively prorogues its elected government. Like Camden, Benton Harbor is a predominantly minority community (approximately 90 percent African American versus Camden, which is roughly 55 percent African American and 35 percent Latino). Whirlpool Corporation is Benton Harbor's version of Campbell Soup Company, maintaining a headquarters while moving manufacturing facilities outside the United States in pursuit of lower labor costs and helping to gut the municipal tax base in the process. The government and schools of Benton Harbor, similar to Camden, lack the capacity to deliver acceptable levels of service. As with Camden, the state appointed a management czar, in this case with even more far-reaching powers than the Camden COO position: the state manager may void existing labor contracts, sell city assets, and unseat local pension boards. No spending, taxing, or capital actions, moreover, could be taken without his approval. East St. Louis, Illinois, provides another good example of a small, distressed city, deindustrialized and devoid of adequate fiscal capacity. As in the cases of Camden and Benton Harbor, a major multinational corporation, Monsanto, once part of the political-economic fabric of the city, has pulled out, but not by closing its manufacturing plant. In this instance, Monsanto employed the strategy of working with the state legislature to incorporate a separate municipality, Sauget, Illinois, which it occupies with processing facilities for a copper company and a zinc manufacturer.[18] Sauget abuts East St. Louis, insulated from its taxing authority and any accountability to the city for the substantial environmental externalities it inflicts on that community. East St. Louis, like Camden and Benton Harbor, has regressed to a relationship with the state amounting to financial receivership. It is ultimately dependent on aid from Springfield for basic functions. Illustrative of this dependency, in 1989, then-Governor James Thompson insisted that the mayor and city council resign as a condition of receiving emergency state aid. Cities such as these clearly fall into Elkin's category of "financial wards of the central government" and are far beyond the chance of any local initiative improving their economic vitality; we are as likely to find a unicorn as an urban growth machine in such communities.

State interventions in Camden and comparable cities are merely a logical response to long-simmering structural problems that, for all intents and purposes, make such cities de facto financial wards of the state, even without direct political takeover. Once a municipality depends substantially on state aid and federal grants for providing basic services, the concepts of a commercial republic or the classical urban regime with its attendant growth machine become much less relevant to our understanding of urban governance. While Elkin's caveat is crucial for precisely this reason, it need not be asserted in stark, either/or terms. The mutual dependence between business and local government that classically defines an urban regime turns, of course, on the presence of a robust private sector. If the private sector is not eviscerated and government capacity is not drastically compromised, as they were in Camden, Benton Harbor, and East St. Louis, vestiges of a classic urban regime may persist. In larger cities with substantial and diverse private sectors, business may in fact remain part of an urban growth machine, helping to reinvent and reinvigorate the urban economy. Thus, we may think of a continuum of urban governance ranging from the urban growth machine model at one extreme to a community development regime model at the other, with room in between to situate cities with varying degrees of business well-being and governmental capacity. In smaller, manufacturing-centered cities, though, where private enterprise exercises its "exit" option over its "voice" or "loyalty" options and elected officials have lost credibility in the delivery of basic public services, communities and anchor institutions must look elsewhere for resources to support their preferences and objectives. When this happens, the character of the urban regime is transformed into something qualitatively different from the one commonly understood in the commercial republic or growth machine models; the foundation is laid for the emergence of a community development regime.

Contours of a Community Development Regime

In smaller cities facing the challenges of eroded public and private sectors, but with relatively vigorous community-based organizations and nonprofit anchor institutions, the conditions are ripe for a community development regime to form and coalesce. Under this new regime, major initiatives not only in children's health, but also public safety, and physical development of hospitals, universities, or public amenities include local government less as a crucial partner in agenda setting and policy design than as an environmental factor in the calculations of strategic alliances. With local government capacity strained to the point of being ineffectual, both private-sector actors and higher levels of government are drawn to these alliances as effective partners. Perhaps more importantly, citizen participation, let alone meaningful opportunities for holding such alliances publicly accountable, are severely circumscribed. While it is noteworthy that a community development regime effectively freezes the citizenry out of both ends of the political process—agenda setting and accountability—it is equally noteworthy that, unlike the case of the urban growth machine, there is no evidence of any nefarious designs to make decisions behind closed doors. Quite the contrary, collaborations such as NJPHK-C, with the explicit encouragement of their external funders, consciously devote scarce resources to engaging community-based organizations and residents. Indeed, early phases of such initiatives place great emphasis on outreach through neighborhood meetings to explain programs and recruit resident support. Such sincere efforts notwithstanding, under the community development regime, agendas are set and programs are designed ex ante. Only after the higher-level alliance organizers have framed an initiative is the citizenry or local government deeply engaged. In terms of composition, the upper echelon of these alliances includes some combination of external resource suppliers—states, counties, and philanthropies—and internal stakeholders—community and high-capacity faith-based organizations and "anchor institutions."

The concept of anchor institutions requires some elaboration to connect it with the concept of a community development regime. According to the University of Pennsylvania's Netter Center for Community Partnerships:

> Anchor Institutions are place-bound and provide significant employment and/or social capital in a community. Hospitals, universities, utilities, and churches are often cited as examples of urban anchors. Since the mid 1990s, there has been increasing recognition of the role that "eds and meds," i.e. institutions of higher education and medical facilities, play in the urban economy and the life of their cities generally. These institutions reflect a knowledge-based economy that is now dominant in American cities. These institutions have been thrust to the forefront as the "anchors" of their communities—anchors that can rethink their range of resources to contribute more directly to the improvement of their communities, cities and regions.[19]

Based on the findings of urban praxis as well as community-based and action research, a consensus has formed among community development experts and national foundations concerned with urban issues that anchor institutions, especially hospitals and universities, are critical players in the revitalization of cities. In larger cities, foundations interested in investing in distressed communities can work with government and business to partner with neighborhood-based anchor institutions at the point of service. In smaller cities, anchors are even more critical because the public and private sectors are so weak. In either case, anchor institutions are at the center of community development regimes. Indeed, consensus on the centrality of anchors to ameliorating urban distress led to the formation of a national network, the Anchor Institutions Task Force (AITF). As explained on the Web site of MARGA, Inc., the consulting firm providing management and administration to the AITF, anchor institutions are key to "complementing philanthropic strategies to support and strengthen vulnerable communities." AITF brought together anchors, funders, and urban researchers to exchange information, expand knowledge, and extend best practices for anchor institutions in urban areas. The organization also focused on how the Department of Housing and Urban Development (HUD) could increase its impact by strategically leveraging anchor institutions with philanthropic and other resources to better carry out its mission to "create strong, sustainable, inclusive communities and quality affordable homes for all."[20] As a report from a recent AITF conference explained:

> The U.S. Department of Housing and Urban Development (HUD) was recently advised . . . on how HUD could increase its impact and strategically leverage anchor institutions . . . to improve communities and help solve significant urban problems. . . . Communities cannot be revitalized and redeveloped without greater alignment across policy, institutions, civil society organizations (such as community based nonprofit organizations), and private resources (such as philanthropy). A new administration with a fresh vision presents an opportunity to develop and implement new strategies emphasizing partnerships that cross traditional boundaries.[21]

Embedding anchor institutions in urban revitalization policy is now shaping federal policy and funding, and while the AITF strategic vision essentially maps the contours of a community development regime for housing and economic revitalization, the model applies with equal force to a broad array of social policy as well.

While anchors exist in all cities, they play an especially crucial role in governance regimes of smaller distressed ones, filling many of the functions attributed to private enterprise in classical regime theory: conceiving and driving capital development, exercising outsized influence on land use policy, attracting external investment, and providing technical and strategic support for local political leadership. When city government does not have the slack resources to engage anchor institutions on strategic development issues, there is a natural tendency for these institutions to partner with foundations, other levels of government, and effective nonprofits interested in addressing the problems of these cities.

This marginalization of city government in smaller cities does not necessarily reflect a lack of concern on the part of elected leaders or department directors. More often than not, the disengagement of anchors and high-capacity nonprofits from city leadership illustrates the hollowing out of urban government that has paralleled the hollowing out of social and economic infrastructure in older urban communities subjected to sprawl.[22] The mutually reinforcing processes of sprawl and deindustrialization in these smaller urban centers, it bears repeating, have stripped them of both a tax base to sustain basic government functions and the capacity to formulate and drive a policy agenda or attract external investment. With a feeble property tax base, a weak private sector, and concentrated poverty, cities like Camden, East St. Louis, and Benton Harbor are caught, as David Rusk puts it, "running up a down escalator." They simply do not have the administrative, economic, or financial capacity to devote to serious strategic planning or wicked policy problems when they require significant state aid merely to sustain minimal municipal services. Rounds of state budget cuts imposed since the 1980s have only exacerbated this already dire set of circumstances for Camden and similar small urban governments, the end result being an unraveling of urban growth machines and a deficit in governing capacity and public confidence.

Frustrated by the inability of their local government to focus on the long-term planning necessary to address wicked policy problems, anchors as well as leading nonprofit and faith-based organizations see collaborations with foundations and higher levels of government as a means of responding to the urgent challenges in their cities. The NJPHK-C exemplifies such collaborations, which, in effect, play the policy/planning role that local government and business used to play in classical regime theory. A critically important function in such coalitions is filled by policy-oriented philanthropies, such as the Robert Wood Johnson Foundation, the William Penn Foundation, the Annie E. Casey Foundation, and the Ford Foundation, which focus on urban issues and engage academics and think tanks to define efficacious policy and best practices. Where local government capacity is found lacking, local institutions may, independently of local government, seek out these foundations to support community-building efforts. In such cases, the locals must, of course, make their requests conform to the foundations' policy goals and programmatic aims, which have been worked out carefully, with the help of academic consultants, like-minded philanthropic funders, and state or federal governments that can provide resources. As a practical matter and quite understandably, the local partners must adopt the policy priorities of foundations or other levels of government and must align their activities with prescribed programmatic models to acquire needed funds and technical assistance. Conversely, foundations may initiate contact directly with anchor institutions, faith-based and social service providers, and community leaders, inviting funding applications for programs and initiatives that pilot or implement policy and practice developed by the foundation and its consultants. In either case—local anchor institutions and other nonprofits looking for external partners with resources to support community development or foundations prospecting for partners in cities where the well-researched socioeconomic policies they support may be of use—neither government nor the citizenry has a noteworthy voice in formative discussions or postimplementation accountability.

Under this new kind of urban governance, community development corporations, faith-based organizations and neighborhood associations, and anchor institutions develop policy, programmatic, and financial ties to organizations controlling resources outside the city, and they do so quite independently of local government leaders. Concomitantly, external actors at higher levels of government or from the philanthropic sector reach out directly to local nongovernmental actors.

These connections and modi operandi were set in place during the 1990s, in large part as a response to the Reagan administration's laissez faire urban agenda. Described aptly by Neal Cohen, the Reagan urban policy was to remove the federal government from the equation, pegging cities' well-being to the performance of the free market and consigning responsibility for the cities to state government:

> At midsummer [1982] and several months after a congressionally mandated completion date had elapsed, the Reagan Administration issued its national urban policy report. It stated explicitly what the Administration's foot dragging had implied: minimal federal direction would be forthcoming for cities and urban America would improve and prosper only if the Reagan economic and federalism reforms succeeded. Thus U.S. urban policy, such as it is, exists only as a derivative of these larger domestic initiatives.[23]

A key response to the federal government's eschewing a lead role in urban policy in the 1980s took the form of the community development model championed by community-oriented research and urban praxis. That response planted the seeds of the community development regime that is now reconnecting with federal policy makers under terms exemplified by the AITF. As Neil Bradford put it in a review of urban policy in the United States and Great Britain,

> the urban policy activism of the 1990s contributed to the consolidation of a robust community-based development paradigm that joined actors at different scales in a common discourse. . . . Influenced by the ideas of Amarta Sen, John Kretzmann and John McKnight; the new paradigm emphasized building the assets of individuals and communities. Under the rubric of Comprehensive Community Initiatives, once divergent streams of community activists (most prominently, Community Development Corporations, Industrial Area Foundations, and neighborhood associations) came together in cities behind multi-sectoral projects.[24]

Thus, the basics of the community development regime were forged of necessity as the federal government withdrew its support for a robust urban agenda. By the time the Clinton administration breathed life into urban policy with its empowerment zone initiative, the community development regime model was well understood. In the George W. Bush administration, the model aligned nicely with the mission of the White House's Office of Faith-Based and Community Initiatives. The Obama administration built on this model, renaming the executive office agency the Office of Faith-Based and Community Partnerships, reflecting even more precisely the approach of community development we have been describing. The Obama Strong Cities, Strong Communities program added yet more legitimacy to the community development regime model. As the White House Web site notes:

> Strong Cities, Strong Communities is a new interagency pilot initiative that aims to strengthen neighborhoods, towns, cities and regions around the country by strengthening the capacity of local governments to develop and execute their economic vision and strategies. Strong Cities, Strong Communities bolsters local governments by providing necessary technical assistance and access to federal agency expertise, and creating new public and private sector partnerships. By leveraging existing assets, providing new resources, and fostering new connections at the local and national level, Strong Cities, Strong Communities will support towns and cities as they develop comprehensive

plans for their communities and invest in economic growth and job creation.[25]

In addition to the recognition of the lack of capacity in urban governments, especially acute in smaller cities, note the emphasis on "creating new partnerships" and "fostering new connections." The Strong Cities, Strong Communities initiative reflects the community development regime, explicitly seeking to expand the partners in urban governance in six pilot cities of various sizes: Cleveland; Detroit; Fresno; Memphis; New Orleans; and Chester, Pennsylvania.

At a 2011 international conference on community change, James Gibson, a senior fellow at the Institute for Social Change, presented a retrospective on urban policy that nicely describes the appearance of this new regime type. Gibson asserted that, by the time of the Clinton administration, urban policy had taken a turn away from the "libertarian embrace" of a market-driven approach to social welfare policy and recognized that "it was the role of the community and the nation to mitigate the raw workings of the economy."[26] He claimed further that this community-building approach (formulated in response to the Reagan agenda) had taken root:

> [D]espite its limitations, community building has brought a new level of integrity and respect, and a qualitative "people" dimension to partnerships and collaborations aimed at improving conditions in poor neighborhoods. Even as its vogue has declined among most major national foundations, entrepreneurial initiative-taking has grown in inner city neighborhoods around the US—with the increasing participation of local government and local foundations . . . More networking among people involved in these initiatives—through the efforts of Local Initiative Support Corporation (LISC), PolicyLink, Enterprise, Neighborhood Works and the Aspen Roundtable have tended to stimulate and support exchange among activists in local projects about effective practice.[27]

Gibson succinctly portrays the philosophical and developmental underpinnings of a new community development regime. His observation about the "increasing participation of local government" clearly implies that an agenda for social justice in urban centers was developed without the participation of local government and, we may safely assume, without business influence or the citizenry either. While it may be too much to expect such municipalities and their residents to develop urban policy models, one may reasonably ask what mechanisms for accountability, beyond evaluation reports required by foundations or government agencies providing funds, these models and their attendant programs provide.

In major cities where public safety initiatives, neighborhood redevelopment, and educational reform have gained national attention, the community-building ethos and paradigm exist alongside and perhaps overlap with the traditionally understood urban regime, as Clarence Stone, Joe Painter, James Davies, and others have observed. In these cases, the business-government coalition that defines the urban regime may cede policy and political space to alternative, social justice–oriented collaborations and may even be induced to support them. For example, Stephanie Pincetl argues convincingly that environmental nonprofits have constructed an alternative governance regime in Los Angeles that has exerted clear influence on land use decision making, traditionally the domain of the old business-government coalition.[28] In these large cities, the traditional urban regime reserves control over the growth agenda and seeks to ensure that community building does not thwart key projects or encroach too much on their agenda control. Yet in smaller distressed cities with a less-than-robust business community, there is no private-sector coalition partner for local government. For their part, local officials might be tempted to turn to external resource partners, and there are individual cases of particularly energetic and articulate leaders who work directly with external partners and personally advance projects with anchors, nonprofits, and local business. However, even in these rare cases, city leaders must buy into policies and priorities established elsewhere. Moreover, the prevailing wisdom generated by university-based urban research as well as think tanks with an urban agenda has directed those external partners, primarily foundations and the federal government, to connect with nongovernmental entities at the community and neighborhood levels. Local government in small, distressed cities, then, careened from the Reagan era, in which serious urban policy was nonexistent, to a period in which renewed attention to urban issues left them on the outside looking in. While the community development regime requires and desires city government's cooperation and acquiescence to advance its agenda, elected officials usually are brought into local initiatives by a coalition that has already determined policy goals, based on financial or technical support from external agencies such as the Local Initiatives Support Coalition, which describes its role as follows:

> Our unique structure enables local organizations to access
> national resources and expertise and our funding partners to
> leverage their investment and achieve an impact that is truly
> remarkable. The Local Initiatives Support Corporation (LISC) is
> dedicated to helping community residents transform distressed
> neighborhoods into healthy and sustainable communities of
> choice and opportunity—good places to work, do business
> and raise children.[29]

Another external actor, the Aspen Roundtable on Community Change,
convenes urban scholars and practitioners, foundations, and supporters
to exchange and disseminate best practices on urban policy and social
justice. As its Web site proclaims:

> Since its founding in 1994, the Aspen Institute Roundtable
> on Community Change has become a core field-building
> organization, helping individuals and institutions improve
> conditions in poor communities. The Roundtable is known
> for its pioneering work on Theories of Change and community
> building evaluation.[30]

There is in fact a national conversation about urban affairs that shapes
agendas, informs decision makers, and mobilizes resources outside local
government in smaller cities but affects policy in those cities. The philosophical and ideational conversation in this network does not include
the elected leadership of small cities but does shape an agenda that is
externally funded and then applied in their municipalities. Importantly,
this conversation influences not only philanthropic institutions but also
federal grants and state policy makers. We now turn to an examination
of cases in three distinct policy domains in Camden, each illustrating the
operational character of a community development regime.

Community Health, Crime, and Construction in Camden

As noted, Camden is in many respects the quintessential small, distressed
city. Once a major manufacturing center with national, indeed multinational, corporations at the head of a thriving business sector and a
political center for county, regional, and even state politics, Camden, by
2006, was ranked the nation's poorest city by the US Census Bureau. Its

unemployment rate, according to the Bureau of Labor Statistics, spiked by more than 25 percent in the early 1990s, is hovering around 20 percent now, and has never dipped far below 10 percent in the last twenty years.[31] Camden also suffers from persistently high crime rates.[32] Moreover, the city's structural fiscal deficit is well documented; key factors in this situation are an exodus of the private sector and the amount of prime land occupied by nonprofit organizations exempt from regular property taxes.[33] Much of this land in the center of town, however, is occupied by faith-based groups, social service providers, hospitals, and universities, which provide potential anchor institutions for community development. Camden therefore offers a good opportunity to glimpse a community development regime in action. We examine in turn how that regime manifested itself in setting Camden's agenda on public health, public safety, and physical development. While this set of case studies is illustrative rather than exhaustive, it does provide insight into the functioning of a community development regime in a smaller distressed city. For ease of comparison, each case is organized around the sources of its support, both financial and technical; the size and composition of the group addressing the particular problem; and the modalities and effectiveness of its outreach and civic engagement activities.

Public Health: Reducing Childhood Obesity

Statistical as well as anecdotal evidence indicates that Camden, like other impoverished urban areas, suffers from widespread obesity, particularly among its children. The key contributing factors to this public health problem are poor eating behaviors due primarily to high cost and low availability of nutritious foods, and lack of physical activity due to a paucity of public parks or neighborhood playgrounds, and ubiquity of drug-related criminal activity making neighborhoods unsafe.[34]

Recognizing this problem, the Robert Wood Johnson Foundation (RWJF) has made a commitment to addressing obesity and reversing its effects by 2015. As its Web site explains, "RWJF funds efforts at the local, state and federal level to change public policies and community environments in ways that promote improved nutrition and increased physical activity—both of which are critical to reversing the childhood obesity epidemic." In the foundation's home state of New Jersey, the vehicle for advancing this strategic goal is the New Jersey Partnership for Healthy Kids, which predictably has sought to set up an operation in Camden. As its grant-making guidelines explain, "RWJF does not accept unsolicited proposals for its work to prevent childhood obesity. We issue specific solicitations for proposals and ideas throughout the year." Indeed, RWJF developed its own ideas of where it would like to pilot its Healthy Kids programs, namely New Jersey's most distressed cities, and understood that if the program were to have a chance of success, it would need to make grants to partnerships that could muster the requisite organizational, policy, and administrative resources to tackle a complex problem like childhood obesity.

The quandary confronting RWJF, and a challenge facing any would-be private or nonprofit investor in Camden, was finding the right partners given the weakened state of local government. In this case of childhood obesity, the lack of capacity and responsiveness of the school system also presented a problem, because any programming focused on childhood nutrition logically would link to the schools. Its strategy in addressing this problem mirrored the approach of many external funders dealing with smaller distressed cities: it identified nonprofits and anchor institutions with the capacity to adopt and implement a complex social policy initiative and leveraged its funding to those partnerships. In this case, a critical partner identified was the Campbell Soup Company, whose foundation activities and funding priorities related to nutrition and consequently matched the goals of the NJPHK-C. Of equal importance, RWJF partnered with the regional YMCA serving Camden and the County United Way to co-chair the project. The United Way provided an entrée not only to county and nonprofit social services and community development corporations, but also to anchor institutions, particularly Rutgers University–Camden and Cooper Medical Center/University of Medicine and Dentistry at Rowan University, all serving Camden. From this group, a planning team was forged that included the set of participants noted at the outset of this chapter. As we also noted, local government was not a party to this effort. A strategic planning document prepared for NJPHK-C noted:

> The main barriers the partnership foresees deal with the staffing and budget constraints of municipal government and the public school district. The Camden City government faces many urgent issues at this time, including major staff and budget reductions, police department restructuring and staff reductions, and the redevelopment of the City in order to attract ratables. The Mayor, however, has indicated that one

of her priorities is Youth Development, including the overall
health of the city's youngsters.[35]

Local government, then, was excluded from the core planning team and
direct implementation not because it lack motivation or concern, but
because it lacked capacity; indeed the mayor was deeply and personally
supportive of the effort. The core planning group also employed university-based research on the incidence of childhood obesity and exercised
its own judgment on neighborhood social capital to identify two communities in which to launch the program. While the NJPHK-C approach
is entirely rational from a policy analytic perspective, the agenda setting
and decision making were clearly not processes characterized by wide
participation or public debate. The people of Camden did not have a voice,
much less a vote, in the framing or siting of the project. The long-term
legitimacy as well as the short-term efficacy of this effort both depended
on civic engagement activities built into the NJPHK-C strategic plan.

Once the NJPHK-C core planning team fixed its mission (To mobilize the Camden City community to reverse childhood obesity) and its
vision (To be a key change agent and advocate to significantly improve
the health and wellness of the Camden City community), it set about
recruiting in its two target neighborhoods advisory teams representing
health care and social service providers, community and faith-based nonprofits with a solid record in community organizing, teachers, parents and
leaders from government and business. With this organizational infrastructure in place, the project next identified six pilot sites (schools, day
care providers, churches, etc.), three in each neighborhood, to engage the
local residents and sent the project site teams to begin building trust and
relationships at these sites. A critical objective of these initial contacts was
to "ensure that the appropriate organizations (internal) and neighborhood
individuals (external) were a part of the team."[36] Only then were plans
implemented to directly work with community residents through three
planned "community engagement sessions," which provided an orientation, brief history, information on funders and the core planning team,
strategies for improving family nutrition, and data on childhood obesity.
Through these meetings, residents were aided in the development of cus-
tomized plans (subject to review by the NJPHK-C Core Planning Group)
to improve nutrition and create opportunities for exercise in their neighborhoods. Through this process, the project engaged residents and community leaders in an effort to address a critical public health issue, and
from a standpoint of programmatic design the strategy and tactics used

were both realistic and cogent. The community's participation, however, was confined within the policy box built by the NJPHK-C Core Planning Group. Inside that box, members of the community exercised their own judgment, albeit subject to the review of the Core Planning Group, as to the specific activities and delivery mechanism employed in their neighborhood. The policy agenda and external funding were set outside the community just as surely as they would have been under the old urban growth machine. Even though the NJPHK-C goal of improving community wellness builds on the use value rather than the exchange value, consciously seeks to enhance residents' quality of life rather than expropriate or impinge on their homes, and promotes transparent engagement rather than secretive decision making, it reflects a pattern of urban governance in which the voting public remains in a politically reactive posture rather than enjoying what one prominent Camden resident described as "a real seat at the table."[37]

Public Safety: Reducing Community Violence

Although there are legitimate statistical disputes about the crime rate in Camden and whether it ranks as "America's Most Dangerous City," according to one source, or not in the top ten, as others report, there is no question that drugs and drug-related violence take a terrible toll on the quality of life of Camden residents, especially those who live outside the relative safety of the Center City and Waterfront areas. Like many of Camden's problems, its crime is driven by outside forces as well as the city's internal challenges. The highly lucrative drug trade serves suburban users, who come into the city to make their purchases. Guns from Pennsylvania, which has more lax firearms laws than New Jersey, flow across the Delaware River arming organized drug dealers, which operate in areas of communities where storefronts and open-air drug markets exist. The level of crime in Camden attracted the attention of the state, which has, over time, responded to pleas for assistance from anchor institutions, faith-based leaders, and other stakeholders. The New Jersey Office of the Attorney General (OAG), at various times in the first decade of the 2000s, deployed state police to bolster the local Camden Police Department (CPD), endowed the county prosecutor with "supersession authority" over the CPD, and impaneled a blue ribbon commission led by national experts to reevaluate public safety policy and reorganize the CPD. The OAG also explored violence reduction strategies developed by the National Institute for Justice (NIJ), foundations focused on criminal justice issues, and academic research on communities and urban crime.

It was largely on the basis of these explorations that the OAG became interested in funding a community-oriented public safety program in Camden, the Camden Safer Cities Initiative (CSCI). The approach of CSCI was to use data-driven analysis and collaborative problem solving among an alliance of police, prosecutors, courts, supervisory agencies (parole, probation, and juvenile parole), faith-based leaders, social service providers, "eds and meds," and community leaders. Following the findings of best-practice research, this alliance was to determine the subset of offenders on parole or probation most likely to "kill or be killed" and provide them with intensive supervision as well as access to employment training, drug rehabilitation, mental health services, housing, reintegration into communities, educational opportunities, and faith-based mentoring. Again we see the pattern of external resources being brought to bear on an urban problem with the broad policy outlines preestablished. Although it would not be fair to say that the OAG put public safety on Camden's agenda—citizens and institutional actors were asking for help because they judged local authorities incapable of addressing the drug and violence problems in the city—there is no doubt that the specific approach came from outside and, as indicated below, often clashed with the preferences expressed by residents.

Much like the launch of NJPHK-C, the OAG determined early on that city government, then in the early stages of the MRERA and the COO's tenure, would not have the organizational slack to partner on CSCI. While the COO and elected officials were informed of the project and periodically sent representatives to steering committee meetings, there was no expectation that city government would be a central player. Outreach and engagement followed a similar blueprint as well. With OAG funding, a small steering committee of public agencies recruited a few citizens who had been involved in public safety issues and, with the assistance of Rutgers University and the University of Medicine and Dentistry–New Jersey, analyzed crime data, determining that the target group would be 18- to 24-year-olds who were under supervision and had committed aggravated assault. The group then recruited a set of social service agencies, community groups, and faith-based organizations that could connect with residents and provide the required services to the target group. The expanded steering committee reviewed experiences of similar efforts across the country and replicated, with some modification, a case management model in which a group of supervising agencies and service providers would share information on cases to identify systemic problems and report back to the larger steering committee to solve those problems. Next, community, public education meetings were held in neighborhoods across the city in which the project was explained and residents were asked to serve on the project steering committee to ensure input from residents. It is important to note that at these meetings, residents generally were very suspicious of, even resistant to, the program, particularly the idea that convicted felons would get what they perceived as privileged access to an array of social and educational services that law-abiding citizens needed as well. Many expressed the view that what was needed was simply more police, preferably State Troopers patrolling their particular neighborhoods. Sincere efforts were made to explain resource constraints and the efficacy of the case management and problem-solving strategy focused on the relatively small set of offenders most responsible for violence. The meetings however were organized to explain how the program would work not to solicit alternative idea for how to reduce violence. Again the agenda and policy design were described, not debated. CSCI was predicated on civic engagement, but with a programmatic model and on terms that were set in advance. As in the case of the childhood anti-obesity campaign, neither local government nor residents had a "real seat at the table."

Physical Development: Reducing Urban Blight

While public health and public safety appear to reflect the operation of a community development regime in Camden, a truer test of whether the urban growth machine maintains control over agendas and policy making lies in decisions about land development. In fact, Camden illustrates how a major development project conceived and put forward as if the classic urban regime were operational was derailed and reinvented under the norms of an emergent community development regime. Under the MRERA, the state, along with the city leadership, mayor, and City Council as well as the COO, engaged Cherokee Partners, a private development firm, in discussions on the redevelopment in Camden. Cherokee identified the City's Cramer Hill neighborhood, which boasted a significant stretch of waterfront on the Delaware across from Philadelphia, as the best location to attract redevelopment investors. The governor of New Jersey came to a Camden meeting in January 2004 to announce, with great fanfare, Cherokee's $1.1 billion plan for Cramer Hill. Citing scripture, he proclaimed, "The stone the builders rejected has become the capstone . . . the Lord has done this and it is marvelous in our eyes." The actual proposal was described in one urban development publication as follows:

> Cherokee aims to transform Cramer Hill into a city within a city. The company will convert the neighborhood's 450 acres (180 hectares) into a mixed-use development that will include 5,000 new homes; more than 500,000 sq. ft. (45,000 sq. m.) of retail space; a new marina, parks and trails; and an 18-hole golf course created from a closed 89-acre (36-hectare) landfill.[38]

To assemble the land necessary for this planned redevelopment, Cherokee would have to gain control of approximately 1,200 homes via the City asserting eminent domain under New Jersey's redevelopment statutes. In this instance, the powers that be were acting as if the governing model of the old urban growth machine were still in effect. Cherokee clearly evaluated the Cramer Hill neighborhood in terms of its exchange value rather than its use value. The ensuing years of legal and political wrangling followed by the scrapping of the Cherokee plan for one based on a human capital analysis and funded by major foundations demonstrate the shift to a community development regime.

The Cherokee project succumbed to combined pressure from community organizing, opposition from high-capacity nonprofit and faith-based groups, and lawsuits prepared by Legal Services of New Jersey attorneys representing residents and small businesses facing eminent domain proceedings. Initially the city and the developer sought to proceed by working with the City Council to approve a redevelopment plan for the Cramer Hill neighborhood, an approach that would facilitate the use of eminent domain rather than lot-by-lot acquisition of the land required for the project. The City Council, under the eye of the state-appointed COO, duly approved a redevelopment plan, but the plan was immediately and successfully challenged in court. The plan was overturned on a technicality—that there was inadequate notice provided for a statutorily required public hearing. Subsequently, the city and Cherokee attempted to rely on the state's Fair Housing Act (N.J.S.A. 52:27D-325), which allows the use of eminent domain. This time the trial court found for the city, but was reversed on appeal. As the Appellate Division of the State Court found:

> We are nevertheless compelled to remand this matter for the trial court to conduct a fact-finding hearing to determine if

the ordinance passed under N.J.S.A. 52:27D-325 will assist the City in meeting its fair share housing obligation under the FHA . . . the trial court must determine whether the proposed land acquisition plan authorized by the ordinance actually increases the number of affordable housing units in the City.

In going about this task, the trial court should be guided by the overarching public policy supporting the City's authority to take private property by eminent domain under N.J.S.A. 52:27D-325: the exercise of the power of eminent domain granted to municipalities . . . is expressly predicated upon a finding that the proposed land acquisition is "necessary or useful for the construction or rehabilitation of low or moderate income housing." . . . Absent such a finding, the City lacks the legal authority to proceed. . . .[39]

The standard of demonstrating that the "the ordinance actually increases the number of affordable housing units in the City" proved too difficult to meet. However, the narrative in this case is not simply a version of the Erin Brockovich/David and Goliath story of a wronged individual and a crusading attorney besting the establishment. It reflects the clout of long-established nonprofit and experienced faith-based organizations as well as the involvement of national foundations that had been investing in Camden. The court cases were really only one weapon in the arsenal of community opposition to what initially appeared to be a great coup for city government: attracting a billion-dollar investment to the nation's poorest city. Public meetings, sometimes facilitated with input from foundations, and political pressure brought to bear on state as well as local officials ultimately mobilized enough opposition that the Cherokee redevelopment plan was scuttled. If that community victory had been the end of the Cramer Hill story, it could have been considered a defeat of the urban growth machine, but not necessarily a signal that it was being superseded by a community development regime. As it turned out, though, chapter two of Cramer Hill's redevelopment looked a lot like a community development regime in action.

The failure of the Cherokee plan provided an opening for the Annie E. Casey Foundation and the Ford Foundation, both of which had been trying since the enactment of the MRERA to help shape redevelopment and community revitalization in Camden. They had been connecting with anchor institutions, faith-based groups, and community organizations for some time, funding various projects, inviting applications for their RFPs,

and providing consultation and technical assistance to the COO. After
the Cramer Hill debacle, they worked with a new COO and the eds and
meds coalition on a strategic redevelopment plan for the Lanning Square
neighborhood, which surrounded the Cooper Hospital and its affiliated
medical school, UMDNJ. The approach was to fund a nationally known
consulting group, Urban Strategies, to lead the human capital planning
process. According to Urban Strategies' mission statement:

> Urban Strategies rebuilds the physical and human infrastruc-
> ture of redeveloping urban communities by partnering with
> neighborhood organizations, residents, developers, policy
> makers, institutional stakeholders and funders to transform
> public and private systems and support strong, self-sustaining
> people, families and communities.[40]

Clearly the approach would be to start from a conception of use value rather than exchange value. Of equal importance, Urban Strategies
deployed a civic engagement and outreach approach that mirrored those
used in CPHK and CSCI. Unlike Cherokee, they engaged residents directly in identifying opportunities and programmatic specifics. Indeed, the
final plan grew out of a labor-intensive effort to create a "human capital
plan" for the neighborhood. The success of this project led to a commitment on the part of the COO's office that all future redevelopment plans
would have to be built with a human capital plan as their foundation.
And the next community that Urban Strategies engaged was Cramer Hill.
The old urban regime approach of assembling land to repurpose it based
on a private-sector analysis rooted in exchange value was gone, replaced
by a new governing and decision model predicated on the concept of use
value and revitalizing the community in place.

In a sense, the recent history of physical revitalization in Camden
represents the triumph of a more inclusive and progressive approach to
redevelopment. Yet, just as in the cases of childhood obesity and urban
violence, agendas were set and policy models created ex ante from national conversations and exchange of evidence-based research among social
policy experts, think tanks, consulting firms, state and federal government, and foundations. External resources drove socioeconomic agendas
and models developed through these conversations, and while human
capital planning seemed, on its face, a preferable basis for revitalization
than neoliberal, market-driven plans for offices and golf courses, local
government and residents essentially had no say in creating the blue-

prints for these plans. The community development regime provided the architecture and engineering for Camden's urban initiative while elected officials and voters merely got to select furniture and color schemes. This is not to say that the community development regime is not an improvement over the old urban growth regime. However, the principal normative problem identified with the urban growth machine—the disenfranchisement of citizens from basic agenda setting and policy decisions—has not been resolved.

Representation without Voting?

Clarence Stone reminds us that the reason urban regime analysis has gained so much theoretical traction is that it unmasked the pluralist myth that voting and elections provide an effective nexus between citizens and policy decisions in cities. As he concludes, "[a]t best, electoral accountability reaches only part of the process of shaping public policy, and for that part, electoral accountability is in reality very far from being a robust process."[41] Undoubtedly, urban regime analysis informed the community development paradigm insofar as the latter aims to connect residents to real decisions that directly affect their lives—to move from what new leftists used to deride as "mere representation" to participatory democracy. The critical observations presented about a new community development regime are not intended to diminish the power of the original critique offered by Stone and other urban regime theorists. Nor are they intended to denigrate the positive effects of education reform, neighborhood revitalization, community policing, programs for at-risk youth, and numerous other urban policy initiatives brought to smaller distressed cities by external actors connecting with local nongovernmental stakeholders. Often, in these cities bereft of both high-functioning public management and a robust business sector, the collaborations of a functioning community development regime are salutary.

These benefits, however, should not deter students of urban politics from a critical consideration of how well this new governing paradigm addresses the normative challenge originally posed by urban regime theory. If local elections are ineffective mechanisms of popular sovereignty and, by extension, little more than fig leaves for legitimating urban policy, how successful is the community development regime in redressing this grievance? Based on this initial assessment, it is not ultimately successful. If one judges the democratic character of urban policy making by the

nature and neighborhood location of investment, the community development regime has clearly shifted the urban agenda in a more egalitarian
direction, substituting use value for exchange value and inserting what
Jim Gibson called a "people dimension" into the policy process. However,
the participatory and deliberative nature of the process itself remains limited, even corporatist. In each of the three cases we examined, there is
a remarkable degree of institutional overlap in the community development partnerships: eds and meds, state and county government, the same
high-functioning nonprofits and faith-based groups. Like the old urban
growth machine, there is not a formal governing body, but the membership and contours of the community development regime in Camden are
discernible. Ideas, priorities, and resources shaping urban policy develop
in a national network of foundations, think tanks, university research
centers, and federal as well as state agencies. These ideas and priorities are
imported to cities, and the resources attached to the ideas and priorities
serve as inducements to mobilize local nonprofits around a community
development agenda. The principles of civil society and civic engagement
are intended to connect people to projects, but there is no accountability
to the voting public. Local government is relegated to an environmental
factor to be managed, co-opted, or bypassed. In smaller distressed cities, this new urban regime attracts both the entrepreneurial energy of
talented individuals who, in other settings, might help rebuild the private
sector and the public-spiritedness of individuals who might otherwise
engage in electoral politics. What remains are millions of dollars invested
in initiatives, demonstration projects, and social services that are aimed at
alleviating the problems put in place by the old urban regime but but do
not invite local government or residents to sit at the agenda setting table.

Notes

1. In the interest of full disclosure, Richard A. Harris directed Rutgers-
Camden's Walter Rand Institute for Public Affairs (WRI), which provided the
technical support for this strategic plan. Moreover, the portfolio of projects the
Institute has undertaken in Camden over the last decade, ranging from government capacity building to public safety, has provided a number of vantage points
from which to observe institutional, philanthropic, organizational, and intergovernmental relationships in Camden.

2. Stephen L. Elkin, "Business State Relations in the Commercial
Republic," *Journal of Political Philosophy* 2, no. 2 (2006): 115–139, 133; Clarence

Stone, "Looking Back to Look Forward: Reflections on Urban Regime Analysis," *Urban Affairs Review* 40, no. 3 (2005): 309–341.

3. Charles E. Lindblom, *Politics and Markets: The World's Political-Economic Systems* (New York: Basic Books, 1977).

4. Harvey Molotch, "Growth Machine Links: Up, Down, and Across," in *The Urban Growth Machine: Critical Perspectives Two Decades Later*, ed. Andrew E. G. Jonas and David Wilson (Albany: State University of New York Press, 1999), 247–265.

5. Peter Bachrach and Morton S. Baratz, "Two Faces of Power," *American Political Science Review* 56, no. 4 (1962): 947–952.

6. Campbell Soup Company closed its manufacturing facility (eliminating thousands of jobs), but it kept its world headquarters in the city.

7. Howard Gillette Jr., *Camden After the Fall: Decline and Renewal in a Post-Industrial City* (Philadelphia: University of Pennsylvania Press, 2004).

8. With a current population of approximately 80,000, the victor in the last mayoral election garnered fewer than 5,000 votes.

9. The MRERA provided that disputes between the COO and the mayor would be resolved by the assignment judge of the Camden Vicinage acting in the capacity of a "special master." There was little doubt that any such disputes would be resolved in favor of the COO.

10. WRI was written into the MRERA legislation to provide technical assistance and training, thereby providing us with an inside view of the legislative enactment and implementation. Indeed, WRI provided a key legislative sponsor of MRERA with a needs assessment on government capacity building in Camden; this study's recommendations appear in the law, designating WRI as a lead implementation agency.

11. We cite 2000 data because final urban population data are not published yet, and there is currently a rule making in progress that will alter the way the Census Bureau aggregates urban populations.

12. Richard Feiock and Hee-Soun Jang, "The Role of Nonprofits in the Delivery of Local Services," paper presented to the National Public Management Research Association Meeting, Washington, DC, October 9–10, 2003.

13. For a political science discussion of the concept of civic engagement, see especially Theda Skocpol and Morris Fiorina, eds., *Civic Engagement in American Democracy* (Washington, DC: The Brookings Institution Press, 1999).

14. On this point, see especially Joe Painter, "Regulation, Regime and Practice in Urban Politics," in *Reconstructing Urban Regime Theory, Regulating Urban Politics in a Global Economy*, ed. Mickey Lauria (Thousand Oaks, CA: Sage, 1997).

15. Clarence N. Stone, "Looking Back to Look Forward: Reflections on Urban Regime Analysis," *Urban Affairs Review* 40, no. 3 (2005): 309–341, 312.

16. Ibid., 326.

17. Stephen L. Elkin, "Business State Relations in the Commercial Republic," *Journal of Political Philosophy* 2, no. 2 (2006): 115–139, 133.

18. Jonathan Kozol, *Savage Inequalities: Children in American Schools* (New York: Crown, 1991).

19. Anchor Institutions Toolkit: A Guide for Neighborhood Revitalization, Report prepared by the Netter Center with funding from the Annie E. Casey Foundation, March 2008.

20. HUD mission statement, http://portal.hud.gov/hudportal/HUD?src=/about/mission.

21. December 15, 2010 AITF Forum, http://www.margainc.com/initiatives/aitf. See also Paul C. Brophy and Rachel D. Godsil, "Retooling HUD for a Catalytic Federal Government: A Report to Secretary Shaun Donovan," prepared by the University of Pennsylvania Institute for Urban Research with funding from the Rockefeller Foundation, February 2009.

22. See especially Myron Orfield, *American Metropolitics: The New Suburban Reality* (Washington, DC: Brookings Institution Press, 2002); David Rusk, *Inside Game/Outside Game: Winning Strategies for Saving Urban America* (Washington, DC: Brookings Institution, 1999).

23. Neal M. Cohen, "The Reagan Administrations Urban Policy," *The Town Planning Review* 54, no. 3 (1983): 304–315.

24. Neil Bradford, "Place Matters and Multi-Level Governance: Perspectives on a New Urban Policy Paradigm," *Policy Options* 25, no. 2 (2004): 39–44.

25. The White House, "Announcing Strong Cities, Strong Communities," accessed March 15, 2012, http://www.whitehouse.gov/blog/2011/07/11/announcing-strong-cities-strong-communities.

26. James Gibson, "From Community Building to Equitable Development: A Journey from Projects to Policy in the Struggle for Community in Urban America," paper presented at the Global Roundtable on Comprehensive Community Change, Shdemot Center and Oranim College, Israel, February 21–24, 2011.

27. Ibid.

28. Stephanie Pincetl, "Nonprofits and Park Provision in Los Angeles: An Exploration of the Rise of Governance Approaches to the Provision of Local Services," *Social Science Quarterly* 84, no. 4 (2003): 979–1001.

29. Gibson, "From Community Building to Equitable Development."

30. Aspen Roundtable on Community Change, http://www.aspeninstitute.org/policy-work/community-change.

31. Unemployment data in Camden are notoriously unreliable given the large number of undocumented residents in the city.

32. Camden has been ranked as "America's Most Dangerous City" by Morgan Quitno's annual survey, but this ranking is quite misleading, as it does not show trends or break the city into neighborhoods. It also uses an elementary, nonweighted accounting system. Using more sophisticated analytic techniques, neither *U.S. News and World Report* nor the FBI annual statistics place Camden among the top-ten cities in terms of crime rate.

33. On Camden's waterfront, its port facility is operated by a state agency, the South Jersey Port Corporation, and no property taxes are collected on those operations either.

34. New Jersey Childhood Obesity Study: Camden, Rutgers State Health Policy Center, Summer 2010.

35. *Community Strategic Plan: NJ Partnership for Healthy Kids-Camden,* February 28, 2011, 22.

36. Ibid., 11.

37. This oft-repeated quote is from Ms. Sharon Miller, now deceased. Ms. Miller was an indefatigable champion of Camden and its residents and decried what she saw as the power imbalance between those who lived in her city and those who set the agenda for her city, even if those setting the agenda were well intentioned and professed a desire to "empower" the people.

38. Jack Lynne, "$1.1B Redevelopment Targets Camden, N.J., One of Nation's Poorest Cities, *Site Selection,* January 5, 2004, http://www.siteselection.com/ssinsider/snapshot/sf040105.htm.

39. Slip Opinion, *Cramer Hill Residents Association v. Primas* 395 NJ, Super.

40. Mission Statement, Urban Strategies, Inc., http://www.urbanstrategiesinc.org/.

41. Stone, "Looking Back to Look Forward," 311.

5

Counting Bodies and Ballots

Prison Gerrymandering and the Paradox of Urban Political Representation

Khalilah L. Brown-Dean*

It makes eminent good sense to say as a matter of law that one who is in a place solely by virtue of superior force exerted by another should not be held to have abandoned his former domicile. The rule shields an unwilling sojourner from the loss of rights and privileges incident to his citizenship in a particular place, such as, for example, paying resident tuition at a local university, invoking the jurisdiction of the local divorce courts, or voting in local elections.

—Judge Wade H. McCree, *Stifel v. Hopkins* (1973).

American cities have long been the site of contentious efforts to define the boundaries of political community. From New York City's 1863 draft riots sparked by immigrants' opposition to class bias in compulsory military service to the 1992 riots in Los Angeles over police misconduct, cities provide ideal spaces for citizens to express their discontent. At the same time, however, cities have been viable sites for marginalized communities

*I am grateful to Michael Javen Fortner, Richardson Dilworth, Amy Bridges, Rogers Smith, and Jennifer Hochschild for helpful comments on earlier drafts. I also appreciate the skilled research assistance of Christopher Pagliarello.

to contest their disfranchised status by electing candidates to decision-making positions. The widespread efforts of the civil rights movement helped open up the political process and ushered in an impressive cadre of minority voters and elected officials. This is most evident in the election of minority politicians, who first shattered the political glass ceiling at the local level as mayors and city council members. Over the last forty years, Americans have elected minority governors in ten states and many more mayors in cities as diverse as Newark and Denver. All of these indicators suggest that communities of color have overcome their past exclusion and institutionalized their political presence. As a result, cities represent one of the most compelling arenas for evaluating key features of American democracy: power, conflict, federalism, identity, representation, and resource allocation.

The transition from massive acts of insurgency to formalized participation in the electoral process has been well documented and debated among political scientists.[1] Though urban spaces serve as valuable incubators for developing minority political empowerment, various processes (e.g., deindustrialization) have created rapidly changing social and economic conditions that challenge this power. Few issue areas highlight the intensity of the battle for urban power like the expansion of America's criminal justice system. Since the 1970s, the incarcerated population in the United States has increased nearly sixfold. As a result, the United States now holds the unique distinction of being the world's leader in incarceration. Currently, there are 2.5 million US residents behind bars and more than 7 million people under some form of supervision as criminals.[2] More succinctly, 1 in every 32 Americans is involved with the criminal justice system as defendants. America's increasing reliance on and shifting approaches to incarceration have had an especially strong impact on communities of color. Although blacks comprise just 12 percent of the total US population, they comprise 60 percent of all Americans behind bars. In fact, if current trends persist, 1 in 3 young black men will enter prison at some point in his lifetime.[3] As Figure 5.1 indicates, blacks are significantly overrepresented in US correctional institutions. Since the 1950s, the incarceration rate for African Americans has increased by more than 800 percent. Incarceration rates for Latinos have also risen steadily since the 1970s.[4] While the growth of mass incarceration and the collateral consequences of a criminal conviction are part of a national trend, the impact of this trend is felt most directly by urban residents and their representatives.

Each year, more than 650,000 people are released from prison and often return to communities that are already grappling with the effects of

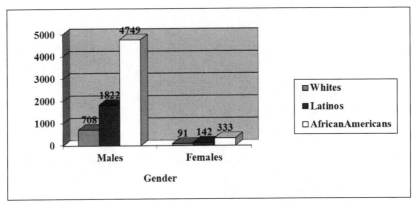

Figure 5.1. Incarceration Rates by Race and Gender, 2010.

crime, poverty, violence, and inferior education.[5] Where urban residents struggle to secure access to housing, education, and employment, this struggle is intensified by the increased presence of those leaving prison and attempting to return to their families. A robust body of work within sociology asserts that the quality of one's life is defined by where one resides based on "neighborhood context effects."[6] Neighborhood context effects are unique to a given neighborhood such that the impact of living in neighborhood "A" is different from the impact of living in neighborhood "B" even for the same individual or group. Neighborhood context effects reflect broader social forces, such as the availability and affordability of housing, family structures, literacy rates, community institutions, and support services. The impact of mass incarceration on neighborhoods is reflected in declining economic opportunities, disrupted family stability, limited education attainment, and often civic retreat.[7] The tremendous social costs of directly removing human capital have been well documented.[8] However, the instability created by concentrated punishment within particular neighborhoods raises even greater concerns that the United States' approach to punishment exacerbates existing cleavages while having a disproportionate impact on groups already struggling to define their place in American society. For example, more than 25 percent of African Americans and about 20 percent of Latinos live below the federally established poverty line. The bulk of these communities, and the bulk of the communities to which the formerly incarcerated return, are in urban areas. For their part, city governments face the increasing challenge of reconciling high demands for service with limited resources.

Mass incarceration has fundamentally redefined the relationship between individuals and the state by rendering invisible those convicted of crimes. To some extent, this invisibility derives from "civil death" statutes that were once used to totally deny the civil rights of those convicted of crimes, particularly those sentenced to life in prison or marked for execution.[9] Civil death was built on the belief that those who had offended the community by breaking the law should no longer enjoy the protections of that community. This included being physically removed from the community during incarceration as well as being denied the right to sue, serve on juries, or engage in political decision making. Over time, these statutes have largely been replaced by attaching collateral consequences to a conviction that limit one's ability to make basic life choices in areas such as employment, education, housing, and parenting. As a result, much of the existing scholarship on mass incarceration focuses on those under direct supervision by the state.[10] Although the focus on those convicted of a crime is illuminating, greater attention must be paid to the impact of punishment policies on the standing of communities as a whole. This is particularly important as we consider how our approach to punishment shapes the allocation and distribution of a finite set of resources. Thus, I offer a revised view of civil death that focuses not just on individual offenders, but on the political standing of underrepresented communities as a whole. Civil death, then, reflects the absence of meaningful opportunities for communities to engage the political process on equal footing. I argue in this chapter that the expansion of America's carceral state further strips resources from urban environments while shifting resources to other areas of the state or to another state. These processes diminish the electoral influence of urban areas within both state and national politics.

The confluence of declining economic, social, and political conditions contributes to a heightened sense of civil death for marginalized communities within US cities. Although certain minority groups have achieved formal standing and are legally recognized as full US citizens, facially neutral public policies continue to challenge or weaken that standing. In turn, these policies create differences between groups (e.g., blacks compared with whites) while also creating cleavages within groups (e.g., setting the urban working class against the rural working class against the suburban working class).

This absence of opportunities for political efficacy may result from direct restrictions such as the disfranchisement of (ex) felons or indirect constraints such as allocation of political and economic resources based on population size and composition. The concentration of civil death within urban spaces compromises the ability of local authorities to address the policy priorities of all citizens, not just particular residents. Civil death also limits the ability of citizens to promote their policy interests within an increasingly competitive political space. Civil death differs from apathy or ambivalence, whereby citizens simply choose not to participate because they feel that their participation makes no difference. Often this ambivalence is a result of being formally pushed to the periphery of political representation. Civil death cautions us to examine the institutional and policy features that limit the political standing of particular communities while undermining the representation of the broader geographical space.

In this chapter, I examine an important process that makes it even more difficult for cities to reconcile residents' demands: the enumeration of American prisoners. Inmates in the United States are counted as residents of the town where they are incarcerated as opposed to their place of legal residence prior to their conviction. Though most inmates come from urban communities, the overwhelming majority of prisons in this country are situated in non-urban areas. The result is that areas with larger prison populations receive a disproportionate share of valuable resources, such as legislative districts and funds for the delivery of social service programs. I argue that the enumeration of prisoners and the accompanying distribution of resources further marginalizes communities with a long history of struggling for inclusion. I begin by examining the historical connection between enumeration and racial representation. From there, I explore the political costs of incarceration and enumeration to demonstrate how the process of counting inmates, who cannot vote, apportions power between urban and non-urban spaces. Finally, I consider the long-term consequences of these counting rules for urban representation and inclusion.

Enumeration and Racial Disfranchisement

Article I, Section 2 of the U.S Constitution mandates that:

> Representatives and direct taxes shall be apportioned among the several States which may be included in this Union, according to their respective members . . . the actual Enumeration shall be made within three years of the first Meeting of the Congress of the United States, and within every subsequent Term of ten Years, in such manner as they shall by law direct (1790).

Article I was based on the assumption that using official census counts would create a fair and consistent standard for apportioning districts. The standard helped ensure that "states' wishes to report few people in order to lower their shares in the debt [incurred by the war for independence] would be offset by a desire for the largest possible representation in Congress."[11] This approach met with tremendous resistance. Because states with larger populations would be granted a greater number of seats in the House of Representatives, Northern delegates feared that counting slaves as full persons would increase the political influence of Southern slaveholding states. The Three-Fifths Compromise was born of this fear. The Compromise stated that only three-fifths of the total population of slaves would count toward the apportionment of House members and Electoral College votes:

> [T]heir respective numbers, which shall be determined by adding to the whole Number of free Persons, including those bound to Service for a Term of years, and excluding Indians not taxed, three fifths of all other persons.[12]

Although blacks were numerically included in the process, their ability to vote and influence electoral outcomes was often defined by region.[13] As a result, the presence of blacks, who could not vote, helped inflate the representation of Southern slaveholding states and the power of individual white votes with it. This inflated influence allowed Missouri to be admitted as a slaveholding state while also giving Thomas Jefferson an electoral advantage in the 1800 presidential election.[14] The Three-Fifths Compromise was eventually superseded by Section 2 of the Fourteenth Amendment. The practice of counting bodies while withholding ballots continues to influence the distribution of valuable political resources. Just as the presence of disfranchised blacks increased the representation of white Southerners under the Three-Fifths Clause, the presence of disfranchised inmates increases the representation of communities with prisons.

Since the first census was taken in 1790, the bureau has used the "usual residence rule" to identify "the place where a person lives and sleeps most of the time."[15] Usual residence, however, is not synonymous with legal residence. In most states, legal residence is defined as the place where "you have your permanent home or principal establishment and to where, whenever you are absent, you intend to return."[16] Usual residence is used to determine where people are counted on Census Day. As Table 5.1 indicates, the usual residence standard is also used to count other groups, such as college students and military personnel. Although this

Table 5.1. Usual Residence Groups by Category

Institutional	Noninstitutional
Nursing Homes	College Dormitories
Hospitals	Military Facilities
Wards	Group Homes
Hospices	Shelters
Prisons	Missions

Source: Your Gateway to Census 2000 (US Census Bureau).

standard has been used since 1790, it has been contested in the courts. For example, Massachusetts argued that counting federal employees working overseas as residents of their home of record unfairly skewed the apportionment process. The resulting case, *Franklin v. Massachusetts* (1992), challenged the 1990 Census, which counted 900,000 overseas employees based on their home of record. As a result of the count, the state of Washington took a congressional seat from Massachusetts. However, the enumeration of prisoners differs from the counting of other groups. In most jurisdictions, inmates are counted toward the population of the town where they are incarcerated rather than their place of legal residence. This distinction has taken on renewed political significance as declining economic fortunes forced many states to explore more profitable strategies for managing citizens.

The Political Costs of Shifting Economic Priorities

Over the last twenty years, the federal government's increased support of devolution has shifted greater responsibility for high-cost citizens to local governments. Federal changes in crime control policy were designed to implement a zero-tolerance approach to crime and criminals. This shift fundamentally altered state and local governments' involvement in punishment.[17] National initiatives such as the War on Drugs, gun control legislation, and even Homeland Security have led to dramatic increases in the number of investigations, arrests, convictions, and incarcerations while shifting public costs from federal to lower-level governments.

In addition to its direct economic impact, the United States' approach to punishment bears important political consequences. The tremendous cost of implementing federal mandates forced many jurisdictions to devise innovative means of addressing the increasingly complex needs of their citizens. As a result, prison construction became a prominent and profitable strategy for boosting states' economies in the 1990s. In states such as Virginia, Texas, Colorado, and Oklahoma, legislators aided economically depressed areas by promoting prison construction as a prime economic development strategy. In response, counties and localities engaged in fierce battles to win construction projects. Counties often offered incentives such as relaxed zoning restrictions, free land, rebates, and other infrastructure improvements. The economic benefit of hosting prisons is quite apparent to public officials, who believe that "in my mind there's no more recession-proof form of economic development. Nothing's going to stop crime."[18] In referencing the success of prison building as an economic strategy, Peter T. Kilborn writes,

> [M]ore than a Wal-Mart or a meat-packing plant, state, federal, and private prisons, typically housing 1,000 inmates and providing 300 jobs, can put a town on solid economic footing. As communities become more and more familiar with the benefits that prisons bring, they are also becoming increasingly adept at maximizing their windfall through collecting taxes and healthy public service fees.

Examples of such fees include sales taxes on food, clothing, and toiletry items bought from the prison commissary as well as telephone calls. This last category can prove quite lucrative because all calls are collect. In turn, local government can impose a substantial tax (from 15 to 35 percent) on all calls made from the prison. Clear estimates that each prisoner represents about $25,000 in annual government income for communities where a prison is located.[19] In addition to the money collected directly from prisoners, prisons help to attract other businesses, such as hotels, gas stations, restaurants, and convenience stores that cater to inmates' visitors.

Before 1980, only 36 percent of America's prisons were situated in rural areas. Today, the majority of the country's prisons are based in rural areas. According to Beale, from 1990 to 1999 a new prison opened in the rural United States every fifteen days, totaling 245 new prisons built in rural communities. This trend has permanently reversed previous patterns.[20] In the 1970s, for example, about four new prisons were built in rural areas per year. This expansion in prison building simultaneously increased the number of offenders based in such facilities; the size of the rural incarcerated population increased by more than 120 percent.[21] Prison construction is clustered in particular regions. Table 5.2 highlights

Table 5.2. Top Twenty Prison Counties

State	County	Total Population	Percent Rural	Prison Population	% County Incarcerated
Louisiana	W. Feliciana Parish	15,111	100	4,995	33.1
Texas	Concho	3,966	100	1,299	32.8
Florida	Union	13,442	52.2	4,052	30.1
Illinois	Brown	6,950	41.8	1,912	27.5
Tennessee	Lake	7,954	100	2,090	26.3
Virginia	Greensville	11,560	64.4	3,027	26.2
Texas	Mitchell	9,698	32.0	2,525	26.0
California	Lassen	33,828	58.7	8,367	24.7
Texas	Hartley	5,537	57.6	1,343	24.3
Missouri	Dekalb	11,597	67.1	2,626	22.6
Texas	Jones	20,785	60.9	4,650	22.4
Texas	Waller	61,758	36.3	13,691	22.2
Texas	Bee	32,359	30.6	7,070	21.8
Texas	Childress	7,688	34.0	1,652	21.5
Arkansas	Lincoln	14,492	100	3,003	20.7
Texas	Madison	12,940	69.9	2,681	20.7
Illinois	Johnson	12,878	79.1	2,640	20.5
Nevada	Pershing	6,693	100	1,370	20.5
Texas	Anderson	55,109	41.3	10,750	19.5
Virginia	Sussex	12,504	100	2,370	19.0

Source: Numbers are based on data from the Bureau of Justice Statistics Mid-Year Report (2003); Leah Sakala, "Breaking Down Mass Incarceration in the 2010 Census: State-by-State Incarceration Rates by Race/Ethnicity" (2014), http://www.prisonpolicy.org/reports/rates.html; and by Rose Heyer and Peter Wagner, "Too Big to Ignore: How Counting People in Prisons Distorted Census 2000" (2004), http://www.prisonersofcensus.org/toobig/.

the characteristics of prison populations in the top twenty prison counties in the United States.

From 1990 to 1999, Texas built forty-nine new prisons; one in five rural prisons built in that decade were sited in Texas. The presence of so many prisons in Texas mean the state's counties hold nine places among the twenty counties in the United States with the greatest number of prisoners. Economically depressed areas such as Mississippi (seven new prisons) and Appalachia (nine new prisons) have also relied on prisons to create precious resources such as jobs and revenue. Tracy Huling finds that in many places, rural "penal colonies" have replaced traditional economies, such as oil and coal.[22] In turn, rural communities in Texas, Colorado, California, Illinois, New York, Pennsylvania, Virginia, Arizona, and Florida have all benefited from clustering prisons.

The material benefits of situating prisons in rural areas have been well documented.[23] It is also important to consider how this trend has dramatically affected the descriptive characteristics of rural America. In Pennsylvania, for example, prisoners represent the fastest-growing segment of the state's rural population. The size of the state's prison population increased by 187 percent in rural areas. Nonwhite prisoners now constitute more than half of the total rural nonwhite population. Simply stated, the majority of blacks in rural Pennsylvania are behind bars. Pennsylvania is not unique. For example, 95 percent of Nevada County's black residents are in prison.[24]

According to data from the 2010 Census, a number of rural counties in the West, Midwest, and Northeast have more than doubled the size of their black populations since the 1990s. The majority of those black populations have not moved there by choice. Most of the counties with the fastest-growing young black populations are also home to large incarcerated populations. As a result, in 256 US counties, more than a quarter of the black population is behind bars. In 173 counties, the proportion is more than half.[25] These numbers affirm the geographic bias in prison location. What is the political fallout—for access and incorporation—from this distribution of prisons?

The Political Balance Sheet of Incarceration and Enumeration

Though the Fourteenth Amendment allows states and localities to include inmate populations within their census counts, many have argued that this practice violates the One Person–One Vote Standard. The standard derives from the Supreme Court's 1964 *Reynolds v. Sims* decision, in which justices agreed that state legislative districts must be "as nearly of equal population as is practicable." The One Person–One Vote standard requires that US congressional districts and state legislative districts must be drawn so that their residents have a fair and equal share of representatives in Congress.[26] Congressional districts must conform to an ideal size based on the following formula: total state population divided by number of districts.[27] On average, congressional districts contain approximately 645,000 people. Given the large number of residents in each district, it might be that the impact of including incarcerated populations among the residents is minimal.

Not so, either in states or across states. There is quite a range in the size of state legislative chambers. According to data from the National Conference of State Legislators, the median State Senate and House districts contain 106,362 and 37,562 residents, respectively. The relatively smaller size of state legislative districts increases the possibility that enumerating inmates where they are incarcerated can skew both representation and resources. This is a particularly important consequence of inmate enumeration. Prison overcrowding has forced many states to send their inmates to other states to be housed.[28] Exporting inmates also means that states export resources. For example, Wisconsin houses approximately 10,000 inmates in Oklahoma, Tennessee, and Texas. Faced with the threat of losing a congressional seat, Congressman Mark Green (R-WI) introduced a bill that would allow states to count state and federal prisoners exported to other states as residents of their preconviction place of residence. The bill failed, and Wisconsin lost a congressional seat. It should be noted that Wisconsin's total population loss was greater than the number of out-of-state inmates. However, Green argued that the issue would become increasingly important given the state's incarceration projections for the next ten years.

The Wisconsin example highlights the important connection between inmate enumeration and the distribution of political resources. As further evidence of this importance, Wagner finds that most of New York's legislative districts are inflated by the presence of prisoners.[29] Table 5.3 on page 170 provides information on New York's ten rural districts.

Although only one district is reported as being below the ideal size, removing the disfranchised population reveals that 90 percent of the districts are actually underpopulated. In fact, the state has four Senate districts and ten Assembly districts where more than 2 percent of the residents are incarcerated. New York provides a particularly compelling case for examining the flaws of this practice. Since 1982, all of New York's new prison facilities have been built in rural areas upstate. As a result, while 66 percent (approximately 43,470 people) of the state's inmates are from New York City, 91 percent are housed in upstate facilities. The result is a substantial transfer of both human and political capital from New York's urban, mostly minority neighborhoods to rural, predominantly white communities.

Overall, 52 percent of New York State's prison population is African American; Hispanics account for 30 percent. Though the public may be unaware or indifferent to these discrepancies, legislators seem quite aware

Table 5.3. Selected Characteristics of New York's Rural Assembly Districts

Representative (District)	Reported Population	Number of Prisoners	% District Incarcerated	Number of Black Prisoners	% Blacks Disfranchised	Reported Deviation (%)	Actual Deviation (%)
Kirwan (100)	129,732	3,650	2.8	1,934	11.8	2.5	-.3
Manning (103)	128,212	2,793	2.2	1,436	34.1	1.3	-.9
McDonald (112)	129,570	3,611	2.8	1,849	**96.1**	2.4	-.4
Ortloff (114)	132,349	9,251	7.0	4,623	**82.6**	4.6	-2.7
Destito (116)	127,574	6,187	4.8	2,986	33.5	.8	-4.0
Nortz (118)	128,234	4,245	3.3	2,238	**68.7**	1.4	-2.0
Winner (137)	126,784	3,033	2.4	1,665	40.0	.2	-2.2
Nesbitt (139)	127,916	2,851	2.2	1,528	41.3	1.1	-1.1
Smith (146)	131,864	3,864	2.9	1,767	56.3	4.2	1.2
Buring (147)	125,572	6,386	5.1	3,269	**78.4**	-.7	-5.8

Note: Numbers are based on the Bureau of Justice Statistics Mid-Year Report (2003). Percent Black Disfranchised represents the percentage of blacks in the district who are incarcerated. The Court allows the size of each district to deviate from the standard by 5 percent. By removing the prison population from census figures, we see that nine of New York's Assembly districts fall far short of the allotted size.

of the political dynamics. New York State Senator Dale Volker stated, "It's a good thing these inmates can't vote because if they could they would never vote for me."[30] Volker's district is the site of eight facilities (including Attica) and more than 11,000 inmates. This means that more than 10 percent of his district's residents are disfranchised. This also means that the voting power of 90 percent of a rural prison district is equal to the voting power of 100 percent of an urban district. This inflation holds powerful implications for electoral strength as well as claims of representation. In particular, it prompts us to question whether constituents choose their representatives or representatives choose their constituents. Ironically, Volker also serves on several Senate committees that shape crime policy, including the Crime Victims Committee and the Crime and Corrections Committee. As chair of the Judiciary Committee, Volker led a review of New York's notorious Rockefeller Drug laws.[31] Given that most criminal justice policy is made in the states, inmate enumeration provides a greater incentive for legislators who represent districts with large prison populations to endorse policies that help sustain mass incarceration.

Table 5.4. Top Fifteen Federally Funded Programs That Rely on Census Data

Program	Annual Budget (in Billions)
Medicaid	$104.4
Highway Construction	$19.7
Title I Grants	$3.7
Foster Care	$3.7
Federal Mass Transit	$3.1
Community Development Block Grants	$3.0
WIC (food assistance)	$3.0
Social Services Block Grants	$2.4
Rehabilitation Services	$2.2
Employment and Training	$1.4
Substance Abuse Treatment	$1.4
HOME Investment	$1.3
Community Development	$1.2
Job Training, Title II-A	$1.1
Childcare and Development Block Grants	$1.0

Source: Formula Grants: Effects of Adjusted Population Counts on Federal Funding to States. General Accounting Office.

The Constitution only mandates the use of census data for apportionment. However, census data have become critically important for distributing other political and economic resources. A recent report released by the Brennan Center documents that more than $175 billion in federally funded programs were allocated based on census data. In its "Guide to Census 2000 Redistricting Data," the Bureau aptly suggests that "the imagination is the only limit upon the uses of the stats that come out of the Census."[32]

Table 5.4 documents the top fifteen government programs that rely on census data. These programs target some of the most vulnerable members of our communities, including the poor, children and youth, the unemployed, and individuals battling addictions. Cities have long contended with meeting the needs of such groups. Existing studies suggest that communities of color are often disproportionately represented among such populations. For example, more than 25 percent of African Americans and 22 percent of Latinos nationwide live below the poverty line, the majority of them in urban areas.[33] These figures suggest that communities of color have a greater need for such programs, so a greater share of the available resources should be allocated to urban communities.[34]

In light of these shifting patterns, the Census Bureau argues that "it is even more important now than it was in 1790 that every person . . . be counted and that the information about each be accurate and complete."[35] Accurate enumeration takes on increased significance when we consider that census data shape how states draw political districts and allocate valuable political resources such as general funding, voting machines, and distributive programs. The distribution of these resources holds powerful consequences for the policies that may be enacted.

Consider Connecticut. Although Connecticut ranks twenty-ninth in population among US states, it has one of the highest incarceration rates in the country. The distribution of prisoners reveals great imbalance. More than half of Connecticut's inmates come from a few neighborhoods in the cities of New Haven, Hartford, Waterbury, Bridgeport, and New Britain. Not surprisingly, these five cities are also the most racially and ethnically diverse in the state. For example, African Americans and Latinos comprise approximately 40 and 20 percent, respectively, of the total population of the city of New Haven. Like many other central cities, the bulk of the city's minority groups are concentrated in a few residential neighborhoods, the Hill, Fair Haven, Dixwell, and New Hallville. Within these neighborhoods, 1 in 7 black men (ages 18–49) has a criminal conviction. The same four neighborhoods accounted for 75 percent of New Haven's total incarcera-

Table 5.5. Connecticut's Inmate Population by Town of Origin

Town	Number of Inmates	Percentage of Total
Bridgeport	2,364	12.4
Hartford	2,729	14.2
New Haven	2,882	15.0
Waterbury	1,326	6.9
New Britain	749	3.9
Stamford	500	2.6
Meride	461	2.4
East Hartford	346	1.8
Norwalk	346	1.8
New London	307	1.6
West Haven	307	1.6
Non-Connecticut Residents	1,672	8.7

Source: Christopher Reinhart. "Town of Residence of Incarcerated Inmates," Office of Legislative Research, Connecticut General Assembly, 2010, http://www.prisonsersofthecensus.org/ct/ct_town_of_residence_031002010.pdf.

tion expenditure for 2010. Yet there are no prisons located in the state's metropolitan areas. Table 5.5 presents data on the urban concentration of Connecticut inmates.

Data from the 2010 census also shows that the city of New Haven had a higher proportion of families living below the poverty line (about 19 percent) than both the state of Connecticut (about 8 percent) and the entire nation (about 9 percent). The bulk of New Haven families living below the poverty line are concentrated within the same four neighborhoods. Most of New Haven's inmates originate from diverse communities with diverse socioeconomic needs. However, the communities in which inmates are housed are demographically distinct. The state's largest prisons are located in rural areas—Niantic, Cheshire, Uncasville, and Suffield. The reported population of those areas has increased by nearly 42 percent since 1990. Much of this growth can be attributed to the increasing size of the incarcerated population. The transfer and accompanying enumeration of offenders from urban neighborhoods to Connecticut's rural environs further marginalizes the voters in the neighborhoods prisoners left behind. For example, inmates comprise more than 10 percent of the population in four of Connecticut's state house districts. By removing inmates from the count, we find that these districts are actually underpopulated, hence overrepresented. Former Connecticut State Representative Bill Dyson, who represented a large swath of New Haven's disfranchised urban communities, argues that this transfer process permanently relegates his constituents to the political periphery.[36]

Counting on Civil Death

The decreased size of the electorate in cities coupled with their muffled political voice makes it difficult for urban communities to successfully pursue change. The enumeration process institutionalizes civil death by promoting greater apathy on the part of urban voters and their neglect by elected officials. In this way, the United States' approach to punishment and the distribution of political resources further imperils American cities. Cities become more vulnerable to changing socioeconomic conditions while also being stripped of many of the resources necessary to address the root causes and consequences of economic and social instability. What then is the incentive for a political candidate or public official to respond to the needs of citizens in Newark's Central Ward given the relatively few number of votes and value of campaign donations? Given the rising costs of running a political campaign, can residents of North Philadelphia expect political leaders to consider their interests if they are not viewed as members of their actual or potential governing coalition? Punishment seems to be one of the few issue domains that both Democrats and Republicans agree on. How might this consensus further widen the gap between the principle and the practice of democratic inclusion? The United States' approach to punishment imperils the ability of urban spaces to properly serve and represent their inhabitants. The disproportionate rates of crime, violence, and poverty embedded within cities translate into a direct loss of human capital while also displacing valuable economic and political resources. In essence, the socioeconomic inequality that plagues America's cities both heightens and is heightened by political inequality.

Judith N. Shklar argues that the ballot serves as a certificate of full membership in society because it separates citizens from outsiders and affirms their worth.[37] "[P]eople who are not granted these marks of civic dignity feel dishonored, not just powerless and poor. They are also scorned by their fellow citizens. The struggle for citizenship in America has, therefore, been overwhelmingly a demand for inclusion in the polity, an effort to break down barriers to recognition. . . ."[38] The ability to participate in the political process serves both instrumental and symbolic purposes. The high concentration of citizens who are legally barred from participating, coupled with their diminished socioeconomic status, poses a formidable challenge to urban political representation.

Conclusion

The increase in mass incarceration and the extension of its collateral consequences intensify concerns for the continued ability of urban communities to affirm their political presence. Often the scholarly focus on the Tenth Amendment centers on the battle between states and the federal government about who has primary responsibility to provide for the health and welfare of high-cost citizens. How do the cities that are most often home to high-cost citizens address the day-to-day challenges that arise from their presence? Mass incarceration directly removes human capital from urban communities, while the collateral consequences of a conviction significantly reduce the number of eligible voters. In turn, mass incarceration and its consequences constrain the community's ability to make electoral gains. For example, African Americans represent 40 percent of the 5 million Americans who are permanently barred from voting because of a felony conviction.[39] In Alabama, Florida, Mississippi, and Virginia, one in four black men is permanently disfranchised. Further, the rate of black voter disfranchisement is nearly seven times the national average.[40] In this chapter, I have argued that the incarceration of African American citizens holds powerful consequences not only for individual voters but also, and more importantly, for the communities to which they belong.

Todd Clear writes that "the hard-and-fast assumption of incarceration as a tool of public safety is that removing these people from their communities subtracts the problems they represented for their places, and thereby leaves these places better."[41] The problem with this logic is that it overlooks the assets that are transferred by moving people away from their communities. Mass incarceration disfranchises individual voters while simultaneously diluting the electoral power of the broader communities, both residential and descriptive—towns, neighborhoods, cities, and African Americans and people of color collectively—to which they belong. Although inmates are prohibited from casting ballots in all but two states, their bodies are still counted in the census of the state where they are imprisoned. Just as the presence of disfranchised blacks increased the representation of white Southerners under the Three-Fifths Clause, the presence of disfranchised inmates increases the representation of rural communities while undercutting the representation of urban communities. The overrepresentation of marginalized communities within the criminal justice system leads to their greater underrepresentation in the political process.

Notes

1. Katherine Tate, *From Protest to Politics: The New Black Voters in American Elections* (New York: Russell Sage Foundation, 1993); Ronald W. Walters, *Freedom Is Not Enough: Black Voters, Black Candidates, and American Presidential Politics* (Lanham, MD: Rowan & Littlefield Publishers, 2005); J. Morgan Kousser, *Colorblind Injustice: Minority Voting Rights and the Undoing of the Second Reconstruction* (Chapel Hill, NC: University of North Carolina Press, 1999); Richard M. Valelly, *The Two Reconstructions: The Struggle for Black Enfranchisement* (Chicago: University of Chicago Press, 2004).

2. Khalilah L. Brown-Dean, "Permanent outsiders: Felon disenfranchisement and the breakdown of black politics," *National Political Science Review* 11 (2007): 103–117.

3. Marc Mauer and Ryan S. King, *Uneven Justice: State Rates of Incarceration by Race and Ethnicity* (Washington, DC: The Sentencing Project, 2007), http://www.sentencingproject.org/doc/publications/rd_stateratesofincbyraceandethnicity.pdf.

4. Hispanics were first accounted for in the US Census beginning in 1970. Before that time, the Census along with the Bureau of Justice Statistics simply "assigned" members of this ethnic group to one of the traditional racial groups.

5. Loic Wacquant, "Deadly Symbiosis When Ghetto and Prison Meet and Mesh," *Punishment & Society* 3, no. 1 (2001): 95–133; Bruce Western, *Punishment and Inequality in America* (New York: Russell Sage Foundation Publications, 2006); Todd R. Clear, *Imprisoning Communities: How Mass Incarceration Makes Disadvantaged Neighborhoods Worse* (New York: Oxford University Press, 2007).

6. Tama Leventhal, Jeanne Brooks-Gunn, "The Neighborhoods They Live In: The Effects of Neighborhood Residence on Child and Adolescent Outcomes," *Psychological Bulletin* 126 (2000): 309–337; Robert J. Sampson, *Great American City: Chicago and the Enduring Neighborhood Effect* (Chicago: University of Chicago Press, 2012); Jeffrey D. Morenoff, Robert J. Sampson, and Stephen W. Raudenbush, "Neighborhood Inequality, Collective Efficacy, and the Spatial Dynamics of Urban Violence" *Criminology* 39 (2001): 517–559; Maria Velez, "The Role of Public Social Control in Urban Neighborhoods," *Criminology* 39 (2001): 837–863.

7. Christopher Uggen, Jeff Manza, and Melissa Thompson, "Democracy and the Civic Reintegration of Criminal Offenders," *Annals of the American Academy of Political and Social Science* 605 (2006): 281–310.

8. Todd Clear, "The Effects of High Imprisonment Rates on Communities," *Crime and Justice* 37, no. 1 (2008): 97–132.

9. Harry David Saunders, "Civil Death: A New Look at an Ancient Doctrine," *William and Mary Law Review* 11 (1970): 988–1003.

10. Brown-Dean, "Permanent Outsiders"; Michel Foucault, *Discipline and Punish: The Birth of the Prison* (New York: Pantheon Books, 1977); Marie Gottschalk, *The Prison and the Gallows: The Politics of Mass Incarceration in America* (New York: Cambridge University Press, 2006); Barbara Owen, *In the Mix: Struggle and Survival in a Women's Prison* (Albany: State University of New York Press, 1998); Michelle Alexander, *The New Jim Crow: Mass Incarceration in the Age of Colorblindness* (New York: New Press, 2010); Traci R. Burch, *Punishment and Participation: How Criminal Convictions Threaten American Democracy* (Chicago: University of Chicago Press, 2013).

11. The creation of the personal income tax in 1913 erased the census' attachment to tax collection. However, the census continues to play a prominent role in apportionment.

12. Article I, Section 2 of the US Constitution.

13. The Thirteenth Amendment (1865) abolished slavery, while the Fifteenth Amendment (1870) extended the franchise to African American *men*.

14. Alexander Keyssar, *The Right to Vote: The Contested History of Democracy in the United States* (New York: Basic Books, 2000). The 1800 election was highly contested and resulted in a tie vote in the Electoral College. The Three-Fifths Clause gave slaveholding states more seats in the House of Representatives and helped Jefferson secure victory.

15. US Census Bureau, Population Division, "Plans and Rules for Taking the Census, Residence Rules," http://www.census.gov/population/www/census-data/resid_rules.html.

16. US Department of Defense, Federal Voting Assistance Program, http://www.fvap.gov/laws/legal.html.

17. Lisa L. Miller, *The Perils of Federalism: Race, Poverty, and the Politics of Crime Control* (New York: Oxford University Press, 2008).

18. City manager of Sayre quoted in Kilborn (2001). Peter T. Kilborn, "Rural Towns Turn to Prisons to Reignite Their Economies," *New York Times*, November 24, 2010.

19. Todd R. Clear, "The Problem with 'Addition by Subtraction:' The Prison-Crime Relationship in Low Income Communities," in *Invisible Punishment: The Collateral Consequences of Mass Imprisonment*, ed. Marc Mauer and Meda Chesney-Lind (New York: New Press, 2003), 181–194.

20. Calvin L. Beale, "Cellular Rural Development: New Prisons in Rural and Small Town Areas in the 1990s," paper presented at the annual meeting of the Rural Sociological Society, Albuquerque, New Mexico, August 18, 2001, as cited in Tracy Huling, "Building a Prison Economy in Rural America," in *Invisible Punishment*, ed. Mauer and Chesney-Lind, 197–213.

21. http://www.brennancenter.org/programs/cj/Home%20in%202010.pdf.

22. Huling, "Building a Prison Economy," 206–207.

23. David Shichor, "Myths and Realities in Prison Siting," *Crime & Delinquency* 38, no. 1 (1992): 70–87; Lois M. Takahashi and Sharon Lord Gaber, "Controversial Facility Siting in the Urban Environment: Resident and Planner Perceptions in the United States," *Environment and Behavior* 30, no. 2 (1998): 184–215; Randy Martin and David L. Myers, "Public Response to Prison Siting: Perceptions of Impact on Crime and Safety," *Criminal Justice and Behavior* 32, no. 2 (2005): 143–171.

24. The following states have counties where more than 50 percent of the black population is incarcerated: Illinois, Iowa, Indiana, Kansas, Kentucky, Louisiana, Maryland, Michigan, Minnesota, Missouri, Nevada, New Jersey, New Mexico, New York, North Carolina, Ohio, Oklahoma, Oregon, Pennsylvania, South Dakota, Tennessee, Texas, Virginia, Washington, West Virginia, and Wisconsin.

25. Rose Heyer and Peter Wagner, "Too Big to Ignore: How Counting People in Prisons Distorted Census 2000," http://www.prisonersofthecensus.org/toobig.

26. The Court ruled in *White v. Regester (1973)* that state legislative districts may not deviate from the "ideal size" by more than 10 percent.

27. Although Article I, Section 2 only addresses federal apportionment, the Equal Protection Clause applies the one person–one vote standard to the states.

28. Virginia and Texas are two of the most popular states for receiving out-of-state inmates. A report issued by the Connecticut Department of Corrections estimates that the state spends approximately $40,000 per inmate who is housed in another state. In 2003, 500 Connecticut offenders were housed in Virginia prisons.

29. Peter Wagner, "Importing Constituents: Prisoners and Political Clout in New York" Prison Policy Initiative, 2002, http://www.prisonpolicy.org/importing/importing.html#sec1.

30. Quoted in Jonathan Tilove, "Minority Prison Inmates Skew Local Populations as States Redistrict," *Newhouse News Service*, March 12, 2002.

31. The Rockefeller Drug Laws mandate that anyone convicted of possessing four ounces, or trafficking two ounces of narcotics, is subject to a fifteen-year prison sentence. The Rockefeller Laws have become an influential model of determinate sentencing for other state and federal jurisdictions. Consider, for example, the sentencing disparities for crack versus powder cocaine.

32. US Census Bureau, *Strength in Numbers: Your Guide to 2010 Census Redistricting Data from the U.S. Census Bureau* (Washington, DC: US Dept. of Commerce, Economics and Statistics Administration, US Census Bureau, 2010), http://www.census.gov/clo/www/strenghth2.pdf.

33. US Census Bureau, Income, Poverty, and Health Insurance Coverage in the United States: 2009, Current Population Reports, series P60–238, and Historical Tables—Tables 2 and 6, September 2010. See also http://www.census.gov/hhes/www/poverty/poverty.html and http://www.census.gov/hhes/www/poverty/data/historical/people.html.

34. The terms "African American," "communities of color," and" urban" are not used interchangeably. Rather, this association is based on existing data

that show that African Americans and Latinos are more likely to reside in urban areas than rural ones.

35. US Census Bureau, *Strength in Numbers.* http://www.census.gov/clo/www/strenghth2.pdf.

36. Personal interview, March 4, 2006.

37. Judith N. Shklar, *American Citizenship: The Quest for Inclusion* (Cambridge: Harvard University Press, 1991).

38. Ibid., 3.

39. Khalilah L. Brown-Dean, "Trading *Brown* for Prison Orange: Reflections on Racial Justice Fifty Years after *Brown v. Board of Education*," *Journal of the Institution for Social and Policy Studies* (2005); Khalilah L. Brown-Dean, *Once Convicted, Forever Doomed: Race, Crime, and Political Inequality*, unpublished manuscript, 2006.

40. Jamie Fellner and Marc Mauer, "Losing the Vote: The Impact of Felony Disenfranchisement Laws in the United States" (Washington, DC: Human Rights Watch and The Sentencing Project, 1998).

41. Todd R. Clear, "The Problem with 'Addition by Subtraction.'"

6

Crime, Punishment and Urban Governance in Contemporary American Politics

*Lisa L. Miller**

Camden, New Jersey, and Philadelphia, Pennsylvania, share many common characteristics. Both urban locales have large African-American populations, high concentrations of poverty, alarming murder rates for blacks and Latinos, and vastly disproportionate arrest and imprisonment rates for racial minorities in contrast to whites.[1] The two cities are separated by the Delaware River, which marks the eastern edge of Pennsylvania and the western border of New Jersey. Barely a mile wide, the river represents an iconic moment in American history. George Washington's crossing at Trenton anchors the American mythology as one of a tyrannized people banked down on a snowy riverbank, rising up against an empire, and eventually emerging victorious from a bloody, seven-year war for liberty. The story, of course, masks many realities, including the tyranny that the colonies themselves were perpetrating on another people. The horror of slavery stands as an irreconcilable contradiction to the picture of colonists fighting for liberty that emerges in American civics classes.

But Washington's crossing should also remind us of another oft-misunderstood element of the American founding: the federal political

*I am deeply indebted to participants in the Seminar on the City: American Government as Urban Government at Drexel University, June 13, 2011, as well as to Amy Bridges and Michael Javen Fortner, for their insightful commentary on earlier drafts of this paper.

structure that the American Revolution wrought, due at least in part to
the very cleavages that slavery created for the new nation. The temporary
cooperation between the states that forged the battle for independence
was quickly complicated by the conflicting needs of the new Republic,
and the boundaries between the states took on even greater significance as
the nation's founders struggled to find common ground on which to hold
the country together. The federal structure of the American Constitution
meant that slavery continued and that states and localities remained the
primary venue for governing the day-to-day lives of citizens.[2]

What does this multitude of jurisdictions look like today, and what
are the consequences for contemporary urban governance? In this chapter, I suggest that contemporary federalism shapes the quality of urban
life in important ways, most significantly in the challenges it poses to
the *efficacy* of the political mobilization of marginalized citizens. These
obstacles are particularly acute for African-Americans because they experience disadvantage of a different magnitude from whites in most cities.[3]
Though often lauded as a democracy-enhancing political structure that
promotes political engagement in many forms, I argue that the current
configuration of the multitiered structure of American federalism distorts
urban political priorities and contributes to a governing system that provides punishment, rather than prosperity, for a disturbing proportion of
its marginalized citizens. It does so by diluting the power of urban citizens
in the vertical structure of governance and by Balkanizing natural urban
allies across the array of horizontal jurisdictional authorities.

As Michael Javen Fortner notes in this volume, while city limits are
not inherent to urban governance, deindustrialization and the expansion
of federal lawmaking have constrained cities in important ways in the
second half of the twentieth century. Here I want to add the dramatic
increase in violence and the proliferation of venues for political action
to these other changes that further decreased urban capacity to address
major social problems in the post–World War II period. In a great irony
of the late twentieth century, as legal obstacles to black progress were
being dismantled and blacks began to gain a political foothold in urban
political spaces, the waning power of urban governments within state
legislatures and national politics and the challenges to collective action
across urban localities made it difficult for this new authority to be exercised in meaningful and transformative ways. Increasingly, the primary
social policy tool in the urban arsenal to confront violence and social
disorder became policing, a reactive and repressive tool made even more
so by the declining economic and social capacities of urban governments.

I take as my starting point that the bargain struck through American-style federalism has changed its character and shape over two centuries and continues to be important for understanding the capacity of racial and ethnic minorities to exercise political power in the twenty-first century. The extant literature on federalism and cities has generally focused on the economic incentive of cities to limit taxation and redistribution,[4] the internal race and class dynamics of cities,[5] and the temporal variations in power and authority between local and centralized governments.[6] Here, rather than treat the place of cities in the modern federal system as alternately independent or constrained, I explore the ways in which the federal system carves up and dilutes political power and authority more generally. My focus is the contemporary spatial location of cities in the vertical and horizontal hierarchy of power and authority in the American federal system and the implications of this location for the efficacy of urban political mobilization aimed at confronting and addressing serious problems of poverty, violence, and punishment today.

It is worth noting that the structure of American federalism has long made it difficult for African-Americans suffering from violent victimization to find political recourse.[7] Most obviously, slavery itself was protected by the original constitutional design.[8] But even after the Civil War, the states of the former confederacy ensured that violence toward blacks, especially if it was perpetrated by whites, would remain exclusively the legal terrain of the states. From the use of federal courts to constrain congressional authority in the late 1800s (e.g., *Civil Rights Cases*, *U.S. v. Cruikshank*), to the blocking of anti-lynching legislation in the Senate[9] and the use of state juries to nullify guilty verdicts of murderous white defendants (e.g., the case of Medgar Evers and the two hung juries for defendant Byron de la Beckwith), the decentralized and fragmented federal system provided numerous obstacles to the protection of African-Americans from violence.

By taking account of the political and legal contexts in which cities must govern today, I argue that high levels of political mobilization in urban areas around economic inequality, crime and violence, arrest, and punishment run up against the limited capacity of local governments to ameliorate them and generate substantial limitations on the political efficacy of urban mobilization. Despite the decline of city spoils, urban residents continue to mobilize and engage in "street-fighting pluralism"[10] to demand that local governments redress high levels of deprivation, central to which is the exposure to serious violence. Understanding the limited capacity of city dwellers to force lawmakers to address the vast inequities

in both security and prosperity across racial groups in the urban United
States depends, in part, on understanding how the current structure of
the federal political system organizes representation, political capacity,
and accountability both vertically, within state and national capacities, as
well as horizontally, across cities.

Cities and American Federalism in Brief

James Madison's vision of federalism for the new United States was partly
a function of political necessity, but substantive defenses in response to
antifederalists centered largely on the capacity of a federal system to check
power. Multiple spheres of sovereignty in a large nation would guarantee against usurpation of power by one set of interests over another.[11]
Madison, and subsequent defenders of federalism, also championed the
arrangement as one that would enhance the participatory potential of
American democracy by creating multiple layers of legislative venues and
thus allowing for greater checks on the exercise of power that was not in
the public interest.[12] Though there is some debate about the intellectual
origins of federalism, Americans tend to embrace Madisonian defenses
of it.[13] When I teach constitutional law, my students reflexively defend
American federalism as a natural and essential component of democracy.
They accept the basic premise that multiple levels of government across
localities, states, and national venues offer checks on power, and they are
equally persuaded by the idea that democracy is enhanced when popular
sovereignty is multiplied across a variety of venues.

These popular defenses of federalism (and sometimes scholarly
ones[14]), however, overlook the conflicts in which the structure of the
American republic was forged in the late eighteenth century and its implications for how federalism evolved over the course of American history.
Central to the stability of the new republic was a constitutional bargain
with the slave economy, an agreement that was woven into the fabric of its
institutional design. This design ensured that power was sufficiently centralized to hold the new nation together economically and defensively. But
it also divided power across jurisdictional contexts, creating multiple veto
points that would make it difficult for any one side of the slave economy
conflict to gain sufficient governing powers from the center.[15] Thus, in a
very real sense, power under the United States federal system has always
had multiple veto points woven into the fabric of its institutional design.

As scholars of American development have demonstrated, including
many in this volume, the power and authority of the various components

of the federal system—the places of power, contestation and veto, in other words—have been fluid throughout the nineteenth and twentieth centuries. The Civil War generated profound and long-lasting shifts in the balance of power between the states and national government, and these changes grew in nature and scope throughout the twentieth century. For much of the post–Civil War period, white supremacists and racial reformers fought regular battles in and around these fluid and permeable boundaries, and for nearly two centuries whites successfully exploited their state and local police powers (and occasionally their power in Congress) to deny legal protection to blacks—including what Naomi Murakawa refers to as "the first civil right," that of the protection from violence by other citizens—by winning battles to block the increasingly powerful center from making law in support of black rights and interests.[16]

As the civil rights movement grew more powerful, however, racial reformers began to find success in nationalizing racial issues to shield African-Americans from repressive, local white majorities.[17] American political development scholars have described in detail the dramatic changes to the federal political landscape that emerged in the twentieth century, most strikingly in the post–World War II period. Economic, social, and political developments both domestically and globally generated an activist national government that swept away earlier legal and political barriers to policy making, despite the fact that the US Constitution remained largely unchanged.[18] The Civil Rights Act, the Voting Rights Act, prison reform, and rights of criminal defendants, to name just a few, provide evidence that earlier constitutional limitations on national institutions had little practical effect in restricting the scope of national lawmaking power in the twentieth century when powerful social movements exerted sustained pressure for change and exogenous factors helped propel them forward.[19]

As scholars of both racial and urban political development have noted, however, to regard such changes to the scope of federal power as uniformly benefiting African Americans is to overlook the ways in which racial reforms can also reinforce traditional racial orders, diluting the capacity of reforms to promote lasting economic and social equality. American federalism has provided opportunities for just such dilutions.[20]

Implications for Urban Governance

The growth of the national branches of government as dominant players in policy making and the political utility of nationalizing racial issues in the second half of the twentieth century, however, tells only *one* part of the federalism and localism story. Two crucial qualifiers, to which we now turn, are necessary to understand the place of urban politics, power, and punishment today.

First, though the urban political agenda, with its challenges to race and class hierarchies, rose to national prominence quickly and decisively in the 1960s, by the end of the 1970s it had virtually disappeared.[21] Certainly withering attacks from the newly reconstituted Republican Party and interest groups on the right help to explain this outcome. An often overlooked but important additional factor that facilitated the erosion of cities as worthy beneficiaries of national attention at this time was the astonishing increase in the violent crime rate.[22] Between 1950 and 1980, the national homicide rate more than doubled, increasing 122 percent from 4.6 to 10.2 murders per 100,000. In the twenty-year period between 1960 and 1980, the homicide rate increased in every state except Virginia.[23] In states from New Jersey to Hawaii, Massachusetts to California, Pennsylvania to Missouri, and Michigan to North Dakota, the homicide rate increased at an even higher pace than the national average during this time.[24] Violent crime rates also rose at an astonishingly fast pace, growing 270 percent, from a rate of 160 violent crimes per 100,000 in 1960 to 592 in 1980.

The collision of pervasive, random, often lethal violence as a new and dramatic social problem, and the resistance to black progress by both fervent white supremacists and more moderate members of both parties, created additional incentives to limit urban capacity, except where it pertained to policing and punishment. Vesla Weaver, for example, illustrates how the national policies that emerged to confront crime in the late 1960s and 1970s helped to grow the urban law enforcement apparatus in substantial ways.[25] Just as cities were losing their political capacity to claim fiscal support for a wide range of social policies and public services, serious crime and its political utility for opponents of racial progress increased the one area of local politics that had widespread political support—local police, jails, and local antidrug enforcement efforts.[26]

Second, though the institutions of the national government have grown in scope and authority, the policy-making capacity of states and localities has been largely impervious to these changes in terms of the persistence, and even growth, of routine powers of state governing (with a few notable exceptions, such as the enforcement of bans on de jure race discrimination). In other words, while the constitutional structure of American federalism has changed little since 1787—with the exception of the aptly named Civil War Amendments (13th, 14th and 15th)—*in practice*, the national government has grown in size and scope even as states and localities have also remained sites of group mobilization, activity, and pressure on a wide range of issue, including health, environment, transportation, public works, crime, and public safety. In practice, this has been a positive-sum political process with implications for understanding power and politics in cities and, in particular, the limitations on the efficacy of political mobilization by city dwellers today.[27] The political evolution of federalism in the second half of the twentieth century, then, is both a story of power shifting from the states to the national government—which undoubtedly *improved* the living conditions and life experiences of African-Americans—as well as one of power and authority proliferating across many political venues, which *dilutes* the capacity of city dwellers to influence political agendas.

Why might this be the case? American politics scholars have offered a variety of accounts of the power of urban governance in the latter half of the twentieth century. Katznelson focuses on the bifurcation of workplace politics and community politics of urban ethnic groups that eventually fractured African-American political mobilization and limited local patronage to primarily the distribution of public service benefits to blacks.[28] Peterson, by contrast, assesses the economic place of cities in the federal system, examining the capacity of urban governments to control land, labor, and capital and the possibilities of developmental, redistributive, and allocational policy making.[29] Concluding that cities are fiscally limited, Peterson argues that there are few incentives for active and effective organized group interests at the local level because "redistribution is not . . . ordinarily a constituent part of local government policy."[30] Skocpol analyzes the change in organizational structure and membership over the twentieth century and concludes that the growth of national politics facilitated a top-down institutional structure that replaced traditional, federated associations.[31] These new national organizations were disproportionately left leaning and had the effect of "negatively arousing" social conservatives, who then initiated a revival of voluntarism and grassroots political energy opposing social welfare programs and advocating pro-business policies.[32]

These accounts are important, but they all share an assumption that the mobilization of urban groups in contemporary politics is very limited. Such groups are either *diluting* their organizing by cleaving labor politics from neighborhood politics, essentially *demobilized* altogether, or simply *outnumbered* by right-wing, grassroots, membership groups. By contrast, I suggest that urban dwellers, including the poor, remain actively engaged in pluralistic, group politics but that such activity is difficult to render visible in the context of the modern version of American federal arrangements.

Some see the fluid and open jurisdictional boundaries of American federalism, particularly in the post–World War II period, as providing new and valuable opportunities for a mobilized citizenry to find new venues in which to press their claims.[33] But I have found—and I think Skocpol[34] implicitly confirms—that multiple, simultaneous legislative venues can facilitate wide-scale disenfranchisement of the interests of minorities and the poor by dividing and conquering their advocacy efforts and by erecting obstacles to collective action on issues like security, prosperity, and punishment. Certainly the lived experience of many urban minorities is one of substantial economic, social, and political marginalization. But acting in their collective self-interest on these issues is made more difficult by the jurisdictional boundaries that parse cities into different states and currently place cities at the bottom of a vertical hierarchy of power.

This positive-sum state of American federalism can help us make sense of why city dwellers, particularly blacks, have not been more successful in mounting a challenge to the problems of poverty and punishment and connecting social and economic inequities to crime and violence. Here I provide two illustrations of the challenges that cities face under American federalism in the post–civil rights era as they try to address problems of poverty, crime, and inequality. The first explains the location of cities in the vertical hierarchy of federalism and the second focuses on the challenges to horizontal collective organizing for cities in different states.

Cities in the Federalism Hierarchy

The issue of gun violence provides a useful illustration of the contemporary problems of urban governance in American federalism. My research in Philadelphia in the late 1990s and early 2000s uncovered dozens of local groups actively mobilized on issues addressing a wide range of quality-of-life issues.[35] Though a few were formally organized and national in scope (such as the Association of Community Organizations for Reform Now [ACORN] and the National Association for the Advancement of Colored People [NAACP]), the vast majority of them were less formal and entirely local (Mothers in Charge, Men United for a Better Philadelphia, Strawberry Mansion Community Concerns). These groups brought regular and sustained pressure to bear on local lawmakers to ameliorate the gun violence in their neighborhoods. Many of the proposals addressed gun restrictions, such as gun registries, but these proposals were almost always embedded in larger contexts that addressed neighborhood quality-of-life concerns, such as youth education, after-school programs, job programs, and mentoring. Over seven years of local hearings about gun violence in the 1990s, I rarely encountered groups that advocated for harsher penalties for offenders who use guns in criminal actions. To be clear, this was not because these groups held sympathy for lawbreakers, least of all violent ones, but rather because their focus was on keeping guns out of the hands of young people in the first place, rather than responding retroactively to violence.[36] Political mobilization around gun violence was on reducing victimization, and these groups saw victimization as deeply connected to the quality of life in their neighborhoods. The pressure these groups brought to bear on local lawmakers was a clear effort to hold the government accountable for security—the security from violence *and* security from the economic and educational poverty of the inner city.

Meanwhile, however, gun rights advocates were hard at work in the Pennsylvania state legislature promoting passage of a state law that would prohibit localities from enacting gun controls that were stricter than those enacted by the states. The result, known as a preemption law, meant that many of Philadelphia's gun control efforts were unenforceable.[37] In response to preemption laws in several states, a number of cities, including Philadelphia and Camden, joined together to sue gun manufacturers in federal court for the harm caused by gun violence.[38] The lawsuits linked gun availability to "bodily injury and death, and the fear of bodily injury and death," as well as to economic conditions of cities. The city of Camden's lawsuit, for example, noted that gun availability "interfered with the economic advantages which would have been available to the County of Camden and its citizens had the County not been forced to expend its resources to address the harms caused by various firearms introduced into the County of Camden."[39] The lawsuits were frequently joined by citizen neighborhood groups in these cities.[40]

Not to be outmaneuvered, gun rights advocates then lobbied Congress to pass national legislation protecting gun manufacturers from liability lawsuits in federal court, which resulted in the Protection of Lawful Commerce in Arms Act of 2005.[41] While resisting local regulations regarding *access* to guns, gun rights advocates aggressively supported state and national regulations that increased *criminal sentences* for gun crimes, including federal programs that provided for mandatory minimum sentences for certain crimes committed with a firearm.[42] Though a number of organizations at the national level exist that might represent the interests of city dwellers on these questions—the NAACP, MALDEF (Mexican-American Legal Defense Fund), or La Raza, for example—these groups form a tiny fraction of the political pressure groups that have access to members of Congress[43] and are rarely in a position to challenge the gun rights lobby in these multiple forums.[44]

This story reveals the complex environment in which cities must govern in the post–civil rights landscape. How can local communities hold lawmakers accountable for public safety—the very essence of government—when more organized but narrower interests trump their political voice in other venues? While it is true, as Fortner notes in this volume, that urban delegations to state governments can sometimes successfully promote their interests and extract resources from state governments, such delegations are rarely numerically sufficient to overcome sustained opposition. That the gun issue is of particular importance to black Americans, whose lives are lost through gun violence at staggeringly higher rates than whites and who constitute large portions of the urban populace, is of little consequence in a political system that facilitates the ability of narrow but highly organized interests to migrate across political venues to find ones most hospitable to them.[45] The political pressure for greater community and economic development that forms the core of citizen mobilization on gun violence at the local level is almost entirely lost in the upper echelons of American federalism, where policy goals are winnowed to simply enhancing criminal sentencing for gun crimes. Indeed, as the collapse of the urban agenda in national politics in the 1970s demonstrates, sustaining national attention to the more contextualized, socioeconomic, and racialized interests of city dwellers is more difficult than pressing members of Congress for specific legislation in specific areas. Moreover, collective action efforts by large groups, such as those to reduce urban violence, that are unsuccessful can produce a kind of negative feedback loop that discourages future such efforts.[46]

As noted earlier, this is a particularly bitter irony given that the American political system has long made it possible to ignore black victimization, from slavery and election-related violence in the post–Civil War South, to lynchings and white supremacist resistance to integration in the twentieth century. The capacity of urban minorities, and groups sympathetic to their concerns, to mount credible challenges to the race-laden, individualistic narratives of violence cannot be untethered from the federal system that has helped white racial hostilities perpetuate black victimization from slavery to lynching to urban violence. The contemporary urban experience of racial minorities is to suffer disproportionate violence *and* disproportionate punishment with little political recourse.

Of course, Congress can and has enacted substantial gun regulation. But the mere fact that localities and states can and do so as well, and that there is an ongoing political battle as to which level of government will have the last word, generates a perverse political context whereby the hard-won victories extracted by the local political mobilization of marginalized populations can be vetoed at other levels of government, where more organized and resourced groups have moved the fight. The important ways in which higher levels of government have sometimes allied with cities to address social and economic challenges need to be understood in terms of the contemporary challenges to creating the proper alignment of interests, alongside the ability to neutralize the various veto points where local mobilization can be overridden. As policy making has become more diffuse across political venues, such alliances become more difficult and fragile.

Cities and Horizontal Mobilization

The inability of cities to sustain sufficient political support for their proposals to defeat gun advocates in state legislatures and Congress illustrates another problem of American federalism. Recall the Delaware River, which divides Philadelphia, Pennsylvania, from Camden, New Jersey, two cities that experience some of the same economic and public safety catastrophes. According to the 2009 US Census, Camden is approximately half African-American and more than one-third Latino. The family poverty rate in Camden in 2008 was 39.4 percent, nearly four times the national average, and the median family income is barely half the national average, at $24,600.[47] The 2005 homicide rate was 41 per 100,000, more than eight times the national average. Philadelphia, whose black population also makes up nearly half of the city, has sections that reveal strikingly similar demographics. Strawberry Mansion, for example, is nearly 90 percent black and Latino, has a family poverty rate of 35 percent, and a median family income of $20,000. While Philadelphia's homicide rate is around 29 per 100,000, the rates are very clearly unevenly spread across the city's neighborhoods, with African-American neighborhoods, such as Strawberry Mansion, experiencing much higher rates than others. Pennsylvania, it is worth noting, has among the highest black homicide rates in the country,[48] and Camden is routinely regarded as one of the country's most dangerous cities.

Although these two cities are less than a mile apart and share fundamental common interests, the river that separates them is the marker of state boundaries, and these boundaries pose significant obstacles to coordinated political behavior by organized interests in these two cities. The residents of urban neighborhoods have little opportunity or, for that matter, incentive to join forces and act in their collective self-interest because they are under different state jurisdictions. The problem is that such groups could benefit from their natural allies in other urban areas that face similar challenges of security and prosperity. Whereas my research in Philadelphia uncovered more than 100 organizations lobbying local lawmakers on public safety and quality-of-life issues, the same research in the Pennsylvania statehouse revealed virtually none of these groups. Lawmakers indicated that it is very difficult for less formal or less resourced groups to have much of a presence in Harrisburg and that the very highly organized—the National Rifle Association, American Civil Liberties Union, Mothers Against Drunk Driving, District Attorneys Association, and law enforcement—dominate the state agenda on crime and punishment.[49] The simple realities of resource differentials in a political system that requires advocacy in multiple political venues (both horizontally and vertically organized) create disadvantages for those with concerns that require broad public collective action. Furthermore, likely allies, such as neighborhood groups in African-American and Latino communities in Philadelphia and Camden, are hindered in their collective action efforts by the division of power across the states.

Even if local groups focused on changing the conditions of their communities were able to engage in more cross-state mobilization, it is not at all clear where they should go to press their claims. The ten largest states in the country comprise 54 percent of the population. Those states include sixteen of the twenty most populated cities in the country and ten of the cities with the highest violent crime rates.[50] And yet, in the US Senate, these states have only one-fifth (20 percent) of the legislative votes. As we have already seen, Congress has few incentives to tackle the significant social problems that generate criminogenic conditions in cities, but this is compounded by the unequal representation of interests at the national level. As I have noted elsewhere, congressional attention to crime is episodic and fluid, responding to crimes du jour and shifting priorities, with attention often driven by high-profile events and larger political imperatives, little of which has much to do with the criminogenic conditions of urban neighborhoods.[51] Because policies are also enacted at state and local levels, Congress is able to "cherry-pick" crime issues, further enabling policies that decouple the question of what causes crime from the question of what to do about it. Because most crime policy is enacted at the state level, members of Congress have few incentives to consider crime as a more comprehensive social policy issue and confront guns, social and economic inequality, residential segregation, schools, or any other set of policy issues that local political actors connect to crime and violence.

The state level is also shielded from sustained political pressure by low-income urban communities because of the collective action problems that inhere even within state boundaries, thus opening up opportunities for highly organized but narrow interests to pursue their policy objectives with little coordinated opposition. This applies not only to comprehensive antiviolence strategies but also to many other issues facing low-income people, including affordable housing, quality schools, minimum wage, and public transportation, to name a few. Whereas groups across the urban landscape mobilize around these issues, they are only rarely part of larger, federated organizations that can move across the federal landscape to sustain the political demands. In other words, they rarely benefit from their own natural allies across the polity.

In a very real sense, the difficulty of large groups of ordinary people to coordinate their interests and mount sustained pressure on political elites is consistent with the Madisonian model of American democracy. Valuing stability and property over mass democratic action, this model helps to ensure that the fragmented, nationalized but simultaneously decentered, large Republic imposes obstacles to just this sort of action. That the massive ruptures of wars, economic catastrophes, and social movements overcame these obstacles at particular periods in American history should not obscure the fact that fragmentation and veto points are a central feature of American federalism that is difficult to dismantle. Understanding the constraints of urban groups confronting serious problems of crime, violence, repressive policing, and vast inequality reveals the ongoing obstacles to racial progress that have so often found an institutional outlet in American history.

Conclusion

What does this discussion reveal about urban governance, race, and punishment in the twenty-first century? Though federalism is often celebrated as democracy enhancing because it provides so many potential points of entry, this celebration masks a darker side that has made it difficult for cities in the post–civil rights era to address pressing social problems. In the area of crime and punishment, the high levels of activism and mobilization about quality-of-life concerns that routinely take place in urban politics—including activity around security from violence, but also prosperity and economic development—get lost in the larger political venues, because lawmakers at higher levels can cherry-pick issues and agendas with few electoral consequences from the people who experience the most crime. Furthermore, as others have noted, when it comes to addressing crime, congressional incentives favor individualistic, volitional explanations and racialized images of crime,[52] hardly the kind of conditions favorable to policy making aimed at ameliorating the criminogenic conditions of America's cities. Similarly, states are frequently responsive to highly resourced but narrowly focused interest groups with policy preferences that oppose those of urban reformers.

In contrast to the class consciousness framework offered by Katznelson or the purely economic challenges posed by Peterson, I have suggested here that the current form of the American federal system imposes systematic obstacles to the efficacy of political mobilization around persistent racial and economic hierarchies that are so visible and acute in cities. It is possible that the outcomes that Skocpol and others describe[53] that shifted politics to the right in the postwar period are partly a function of the rightward bias built into the many overlapping venues of contemporary American federalism. If cities want to enact legislation on public goods—either to make provisions for them or more equitably distribute them—such action takes regular, sustained, cross-venue mobilization. Blocking such action, however, or enacting legislation with a singular purpose, is facilitated by the current state of American federalism. Though violence, economic despair, and incarceration plague urban minorities, their political power is diluted and blocked by a federal system that exacerbates collective action problems and makes it difficult to sustain attention to broad social problems in national politics. Such an analysis suggests that the national victories of the civil rights movement occurred not *because* of the federal system, but *in spite of it*.

Notes

1. US Census, American Community Survey; Bureau of Justice Statistics; Statistical Abstracts 2011.

2. George Van Cleve, *A Slaveholder's Union: Slavery, Politics, and the Constitution in the Early Republic* (Chicago: University of Chicago Press, 2010); David Brian Robertson, *The Original Compromise What the Constitution's Framers Were Really Thinking* (New York: Oxford University Press, 2013); Robert F. Williams, *The Law of State Constitutions* (New York: Oxford University Press, 2009).

3. Ruth D. Peterson and Lauren Joy Krivo, *Divergent Social Worlds: Neighborhood Crime and the Racial-Spatial Divide* (New York: Russell Sage Foundation, 2010).

4. Paul E. Peterson, *City Limits* (Chicago: University of Chicago Press, 1981).

5. Ira Katznelson and Margaret Weir, *Schooling for All: Class, Race, and the Decline of the Democratic Ideal* (New York: Basic Books, 1985); Ira Katznelson, *City Trenches: Urban Politics and the Patterning of Class in the United States* (New York: Pantheon Books, 1981).

6. Peter B. Evans, Dietrich Rueschemeyer, and Theda Skocpol, eds., *Bringing the State Back In* (Cambridge: Cambridge University Press, 1985); Terrence McDonald, "The Burdens of Urban History: The Theory of the State in Recent American Social History," *Studies in American Political Development* 3, no. 1 (1989): 3–29; Paul Pierson and Theda Skocpol, eds., *The Transformation of American Politics: Activist Government and the Rise of Conservatism* (Princeton: Princeton University Press, 2007); Frank B. Baumgartner and Bryan D. Jones, eds., *Policy Dynamics* (Chicago: University of Chicago Press, 2002).

7. Claudine L. Ferrell, *Nightmare and Dream: Antilynching in Congress, 1917–1922* (New York: Garland, 1986); Vesla M. Weaver, "Frontlash: Race and the Development of Punitive Crime Policy," *Studies in American Political Development* 21, no. 2 (2007): 230–265; Naomi Murakawa, *The First Civil Right: How Liberals Built Prison America* (New York: Oxford University Press, 2014); Megan Ming Francis, *Civil Rights and the Making of the Modern American State* (Cambridge: Cambridge University Press, 2014).

8. Van Cleve, *A Slaveholder's Union.*

9. Ferrell, *Nightmare and Dream.*

10. Douglas Yates, *The Ungovernable City: The Politics of Urban Problems and Policy Making* (Cambridge: MIT Press, 1977).

11. "Federalist #10" and "Federalist #51," Roy P. Fairfield, *The Federalist Papers: A Collection of Essays Written in Support of the Constitution of the United States: from the Original Text of Alexander Hamilton, James Madison, John Jay* (Baltimore: Johns Hopkins University Press, 1981). James Madison's writings are also available from several online sources. See the James Madison Papers from the Library of Congress, http://memory.loc.gov/ammem/collections/madison_papers/index.html and also from the University of Virginia, http://rotunda.upress.virginia.edu/founders/JSMN and Yale Law School, http://avalon.law.yale.edu/subject_menus/madispap.asp.

12. Ian Shapiro, *The Federalist Papers: Alexander Hamilton, James Madison, John Jay* (New Haven: Yale University Press, 2009); Martha Derthick, "Up-to-Date in Kansas City: Reflections on American Federalism," *PS: Political Science & Politics* 25, no. 04 (1992): 671–675; Frank R. Baumgartner and Bryan D. Jones, *Agendas and Instability in American Politics* (Chicago: University of Chicago Press, 1993).

13. William H. Riker, *Federalism: Origin, Operation, Significance* (Boston: Little, Brown, 1964); Allison LaCroix, *The Ideological Origins of American Federalism* (Cambridge: Harvard University Press, 2010).

14. For example, see Heather K. Gerken, "Foreword: Federalism All the Way Down," *Harvard Law Review* (2010): 4–74.

15. The very issue that made the federalism of the US Constitution necessary, of course, eventually became its undoing, as conflicts over slavery could not be resolved under its framework. Mark A. Graber, *Dred Scott and the Problem of Constitutional Evil* (Cambridge: Cambridge University Press, 2006); Paul Finkelman, *An Imperfect Union: Slavery, Federalism, and Comity* (Chapel Hill: University of North Carolina Press, 1981).

16. Murakawa, *The First Civil Right*. See also Robertson, *The Original Compromise*; Graber, *Dred Scott and the Problem of Constitutional Evil*; Finkelman, *An Imperfect Union*; Riker, *Federalism*; Ferrell, *Nightmare and Dream*.

17. Riker, *Federalism*; Kimberley S. Johnson, *Governing the American State: Congress and the New Federalism, 1877–1929* (Princeton: Princeton University Press, 2007); Kimberley S. Johnson, *Reforming Jim Crow: Southern Politics and State in the Age before Brown* (New York: Oxford University Press, 2010).

18. An important exception to the status of the Constitution in the post–Civil War period is the 24th Amendment, ratified in 1962, which rendered illegal the imposition of any tax as a prerequisite for voting in federal elections.

19. Civil Rights Act, July 2, 1964 (Public Law 88-352), Voting Rights Act, August 6, 1965 (Public Law 89–110); *Miranda v. Arizona* 384 U.S. 436 (1966), *Harper v. Virginia* 383 U.S. 663 (1966); Law Enforcement Assistance Administration (part of the Omnibus Crime Control and Safe Streets Act), June 19, 1968 (Public Law 90-351). See also Feeley and Rubin (1998) for an excellent discussion of prison reform during this period. Mary L. Dudziak, *Cold War Civil Rights: Race and the Image of American Democracy* (Princeton: Princeton University Press, 2000); Malcolm Feeley and Edward L. Rubin, *Federalism Political Identity and Tragic Compromise* (Ann Arbor: University of Michigan Press, 2008); Baumgartner and Jones, *Agendas and Instability*; Theda Skocpol, "Government Activism and the Reorganization of American Civic Democracy," in *The Transformation of American Politics*, ed. Pierson and Skocpol; Paul Pierson, "The Rise and Reconfiguration of Activist Government," in *The Transformation of American Politics*, ed. Pierson and Skocpol.

20. Michael Omi and Howard Winant, *Racial Formation in the United States: From the 1960s to the 1990s* (New York: Routledge, 1994).

21. Baumgartner and Jones, *Agendas and Instability*.

22. See Baumgartner and Jones (1993, chapter 4) for a discussion of how the urban agenda, unlike many other political issues that rose onto the national agenda during this time period, failed to become a policy subsystem and carve out routine policy and lobbying space for its concerns, unlike other issues areas at the time (such as pollution, health care, child welfare and so on).

23. Homicide in these states was already higher than the national average in 1960. See Uniform Crime Reports, Data Tool, http://www.ucrdatatool.gov/Search/Crime/State/RunCrimeTrendsInOneVar.cfm.

24. Michigan, 127 percent (4.5–10.2), North Dakota, 140 percent (0.5–1.2), Missouri, 153 percent (4.4–11.1), New Jersey, 156 percent (2.7–6.9), Pennsylvania, 161 percent (2.6–6.8), Massachusetts, 190 percent (1.4–4.1), Hawaii, 260 percent (2.4–8.7), and California, 270 percent (3.9–14.5).

25. Weaver, "Frontlash."

26. For a discussion of support for increasing law enforcement in black, as well as white, communities, see Michael Javen Fortner, "The Carceral State and the Crucible of Black Politics: An Urban History of the Rockefeller Drug Laws," *Studies in American Political Development* 27, no. 1 (2013): 14–35; Michael Javen Fortner, "The 'Silent Majority' in Black and White Invisibility and Imprecision in the Historiography of Mass Incarceration," *Journal of Urban History* 40, no. 2 (2014): 252–282.

27. I have referred to this elsewhere as the *federalization* of issues across the multiple layers of American government (Miller 2007). There are few public policy issues that are not active agenda items for urban legislatures, state legislatures, and Congress. National security and immigration, for example, two issues over which the US Constitution clearly gives Congress power, are also pursued regularly by other levels of government, as illustrated by Arizona's immigration law and Hazelton, Pennsylvania's effort to ban undocumented immigrants from renting housing or being employed (Arizona SB 1070; "Court Rejects City's Efforts to Restrict Immigrants," *New York Times*, September 9, 2010). Similarly, marriage, crime, education, and urban transportation, issues that clearly fall under state and local police powers, have also become congressional agenda items. As issues have been increasingly nationalized, then, they have not necessarily lost their salience on state and local political agendas.

Lisa L. Miller, "The Representational Biases of Federalism: Scope and Bias in the Political Process, Revisited," *Perspectives on Politics* 5, no. 2 (2007): 305–321.

28. Katznelson, *City Trenches.*

29. Peterson, *City Limits.*

30. Ibid., 210.

31. Theda Skocpol, "Government Activism."

32. Ibid., 55.

33. Sarah Beth Pralle, *Branching Out, Digging In Environmental Advocacy and Agenda Setting* (Washington, DC: Georgetown University Press, 2006); Baumgartner and Jones, *Policy Dynamics.* See also Gerken, "Foreword."

34. Theda Skocpol, "Government Activism."

35. Miller, *The Perils of Federalism: Race, Poverty, and the Politics of Crime Control* (Oxford: Oxford University Press, 2008).

36. Ibid., chapters 5 and 6.

37. The Pennsylvania statute is PA C.S. 6101-6124. See also Goss (2010) for a lengthy treatment of the gun issue in American politics.

38. See *Camden County Board of Chosen Freeholders v. Beretta, U.S.A. Corp.* as one example (273 F.3d 536 (3d Cir. 2001). Other cities that joined in the lawsuits included Miami; New Orleans; Bridgeport, Connecticut; New York; Los Angeles; San Francisco; and Chicago, among many others.

39. *Camden County Board of Chosen Freeholders v. Beretta, U.S.A. Corp.*, Civil Action Complaint, United States District Court for the District of New Jersey, 1999.

40. Philadelphia's lawsuit, for example, was joined by ASPIRA, Guardian Civic League, Residents Advisory Board, Northeast Home and School, and Philadelphia Citizens for Children and Youth. *City of Philadelphia v. Beretta U.S.A. Corp.* 126 F.Supp.2d 882 (2000).

41. Protection of Lawful Commerce in Arms Act, P.L. 109-92, October 26, 2005.

42. Robert J. Spitzer, *The Politics of Gun Control* (New York: Chatham House Publishers, 1998).

43. For a detailed analysis, see Miller, *Perils of Federalism*.

44. The NAACP, the Mexican American Legal Defense and Education Fund (MALDEF), the Urban League, La Raza, and the US Conference of Mayors constitute a microscopic portion of witnesses at congressional hearings on crime topics in relation to prosecutors' organizations, law enforcement, and other justice system representatives. See Miller, *The Perils of Federalism*.

45. According to a Violence Policy Center report in 2009, though blacks represent just 12 percent of the US population, they comprise 48 percent of homicide victims. See Fiorina (1999) and Strolovitch (2007) for a discussion of the unrepresentative nature of many highly organized interest groups and McCarthy and Zald (1987) for discussion of resource mobilization.

Morris Fiorina, "Extreme Voices: The Dark Side of Civic Engagement," in *Civic Engagement in American Democracy*, ed. Theda Skocpol and Morris Fiorina (Washington, DC: Brookings Institute Press, 1999); Dara Z. Strolovitch, *Affirmative Advocacy Race, Class, and Gender in Interest Group Politics* (Chicago: University of Chicago Press, 2007); John D. McCarthy and Mayer N. Zald, "Resource Mobilization and Social Movements: A Partial Theory," in *Social Movements: Perspectives and Issues*, ed. Steven M. Buechler and F. Kurt Cylke (Mountain View, CA: Mayfield Publishing, 1997).

46. Lee Cronk and Beth L. Leech, *Meeting at Grand Central Understanding the Social and Evolutionary Roots of Cooperation* (Princeton: Princeton University Press, 2012).

47. Statistical Abstracts 2011.

48. Violence Policy Center, *Black Homicide Victimization in the United States An Analysis of 2004 Homicide Data* (Washington, DC: The Center, 2007).

49. Miller, *Perils of Federalism.*

50. US Census 2010; Statistical abstracts 2011.

51. Miller, *Perils of Federalism.*

52. Stuart A. Scheingold, *The Politics of Law and Order: Street Crime and Public Policy* (New York: Longman, 1984); Doris Marie Provine, *Unequal under Law: Race in the War on Drugs* (Chicago: University of Chicago Press, 2007); Katherine Beckett, *Making Crime Pay: Law and Order in Contemporary American Politics* (New York: Oxford University Press, 1997); Murakawa, *The First Civil Right*; Weaver, "Frontlash."

53. See also Michael Javen Fortner, "Race and Redemption: The Local Roots of Modern Conservatism," Prepared paper for presentation at the annual meeting of the American Political Science Association, September 1–4, 2010, Washington, DC.

7

Two Cheers for American Cities

Commentary on *Urban Citizenship and American Democracy*

Jennifer L. Hochschild

From the beginning, the editors of *Urban Citizenship and American Democracy* identified three provocative themes running through the volume: 1) "urban autonomy is contingent upon the historical development of the American polity;" 2) "when urban actors and public policies are relatively autonomous they can exert a significant effect on American society and politics," and 3) "local politics and policies shape an individual or a group's . . . membership in a broader community, whether defined as political or racial" (all from page 1 of prospectus). Empirically, the book is full of feedback loops, as one would expect from the first and second themes, ranging from the very macro interaction between constitutional federalism and local policy debates through intermediate levels to the very micro question of the associations among parents' involvement in different public arenas. Normatively, as is implicit in the third theme and the book's title, the authors' touchstone for successful urban citizenship is strong democratic control and greater racial or ethnic equality.

In this commentary, I react to individual chapters and, more importantly, to these overarching themes, empirical regularities, and normative commitments. The chapters are all significant, innovative, and analytically rich. My own views do not always concur with those of the authors and editors, but they have been deeply informed by their arguments.

Autonomy and feedback loops initially seem antithetical. Autonomy implies independence and even separation: cities are not legally or economically dependent creatures of the state or federal government, but rather make policy choices and deploy resources as they wish. Feedback loops imply interdependence and connection: cities are shaped by the state or federal government such that their policy choices and resource deployment are constrained, and they in turn shape other important features of American politics.

One can ease the antithesis with a sleight of hand—at some historical moments cities are independent and at other historical moments they are interdependent or merely dependent. That is surely true, but not analytically very interesting unless one goes much further to explain how, when, and why the swings between autonomy and feedback occur. Some chapters in *Urban Citizenship* start to do just that. In Chapter 4, before Richard Harris elegantly shows how small, deindustrialized cities lost whatever governmental control they used to have over development, at least in conjunction with real estate interests, and are now almost wholly the creatures of benevolent dictatorships in the form of foundations, hospitals, and universities. Harris's "farewell to the urban growth machine" reminded me vividly of Tocqueville's famous passage decrying "the sort of despotism that democratic nations have to fear":

> I see an innumerable multitude of men, alike and equal. . . . Over this kind of men stands an immense, protective power which is alone responsible for securing their enjoyment and watching over their fate. That power is absolute, thoughtful of detail, orderly, provident, and gentle. . . . It gladly works for their happiness but wants to be sole agent and judge thereof. . . . Thus it daily makes the exercise of free choice less useful and rarer, restricts the activity of free will within a narrower compass, and little by little robs each citizen of the proper use of his own faculties.

This characterization seems a bit harsh as a description of nonprofit organizations seeking to curb childhood obesity, community violence, and urban blight in a desperately poor and feckless city. Nevertheless, Harris fears that through the community development regime, urban residents have irrevocably lost the capacity to control the direction of their city, whether through electoral politics or direct participation. That the loss is due to transformation of the urban economy rather than intentional racial or class domination does not make it any less poignant. It does make it an example of the first and third themes of *Urban Citizenship* and a poignant illustration of what happens when the second theme does not obtain.

Tom Hulme, by contrast, provides an illustration in Chapter 2 of urban autonomy, or at least of claims to urban autonomy. He focuses on a historical period almost a century earlier than

Harris's, during which American cities were becoming increasingly industrialized, populated, and substantively energetic. I draw no causal inference about the relationship between economic conditions and urban autonomy from these two cases; the empirical materials and analytic purposes of the chapters are too disparate for direct comparison. But Hulme does offer the existence proof that, on occasion, "citizenship was an identity discourse tied explicitly and strongly to this notion of the city and . . . 'community civics.'" Hulme's cities, like Harris's, were deeply engaged in managing "the health of the people" through "everyday routines . . . of administration" and "effective and egalitarian government." But the earlier urban optimism, even boosterism, contrasts sharply with the current urban despair and hollowing out. The former claimed and promoted a city's right and capacity to benefit its citizens; the latter abandons, perhaps even with gratitude, any claim to self-control or to righting the wrongs of its residents.[1]

Hulme is, of course, analyzing textbooks' presentations of urban politics rather than actual urban political activity, so, as he notes, one must take the Progressive city's self-image with a large pinch of salt. Nevertheless, the self-image is revealing, especially in comparison with Harris's urban growth regime or community development regime. "Citizens were envisioned as interlocking parts of local communities," (1); cities engaged in "'aggressive governmental expansion'" (quoting D. Amsterdam); and "the functions and technologies of urban government" could and did promote "a safe, healthy, and virtuous life." Governmental action was the solution to the evils of private enterprise. In Hulme's words, "the situation before municipal ownership was presented negatively, with private companies delivering little water, opposed to the city council's egalitarian goal of 'millions of streams for every emergency.'" In the textbooks' words, "no privileges" were "given to corporations which would cause discomfort to, or increase the danger of, the people." Urban autonomy indeed!

Although Hulme does not discuss the third theme of *Urban Citizenship*, he makes it clear that even the most Panglossian textbooks did not venture to depict a racial and ethnic utopia. Nevertheless, they consistently used phrases such as "the people of the city," "community life," or "people's bodies and minds"—suggesting implicitly that regimes of state-imposed segregation or group hierarchy need not be part of the autonomous, thriving city. Or perhaps it never occurred to textbook writers that anything other than state-imposed segregation or group hierarchy could characterize a city, so that when they wrote about "the people of the city" they did not really mean *all* of the people. On this point, we would benefit from further investigation by Hulme.

In short, while Hulme fills out the contours of the first theme of *Urban Citizenship*, he is silent on part of the third and his argument adds an important amendment to the second. That is, Hulme's cities as presented in textbooks respond to as well as "exert[ing] a significant effect on" American society and politics. In fact, Hulme's textbook cities exert a significant effect on urban residents in part because of their embeddedness in a larger American society and politics. As he puts it, "while perhaps in retreat on the national stage, progressivism in the local arena was very much alive." Similarly, while "Americanization as a social movement and public policy faded from public consciousness' after immigration restriction in the 1920s, the formative ideas . . . remained deeply embedded in the discourse of citizenship [in cities] throughout the interwar years" (quoting Ziegler-McPherson). The influence ran from national political discourse to urban self-presentation, as well as the reverse. In that way, Hulme's analysis bears partial resemblance to that of Harris, who sees cities as more influenced than influencing.

While Hulme adds nuance to the second theme of *Urban Citizenship*'s editors, Lisa Miller actively contests it in Chapter 6, at least for the contemporary era. In her view, modern cities are unable even to exercise local autonomy, never mind to exert a significant effect on American society and politics. The fault lies in James Madison's constitutional design and the long, dark shadow of the United States' origins as a slave society. Miller links the argument that American cities are stymied in their efforts at independent action with acute concerns about the third theme, political and racial inequality. Like the editors, she is very attentive to feedback loops, in her case through three links: cities' and local actors' power or powerlessness, the federal government's ability or inability to act on behalf of blacks' rights, and the promotion or retardation of racial justice. As these variations suggest, she sees the feedback loops operating in several directions at different points in American history, as the contest between local and national power centers develops.

Miller is as discouraged about contemporary politics as Harris, though for different reasons:

> The current configuration of the multitiered structure of American federalism distorts urban political priorities and contributes to a governing system that provides punishment, rather than prosperity, for . . . a disturbing proportion of its marginalized citizens. It does so by diluting the power of urban citizens in the vertical structures of governance and by Balkanizing natural urban allies across the array of horizontal jurisdictional authorities.

It was not always thus. After the Civil War and for a century thereafter "whites successfully exploited their state and local police powers to deny legal protection to blacks . . . by winning battles to block the increasingly powerful center from making law in support of black rights and interests." That is, postbellum local governments were indeed autonomous and did exert a significant effect on American society and politics, but in the service of racial hierarchy and injustice. By the mid-twentieth century, however, the balance of power had shifted in a more positive direction, and "racial reformers began to find success in nationalizing racial issues to shield African-Americans from repressive, local white majorities." That is, post–World War II local governments lost autonomy, and their effect on American society and politics declined, to the benefit of racial justice.

But the contest has shifted again. By the twenty-first century, not only has the urban political agenda on cities "virtually disappeared," but also city dwellers have been unable to mount an "effective and sustained campaign to reduce income inequality and urban poverty." That is, both the national and local governments lost, if not their autonomy, then at least their will or capacity to promote racial and economic justice. At present, whether intentionally or not, the federal government, states, and localities are all "erecting obstacles to collective action on issues like security, prosperity, and punishment."

I find Miller's argument intriguing but not fully persuasive. After all, her core causal structure—the constitutional system of federalism—has persisted more or less intact through all three of her crucial eras: the segregationist postbellum period, the almost revolutionary civil rights era, and the recent decades of conservative retrenchment and local contestation. In some eras and some locations, local activists have battled higher levels of government in the interests of racial and class justice, as her case of mobilizing against gun violence shows. But in other eras and other locations, local activists have battled higher levels of government in the interests of segregation and exploitation of the poor and minorities, as her case of post–Civil War segregation shows.

Thus, in my view, the constitutional location of cities within the complicated American federal structure is almost an empty vessel. Local political systems are waiting to be filled with morally abhorrent sheriffs like Bull Connor or Joseph Arpaio or with morally admirable activists such as Miller's Mothers in Charge or Men United for a Better Philadelphia. Moving politics up to the national level harms the chances of racial justice in some eras: President Woodrow Wilson fostered urban segregation, and for decades Congress and the courts implicitly sanctioned lynching and state Jim Crow laws while refusing to pass or enforce civil rights laws. Moving politics up to the national level promotes racial justice in other eras: President Lyndon Johnson and the Congresses and courts of the mid-1960s promulgated policies to fight urban racial injustice. And moving politics up to the national level may have no impact: Presidents Bill Clinton, George W. Bush, and Barack Obama and their respective Congresses all did their best to ignore cities completely despite their very different ideological and partisan commitments.

The frustrating lesson of American history is that urban autonomy and racial equality are not linked in any clear causal way; the motives and capacities of political actors, who must strive within the contours of particular social and economic contexts, determine whether local governance reinforces or contests injustice. Similarly, the direction in which the feedback loop spins—whether higher-level governments influence the city or vice versa—is indeterminate, or at least we do not yet have a clear and persuasive theory about which trajectory occurs when.

Another source of frustration to the analyst is that empowerment for one local community may come at the expense of empowerment for another. Just as one cannot state that localism always or never favors racial justice, one cannot assume that local communities share interests in racial justice or anything else. That point is made vividly clear in Chapter 5 by Khalilah Brown-Dean. She draws our attention to the representational and policy consequences of putting prisons in rural areas, which means that young, urban black men become, perforce, non-urban men, at least from the perspective of census enumerators and redistricting commissions. The ironic outcome is that small, white towns gain political power, perhaps at the direct expense of large, nonwhite cities.

Brown-Dean has nothing but criticism for this transfer of people and its accompanying transfer of political and economic resources. From the perspective of efforts to promote racial justice in big cities, it is indeed harmful, not to say bizarre. In a few counties, at least a quarter of the population is incarcerated—which suddenly makes the county look racially integrated in aggregate data and which might bring it public resources that flow from the use of census data on population and poverty. But from the broader perspective of the three central themes of the volume, the story is a bit more complicated. First, while empowering predominantly white towns by importing incarcerated people of color retards racial justice, it also works to offset a century of rural disempowerment. That is surely not the right strategy for correcting decades of ignoring or exploiting small towns and rural communities, but it does have an ironic bite for analysts committed to equality for all Americans.

Second, the trajectory of American political development might eventually swing away from the pattern traced by Brown-Dean of ever-increasing rural political and economic growth based on ever-increasing urban jail or prison sentences. This point does not contravene anything in her chapter; it is an invitation to her to consider what happens when trends start to reverse course. That is, in recent years, more states have moved to reinstate the franchise for ex-felons than to disfranchise those convicted of a felony; does her analysis imply that those formal legal changes will increase cities' real political power over the next decade or two? In addition, the rate of increase in incarceration has slowed, and some evidence suggests that the number of incarcerated individuals is actually declining. Reduction in sentences for possession of cocaine should reinforce what might be a decline in the number of incarcerated young men, as should an intriguing new alliance between liberals appalled at incarceration rates and conservatives appalled at the cost of keeping someone incarcerated. If jails and prisons start to empty, or at least if new ones are no longer needed, will rural communities lose their new political and economic standing, absolutely or relatively? In short, if "urban autonomy is contingent upon the historical development of the American polity," as the first theme of this volume puts it, can we say the same thing about rural and small-town autonomy?

The two remaining chapters are, respectively, the most micro- and macro-level. Marion Orr and his colleagues focus in Chapter 3 on local democratic decision making rather than on racial or ethnic justice per se, although their motivation for studying the former undoubtedly includes concern about the latter. They are interested in how the kind of democratic participation that Miller celebrates gets started and builds momentum, especially among newcomers to the American political scene. They find that Latinos and (especially) Latinas who are active in their children's schools are also relatively active in several forms of civic engagement. Positive feedback loops enter the analysis here at the level of individuals; activism in one sphere reinforces activism in another.

As the authors state, they cannot use cross-sectional survey data to make causal assertions (although they find themselves tempted over and over to argue that "involvement in one's local school has an impact on a person's level of political activity"). From the perspective of democratic participation, the analyst's inability to determine which form of political activity leads to which other form, or whether some unspecified third variable[2] promotes political activism in several arenas at once, is a virtue; a system of mutual causation suggests that encouraging participation anywhere will encourage it everywhere, or at least elsewhere. The crucial point for this book is that some newcomers are becoming politically engaged, perhaps through several mutually reinforcing channels and for a variety of reasons, and may thereby revitalize urban democratic practices. If cities are to be autonomous and efficacious actors in the American political system as Tocqueville envisioned and the editors hope, and if urban politics is to have a chance of shaping people's membership in broader racial and political communities, then incorporating immigrants into schools, civic life, and eventually electoral politics will be essential.

Finally, Michael Javen Fortner's chapter seeks to answer some of the questions I have posed to other chapters, that is, to "provide . . . a theoretical basis and historical background for the urban state." He can address this hugely broad goal in a chapter-length essay only through a somewhat curtailed list of considerations. They include the facts that, although local municipalities are embedded in a context of strong states and a strong federal government, nevertheless they are " 'functionally specialized' and operate according to "explicit rules" that enable them to follow their own partisan and political imperatives, at least to some extent. Furthermore, "urban governments extract resources from society and deploy them to create and support their own coercive and administrative organizations," and a city's delegation in a state legislature may be able to corral a disproportionate share of the state's capacities for its own use (quoting Skocpol).

Fortner emphasizes that a city's resources and space for independent action provide no guarantee that it will act in any particular way—which means that a city may, or may not, effectively expend effort to incorporate the disfranchised and reduce inequality. Its effectiveness depends on yet another series of conditions that include the historical period in which the city is embedded, the health of the economic system at a given time, and the nature of electoral conflict. That indeterminacy accords well with the mixed findings within and across the other chapters but does not resolve the question of whether we should cheer or deplore urban independence.

Despite his qualified celebration of the possibilities of urban citizenship, Fortner ends on a curious note of pessimism: "for the last forty years, historical economic, political, and social forces colluded to cripple the capacity of cities and curtail the effectiveness of urban citizenship." Along with Amy Bridges, I am not so sure. Fortner has not shown the extinction of his set of conditions under which a city may be autonomous and influential—why should we assume that cities can no longer use their functional specialization to extract and use societal resources or can no longer promote justice? After all, Orr and his colleagues show that new urban residents are engaging in civic activities; Miller shows that advocacy groups, though frustrated, are still advocating; Harris shows that, in their own way, "eds and meds" institutions remain committed to poor, small cities. The optimism of Hulme's Progressive-era textbooks may no longer be warranted, but then it never was. If increasing incarceration reduced cities' power, as Brown-Dean shows, then maybe reducing incarceration will enable an increase in that power.

One can also point to some cities' recent political and policy activities as grounds for not giving in to Fortner's pessimism, at least across the board. In the face of the federal government's inability to pass immigration legislation, New York City, New Haven, and other urban areas have created identity cards that give undocumented immigrants standing and access to public resources. The city council in Los Angeles, among other places, voted to boycott the state of Arizona in response to its harsh SB 1070 law that promoted "attrition [of undocumented immigration] through enforcement." New Orleans is experimenting with a system of all charter schools in an effort to improve students' attainment and achievement. Researchers at the Brookings Institute recently published a book proclaiming that "we're at the beginning of the wave of growth of innovation districts in the United States. Again not because someone came up with some smart, federal program but because this . . . represents a clear path forward for cities and metro areas." Cities have been the location for African Americans, and more recently Latinos and Latinas, to gain at least some political power, and occasionally to move into broader arenas of power. They are the site for cultural innovations from hip-hop to modern dance to "ethnic" restaurants; immigrants can revitalize dreary neighborhoods.

Some of these initiatives are likely to fail, and some may not promote racial justice. But rejecting excessive optimism need not imply accepting excessive pessimism, just as celebrating the national government's override of segregationist local authorities in the 1960s does not imply rejection of local autonomy a half-century later. As authors in *Urban Citizenship and American Democracy* make clear, cities can be autonomous actors as well as participants in historically based feedback loops, and they can promote as well as retard democratic engagement and racial justice. The questions are, of course, when and how—and this book provides intriguing answers as well as more questions.

Notes

1. Harris notes that "local government . . . was excluded from the core planning team and direct implementation [of the program to reduce childhood obesity] not because it lacked motivation or concern, but because it lacked capacity; indeed the Mayor was deeply and personally supportive of the effort."

2. Possibilities include mobilization by others, a sense of political efficacy and optimism, fury over maltreatment, or a simple desire to get involved and make a difference.

3. http://www.brookings.edu/blogs/brookings-now/posts/2014/06/innovation-districts-clear-path-forward-for-cities-and-metro-areas.

8

American Cities and American Citizenship

Rogers M. Smith

It is striking that many contemporary scholars of citizenship (including me) rarely write about cities. Citizenship, after all, originated in the *poleis* or city-states of ancient Greece and Rome. Perhaps the most influential discussion of citizenship ever written, Aristotle's *Politics*, is about membership in such cities.[1] And during much of European history up to the French Revolution, the term "citizen" was still most often, though not exclusively, applied to the burghers or *bourgeois* who inhabited municipalities with their own distinctive legal prerogatives.[2] Only with the French Revolution and the American Revolution that slightly preceded it did citizenship come instead to have its most common meaning today—membership in national democratic republics, in which cities are legally subordinate parts. Perhaps the most influential modern discussion of citizenship, T. H. Marshall's "Citizenship and Social Class," is exclusively about such national citizenship.[3] It does not mention cities at all, and much subsequent scholarship on citizenship has followed suit.

It is also striking that (with distinguished exceptions, including the contributors to this volume, and especially its pioneering co-editor Amy Bridges), most scholars interested in American political development (also including me) have focused on the national institutions and policies of the American democratic republic—not on its cities. There is, to be sure, much scholarship in political science and other disciplines, past and present, pertinent to the topic of "urban citizenship in American democracy."[4] But as fields, modern citizenship studies and American

211

political development scholarship have not gone far toward developing, much less debating, accounts of that topic. Yet the endeavor is inescapably demanded by their intellectual agendas.

This situation is improving, as shown by the papers in this volume and a related predecessor, Richardson Dilworth's edited volume *The City in American Political Development*.[5] But, so far, scholars who primarily analyze citizenship have contributed little to these discussions (me again included). With, then, a sense of unfulfilled civic duty toward my fellow scholars of citizenship and American political development, as well as toward America's cities and citizens, here I sketch a conceptual framework for the study of cities and American citizenship and suggest what some of its main substantive questions and topics should be. As will be clear, my points build on much in these recent works.

Conceptually, there are three roles that cities have played in the development of the American political system and American citizenship that seem particularly significant. First, cities are important *sites of political life*. As Michael Javen Fortner argues here, though they exist within larger political, economic, and cultural structures that do much to shape and constrain the possibilities for city living, many have sufficient command of economic and political resources to exercise significant powers of autonomous self-governance. But, as he also stresses, the degree of their autonomous power has varied at different points in American history; and, as Richard A. Harris shows, American cities today are arrayed along a spectrum in which smaller, deindustrialized cities may have very little autonomous power at all.

Yet, even for the residents of such cities, the fact that they inhabit a community whose political leaders and institutions do not have much real power is important in shaping their relationship to the political system more broadly, and hence their experience of American citizenship. For some citizens and civic groups, as Harris also documents, the enfeebled condition of their city governments actually provides new opportunities for civic participation. And because in the United States roughly 80 percent of the population now lives in urban areas, cities, or suburbs, all significantly constrained but many possessed of more resources and governing capacities than Camden, New Jersey, most Americans experience their urban citizenship as a significant part of their broader civic lives.[6] So for the numerous scholars of citizenship who focus on political and social participation, the opportunities and barriers American cities pose for effective civic engagement are crucial topics. The same is true for most other nations.

For many Americans, perhaps even more than in some other nations, municipal governments are especially important because they provide their children's schools and police their neighborhoods, workplaces, and recreational districts, among many other vital services. As the chapters here by Marion Orr, Ken Wong, Emily Farris and Domingo Morel, and Lisa L. Miller discuss, city and suburban educational and policing institutions, policies, and practices have enormous consequences for American urban citizens in ways that often interact with ethnic and racial identities and inequalities in troubling fashion. Urban schools and criminal justice systems do much to shape the opportunities and obstacles that different Americans face in ways that sometimes provide channels of mobility but sometimes provide conditions that can credibly be deemed new forms of second-class citizenship.

Second, in addition to being themselves sites of political life, cities are and always have been important *actors in American state and national politics*—though again, their roles have varied significantly in different eras.[7] The United States was founded as an overwhelmingly rural nation, though leaders from cities like Philadelphia and New York, including Benjamin Franklin, James Wilson, John Jay, and Alexander Hamilton, played major roles in creating the new American republic, along with wealthy rural plantation owners like George Washington, Thomas Jefferson, and James Madison. (John Adams, the crusty farmer and lawyer who resided in Quincy and Boston, Massachusetts, represented both)

As Robert Lieberman has noted, with the rise of urbanization in the late Gilded Age through the New Deal, American national leaders came to have predominantly urban origins, and "cities earned a central, if not always honored, place in the American regime."[8] With the further expansion of federal programs in the Great Society era of the 1960s, cities appeared primed to partner with national agencies on a host of initiatives.[9] But, as Lisa L. Miller summarizes here, the recessionary 1970s followed by the rise of Reagan meant that, even though cities organized to lobby the national government (through new associations like the National League of Cities, founded in 1976), their influence waned in the last quarter of the twentieth century. Though the United States' complex system of federalism and separated powers does not prevent large, enduring majority coalitions from shaping governance broadly in the ways they wish, the existence of these institutional structures means that, as political actors, both cities themselves, and especially their more politically marginal residents, face huge obstacles when they are not riding the current of popular causes.[10] That is a reality that must be given weight in the many emerging studies of multilevel citizenship in many locales. For American inner-city residents, the United States' multiple levels of government now mean that their urban citizenship can seem more a liability than an asset in their efforts to realize the full potential of their American citizenship.

Whether or not cities, and some or all urban citizens, are able to achieve political popularity is intertwined with the third role they have played in the development of American politics and American citizenship. Cities have been and remain *political symbols* of what the American political community as a whole should either fear to become or can hope to become. Every account of American political culture recognizes that the opposition between Jefferson's espousal of a decentralized, agrarian republican empire and Hamilton's vision of an urban-centered, manufacturing and finance-based national republic shattered the harmony of Washington's first administration and gave rise to intense partisan politics. The centrality of cities as symbols in this clash is evident in Jefferson's famous remark in his *Notes on the State of Virginia* that the "mobs of great cities add just so much to the support of pure government, as sores do to the strength of the human body," and his similar statement in a letter to Benjamin Rush in 1800 that "great cities" are "pestilential to the morals, the health and the liberties of man."[11]

But though images of large cities as sinks of corruption have never ceased to resonate with millions of Americans, those depictions came to be combated, especially in the first half of the twentieth century, by portraits of municipal life as sanitary, safe, efficient, and pleasurably modern, as Tom Hulme's reading of interwar civic textbooks here demonstrates. That gleaming imagery, always contested, has subsided since the 1960s as controversies over the nation's ethnic and racial transformations and the efficacy of government programs have dramatized the ills of modern urban life. Today "urban" often is used as a euphemism for "nonwhite and poor" and sometimes socially "pathological." Nonetheless, most Americans still reside in and around cities, albeit of a wide range of sizes in many regions. In many regards, many Americans continue to see their cities as positive rather than negative symbols, at least at times. Americans have, for example, probably never been more united in the modern era than when they were moved by the horrors and heroism on display in New York City on September 11, 2001. Perhaps only briefly, but not for the first or last time, virtually all Americans saw New York City as their own grand metropolis, and as a central symbol of the United States as they wished it to be—for some despite and for some because of the fact that it is simultaneously one of the world's "global cities," a cosmopolitan home to a population in which nearly 40 percent are foreign born.[12] In many other modern nations, such as Japan, Korea, Great Britain, Mexico, and Argentina, a significantly higher percentage of the population lives in the country's largest city, which is both the nation's economic and political capital, than is the case for New York City and the United States.[13] In the cases of all such nations as well as the United States, the ways in which their citizenships are and are not symbolically imagined as urban citizenship is again a topic that studies of citizenship today cannot ignore.

Indeed, reflection on these categories and examples suggests a wide range of unresolved, substantive issues concerning the relationship of American cities to the development of American citizenship, as well as American politics more generally, that are pertinent to scholars of citizenship and much more. It is likely that many of these issues can best be addressed by exploring the interrelationships among all three political roles cities play in American democracy: as sites of political activity embedded in larger structures, as political actors in those larger structures, and as political symbols.

I have already noted that the rise of national democratic republics, beginning with the American Revolution, worked to displace cities as the main sites of citizenship, and that Thomas Jefferson, who triumphed over his Hamiltonian opponents in 1800, made derogation of large cities central to his vision of American republicanism. One issue to be addressed, then, is how and why the United States became an urbanized society nonetheless, to the extent that in the heyday of American cities in the mid–twentieth century, it became possible to present American citizenship primarily as urban citizenship.

Perhaps the answer is chiefly an economic one: financial and productive resources and interests located largely in cities proved too valuable to the nation to be foregone, especially with technological innovations that made undreamed-of material wealth possible but also created new military dangers for the United States. Perhaps the story is more one of political power: with the aid of their growing wealth, those same interests simply proved so politically influential that American governments favored their urban homes. But perhaps the cultural dimension was still more salient: it may be that many Americans were in fact always attracted to the urban lifestyles Jefferson saw as corrupt and immoral and that many more became so over time. Tocqueville remarked that in the commercial society without fixed classes among whites that Americans had established, many came to see farming as a less promising path for upward economic mobility than trade and industry; and in the nineteenth and early twentieth centuries, those jobs were most often in cities.[14] Still, the magnets may not have been purely economic: urban-minded public intellectuals, particularly in the Progressive era, may have succeeded in establishing their vision of expertly managed, clean, comfortable, diverse, yet communal modern cities as an attractive image of what American cities and American citizenship were becoming or at least should become.

It is also important to ask, however, why this vision of pristine, apolitical, efficient cities has not endured, along with the related questions of how and why American cities appear to have declined in political and economic power since the 1960s. It seems necessary to recognize that the Progressive apotheosis of well-managed cities was part of a less than fully successful attack on the traditional forms of partisan urban governance they derided as corrupt ethnic machines. Reformers' views were open then and since to charges of seeking to preserve elite governance under the guise of nonpartisan modernization.[15] Their positions also remained in tension with the focus on national citizenship in which the federal government's leaders had a stake, all the more so during the national crises of the Depression and World War II. And, as Hulme shows, even in the heyday of celebrations of modern municipal governments, business advocates denounced them as tending toward socialism at the expense of free enterprise. Those criticisms have never ceased, and in the post-Reagan era, proponents of "neoliberal" policies favoring deregulation and extensive privatization of governmental services have trumpeted such measures as solutions for financially stressed cities and urban school systems.[16]

Perhaps, then, efforts to identify American citizenship with Progressive visions of urban citizenship have simply been overwhelmed by their many political foes—though if the explanation is political opposition, it matters greatly which foes prevailed and why. Alternatively, perhaps technological and economic innovations by themselves made cities obsolete as locations where economic resources, and thus some measure of autonomous power, were concentrated. But political scientists would be wise to consider instead whether the impacts of such innovations have been interwoven with politics in ways we need to grasp. It may well be that modern technological and economic developments would *not* have had the effect of deindustrializing and depopulating many cities in favor of suburban, sometimes rural, and increasingly overseas locations without public policies supporting those shifts.

If so, then if we are to understand modern American citizenship and American politics, we have to ask, which policies fostered those results?

Who supported them? Who opposed them and why? How much of a role did surviving Jeffersonian-style aversions to big cities play in prompting shifts to more green and spacious suburbs, accompanied by public investments in highways and commuter trains that aided those transitions? Did the day-to-day lives of many urban citizens prompt them to affirm Jane Jacobs's famous condemnation of the dehumanizing consequences of modern urban planning in *The Death and Life of Great American Cities*[17] without sharing her commitments to urban reform, so that they chose exit over voice? Or, again, is the story primarily one of more purely economic power and interests? How much of the movement away from the centers of cities can be traced to the interests and influence of corporations without much concern for either urban citizenship or American citizenship?

Finally, what role did the changing demographics of American cities and the popular and governmental responses to them play? For, in all these inquiries, as the foregoing chapters show, we need to come to grips with the relationship of urban citizenship to the contested and changing ethnic, religious, and racial dimensions of American life—dimensions that have greatly shaped American citizenship and political development as a whole.[18] It was, after all, primarily the cities that received the mass European immigration influxes from the 1830s to the 1850s and the 1880s through the early twentieth century.[19] Many of the immigrants were Catholics who redefined urban spaces as parishes, something that old-stock Protestant Americans found threatening to their conceptions of American identity and often to their electoral interests. Consequently, those immigration flows churned up waves of American nativism and immigration restrictions that made citizenship laws into political battlegrounds, eventually producing Chinese exclusions and the race-based national origins quota systems of the 1920s.[20]

It was also the cities north of the Mason-Dixon line that received the "Great Migration" (or migrations) of African Americans from the south to the north beginning in World War I, continuing in World War II, and reaching a peak during the 1950s as southern agriculture completed the transition to extensive mechanization.[21] The presence of growing numbers of urban African Americans required both municipal and national leaders and white citizens to make choices about whether the new arrivals would be met with further extensions of Jim Crow discriminatory practices or greater acceptance as civic equals. The resulting conflicts helped fuel the fierce activism of the civil rights movement that ushered in the modern era of American citizenship, embodied in antidiscrimination legislation and judicial rulings at every level of government.[22] But the modern era also has proven to be one in which first whites, and then middle-class families of all backgrounds, began to leave their transforming northern cities for suburbs, often taking tax revenues and property values with them. More working-class Catholics tied to their parishes, along with some Orthodox Jews who had to be able to walk to services on their Sabbath, often were slowest to move out—though many found it hard to welcome their growing numbers of black neighbors, exacerbating urban tensions.[23]

And even though, from the 1850s to the present, many Asian and Latino immigrants came to do agricultural or rural construction work, many have always either gone directly to cities or ended up in them whenever their more rural job opportunities declined. Those patterns remain true today, though the range of cities that are receiving immigrants has expanded with the coming of the twenty-first century.[24] As a result of these demographic changes, in the modern era American urban citizens have come to be perceived to be, and often actually are, predominantly nonwhite—black, Latino, to a lesser degree East and South Asian—as well as disproportionately poor, interpretable as displaying pathological "culture of poverty" traits. It is all too likely that to many suburban and rural Americans, many of these nonwhite urban citizens do not seem to embody what they conceive as "true American citizenship," even when they possess legal citizenship—a pattern that has counterparts in many other immigrant-receiving advanced societies.[25]

The story of cities as sites of American political life, as actors in American politics, and as American political symbols must, then, inform and be informed by the struggles over race, ethnicity, and civic status that are painfully central to American citizenship as a whole, with religious conflicts playing lesser but still significant roles. And again, though the particulars and dynamics of race, ethnicity, and religion in relation to citizenship vary in other locales, the tensions between these identities and equal civic standing can be found in most modern nations. American urban citizenship also now has a further, even more directly transnational significance. In the twenty-first century, the largest American metropolitan areas increasingly display the class structure of what Saskia Sassen and others have deemed "global cities."[26] Their wealthiest inhabitants often have incredibly busy cosmopolitan lifestyles, pursuing careers and amassing fortunes that mean they effectively live and work in multiple locations around the world. As part of those lifestyles, they fund the growth of low-wage service industry jobs—restaurants, dry cleaners, home and office maintenance workers, childcare providers, taxi drivers, and much more—that are often filled by nonwhite citizens or, still more often, immigrants seeking to secure a foothold in the world's largest national economy. Many do, but many falter; and so these two "global city" classes contribute to rising levels of urban economic inequality. The sources and consequences of these economic patterns among the inhabitants of the nation's largest cities are, again, matters of central concern for scholars of American citizenship and American political development, as well as citizenship studies more generally.

And in recent years, as national institutions have failed to address the many dissatisfactions bred by current national immigration policies, American cities have responded to their growing numbers of immigrant residents in widely different ways.[27] Many large cities, including New York, Chicago, Philadelphia, Baltimore, and more, have insisted they wish to welcome all immigrants, even to be "sanctuary cities," in opposition to what they see as increasingly and unduly harsh national efforts to deny immigrants social services and to deport those who are unauthorized. Other cities, including some major ones like Phoenix but particular- ly smaller ones like Hazleton, Pennsylvania, which only recently have become recipients of immigrant influxes, instead have opted for initiatives to discourage these new arrivals, sometimes with the support of state officials, as in Arizona. Cities are not the only sites in which these latest battles over who will be part of American democracy are taking place, but they are central to current struggles as sites of political life, as actors in broader American politics, and as symbols of what sort of democratic republic Americans want the United States to be. And similar citizenship- centered struggles are taking place in cities and in national politics in most of the nations of northern Europe, in Canada, in Japan, in Australia, and in many other societies seeking to cope with their conflicted responses to immigrants whom they often need and often fear.

In this last, symbolic regard, it is striking, perhaps ironic, that even as the Reagan era brought about the federal distancing of responsibil- ity for much in the life of American cities that several of the chapters here address, Ronald Reagan himself revived John Winthrop's colonial-era phrase, "city on a hill," to portray how Americans should think about their nation.[28] In the context of immigration (as well as other contexts), that phrase has long been subject to very different interpretations. For some, it has meant that the United States should be an asylum for suffering and aspiring people from around the world; for others, it has meant that the United States should be an example to the world, but one kept pure by preventing corrosive influences from entering. I have argued that, in either case, the "city on a hill" image is a dangerous one for Americans to continue to embrace.[29] Either way, it perpetuates a sense that the United States and Americans are fundamentally superior to the rest of the world's regimes. That flattering self-portrait may or may not have done little harm when the United States was a struggling set of former colonies striving to achieve a reasonably stable, peaceful, and prosperous national existence. And it is not unusual—it is indeed probably necessary—for national leaders to support civic solidarity by celebrating their regimes in rhetorically effective ways. But for the world's richest and most powerful nation to do so by means of this providentialist imagery is unwise at a time when the United States' wealth and military power spawn resentments yet remain insufficient to command the multilateral actions needed to address a wide range of global challenges.

It seems far more appropriate for Americans today—and, I venture to say, for the citizens of other nations as well—to strive to see themselves not as the privileged occupants of any "city on a hill" but as egalitarian-minded citizens of a "great metropolis on a plain," one on which the world's other political communities also reside as respected and valued neighbors. The political challenges to winning acceptance for such conceptions of citizenship will vary greatly in different locales. Whether most Americans will come to embrace this sort of self-image may well prove to depend in part on whether most come to see their increasingly diverse and cosmopolitan cities as places that they can enjoy and in which they can take pride or whether they see them chiefly as sources of burdens and dangers. And how Americans as a whole see their cities may well partly depend, in turn, on urban political actors, on how successfully urban citizens and leaders govern themselves, to the extent they have autonomous power to do so, and how effectively they identify and champion economic, educational, and social policies that can improve their circumstances and be more broadly beneficial as well.

There are, then, many vital, substantive issues to address concerning cities as political sites, as political actors, and as political symbols. It is, above all, the great significance of these issues that makes it important to recognize, as the essays collected here do, that urban citizenship and American democracy have always been and remain in the twenty-first century profoundly intertwined, in ways of great consequence for American citizenship, for American political development, and for the wider world in which they are such integral and influential parts.

Notes

1. Aristotle, *Politics*, ed. Ernest Barker (London: *Oxford* University Press, 1958), 92–109.

2. John G. A. Pocock, "The Ideal of Citizenship Since Classical Times," in *Theorizing Citizenship*, ed. Ronald Beiner (Albany: State University of New York Press, 1995), 29–37.

3. Thomas H. Marshall, "Citizenship and Social Class," in *Class, Citizenship, and Social Development* (Garden City, NY: Doubleday & Co., Inc., 1965), 71–134.

4. Clarence N. Stone and Robert K. Whelan, "Through a Glass Darkly: The Once and Future Study of Urban Politics," in *The City in American Political Development*, ed. Richardson Dilworth (New York: Routledge, 2009), 98–118.

5. Dilworth, *The City in American Political Development*.

6. US Statistical Abstract, "Table 29: Urban and Rural Population by State: 1990 and 2000," http://www.census.gov/compendia/statab/2012/tables/12s0029.pdf.

7. Philip J. Ethington and David P. Levitus, "Placing American Political Development: Cities, Regions, and Regimes, 1789–2008," in *The City in American Political Development*, ed. Dilworth, 154–176.

8. Robert C. Lieberman, "The City and Exceptionalism in American Political Development," in *The City in American Political Development*, ed. Dilworth, 18, 24, 38–39.

9. Jerome Hodos, "Against Exceptionalism: Intercurrence and Intergovernmental Relations in Britain and the United States," in *The City in American Political Development*, ed. Dilworth, 55.

10. Neil Brenner, "Is There a Politics of 'Urban' Development? Reflections on the US Case," in *The City in American Political Development*, ed. Dilworth, 126–137.

11. Thomas Jefferson, *Notes on the State of Virginia*, (Charlottesville: University of Virginia, 1993 [1781–1782]), http://etext.virginia.edu/toc/modeng/public/JefVirg.html, 291; Thomas Jefferson, *Political Writings*, ed. Joyce Appleby and Terence Ball (Cambridge: Cambridge University Press, 1999), 28.

12. US Census Bureau, "State and County QuickFacts," http://quickfacts.census.gov/qfd/states/36/3651000.html.

13. Lieberman, "The City and Exceptionalism in American Political Development," 23, 27.

14. Alexis de Tocqueville, *Democracy in America*, trans. Arthur Goldhammer (New York: Library of America, 2004), 642, 645.

15. Jessica Trounstine, "Challenging the Machine-Reform Dichotomy: Two Threats to Urban Democracy," in *The City in American Political Development*, ed. Dilworth, 77–97.

16. Pauline Lipman, *The New Political Economy of Urban Education: Neoliberalism, Race, and the Right to the City* (New York: Routledge, 2011);

Timothy Weaver, "Neoliberalism in the Trenches: Urban Policy and Politics in the United States and the United Kingdom" (PhD diss., Department of Political Science, University of Pennsylvania, 2012).

17. Jane Jacobs, *The Death and Life of Great American Cities* (New York: Random House, 1961).

18. Clarissa Rile Hayward, "Urban Space and American Political Development: Identity, Interest, Action," in *The City in American Political Development*, ed. Dilworth, 141–153.

19. Arstide R. Zolberg, *A Nation by Design: Immigration Policy in the Fashioning of America* Cambridge: Harvard University Press, 2006), 128, 205.

20. Daniel J. Tichenor, *Dividing Lines: The Politics of Immigration Control in America* (Princeton: Princeton University Press, 2002), 46–149.

21. Stewart E. Tolnay, "The African American 'Great Migration' and Beyond," *Annual Review of Sociology* 29 (2003): 209–232.

22. Thomas J. Sugrue, *Sweet Land of Liberty: The Forgotten Struggle for Civil Rights in the North* (New York: Random House, 2008).

23. Gerald Gamm, *Urban Exodus: Why the Jews Left Boston and the Catholics Stayed* (Cambridge: Harvard University Press, 2001).

24. Douglas S. Massey, ed., *New Faces in New Places: The Changing Geography of American Immigration* (New York: The Russell Sage Foundation, 2010).

25. Alastair Bonnett, "The Metropolis and White Modernity," *Ethnicities* 2, no. 3 (2002): 349–366.

26. Saskia Sassen, "Global Migrations and Economic Need," in *Citizenship, Borders, and Human Needs*, ed. Rogers M. Smith (Philadelphia: University of Pennsylvania Press, 2011), 56–91.

27. Christina M. Rodríguez, "The Significance of the Local in Immigration Restriction," *Michigan Law Review* 106, no. 4 (2008): 567–642.

28. Ellen Reid Gold, "Ronald Reagan and the Oral Tradition," *Central States Speech Journal* 39, nos. 3–4 (1988): 159–175.

29. Rogers M. Smith, "From a Shining City on a Hill to a Great Metropolis on a Plain? American Stories of Immigration and Peoplehood," *Social Research* 77, no. 1 (2010): 38–40.

Contributors

Amy Bridges is a professor of political science at the University of California, San Diego. A scholar of city politics, Bridges is the author of *A City in the Republic, Antebellum New York* and *Origins of Machine Politics* (Cambridge, 1984), and *Morning Glories, Municipal Reform in the Southwest* (Princeton, 1997). More recently, Bridges authored "The Sun Also Rises in the West," a study of the Justice for Janitors movement in Los Angeles, for *The City Revisited*. Bridges has served on the editorial boards of *Politics & Society, Urban Affairs Review, Journal of Policy History, and Studies in American Political Development*. Persuaded that for too long political scientists and historians have neglected the western region, writing US history as northern and southern history, Bridges is currently writing a book about the founding constitutions of the western states, *Western Window, Constitutions, Society, and Growth*. This work recently earned her fellowships from the American Council of Learned Societies and the National Endowment for the Humanities.

Khalilah L. Brown-Dean is an associate professor of political science at Quinnipiac University. Brown-Dean was previously the Peter Strauss Family Assistant Professor of Political Science and African American Studies at Yale University and a resident fellow of the Institute for Social and Policy Studies and a research fellow at the Macmillan Center for International and Area Studies at Yale. Dr. Brown-Dean received her PhD in political science from The Ohio State University in 2003 and a bachelor's degree in government from the University of Virginia in 1998.

Emily M. Farris is an assistant professor of political science at Texas Christian University, specializing in American politics on issues of urban politics and racial/ethnic politics. Her research has been supported by awards from the Fund for Latino Scholarship, travel grants from American Political Science Association and Southern Political Science Association, and fellowships at Brown University. She is a recipient of the Stone Scholar Award and the Byran Jackson Dissertation in Ethnic and Racial Politics Research Support Award from the Urban Politics section of the American Political Science Association.

Michael Javen Fortner is an assistant professor and the academic director of urban studies at the Murphy Institute at City University of New York School of Professional Studies. In 2010, he received a PhD in government and social policy from Harvard University. At Harvard, he was a doctoral fellow in the multidisciplinary program in inequality and social policy and an affiliate of the Minda de Gunzburg Center for European Studies. His work studies the intersection of American political development and political philosophy—particularly in the areas of race, ethnicity, and class. He is also the author of *Black Silent Majority: Urban Politics and the Rockefeller Drug Laws* (Harvard University Press, 2015). His scholarly articles have appeared in *Studies in American Political Development*, the *Journal of Urban History*, the *Journal of Policy History*, and *Urban Affairs Review*. He has also been published in the *New York Times, Newsweek, Boston Review*, and *Dissent*, and his research has been covered in major media outlets, such as the *Chronicle of Higher Education*, the *Atlantic*, the *New York Times*, the *New Yorker*, *New York Magazine*, the *Daily Beast*, *Time*, WNYC and NPR. He has been awarded fellowships and grants from the National Science Foundation, the Ford Foundation, the Aspen Institute, the Center for American Political Studies, the American Political Science Association, the New York State Archives, the Rockefeller Archive Center, and the Mortar Board Honor Society. He has also received several teaching awards.

Richard A. Harris teaches and writes in the areas of American politics and public policy, with specializations in business/government relations and environmental policy. In addition to publishing books on these topics with Duke University Press and Oxford University Press, Dr. Harris has received research fellowships from the National Endowment for the Humanities and the Brookings Institution. He also has received support for innovative teaching as well as the Provost's Award for Teaching Excellence at Rutgers-Camden. He currently serves as director of the Senator Walter Rand Institute for Public Affairs, a campus-wide institute for applied research and public service.

Jennifer L. Hochschild is Henry LaBarre Jayne Professor of Government and professor of African and African American Studies at Harvard University. Her most recent book (coauthored with Nathan Scovronick) is *The American Dream and the Public Schools*. Her book (coauthored with Vesla Weaver and Traci Burch) *Creating a New Racial Order: How Immigration, Genomics, Multiracialism, and the Young Can Remake Race in America* will be published in early 2012. Hochschild is currently John R. Kluge Fellow of American Law and Governance at the Library of Congress, where she is conducting research on the development of partisanship and ideological valences around genomic science. She also studies and publishes on the topic of immigrant political incorporation in North America and Western Europe.

Tom Hulme is an Early Career Urban History lecturer at the Centre for Metropolitan History (Institute of Historical Research, School of Advanced Study). In 2013 he received a PhD in urban history from the University of Leicester, funded by the Economic and Social Research Council. Between 2013 and 2015 he was a postdoctoral researcher at King's College London on the Arts and Humanities Research Council project "The Redress of the Past: Historical Pageants in Britain, 1905–2016." He has published on various twentieth-century topics, such as civic education, local government, public housing, school architecture, and historical pageants.

Lisa L. Miller is an associate professor of political science at Rutgers University in New Brunswick, New Jersey. She has a PhD from the University of Washington and a bachelor of arts degree from the University of Virginia. Her interests are at the intersection of law and social policy, specifically the politics of punishment and the legal and political mobilization of racial minorities on crime and justice issues. She has written extensively on the development of crime and justice policy and legal frameworks in the United States and has also published research examining the inner workings of the federal criminal courts. Her most recent book is *The Perils of Federalism: Race, Poverty and the Politics of Crime Control* (2008, Oxford University Press).

Domingo Morel is visiting assistant professor at McCormack Graduate School of Policy and Global Studies at the University of Massachusetts, Boston. He has a PhD in political science from Brown University, a bachelor of science degree in human development and family studies from the University of Rhode Island, and a master of arts degree in counseling from

Rhode Island College. His research interests are in American politics and political theory, with a focus on African American and Latino politics. He is cofounder of the Latino Policy Institute at Roger Williams University and an adjunct faculty member in the African and African American Studies Department at the University of Rhode Island.

Marion Orr is the director of the A. Alfred Taubman Center for Public Policy and American Institutions and the Fred Lippitt Professor of Public Policy, Political Science and Urban Studies at Brown University. He previously was a member of the political science faculty at Duke University. A native of Savannah, Georgia, he earned his bachelor of arts degree in political science from Savannah State College, a master of arts degree in political science from Atlanta University (now Clark-Atlanta University), and a PhD in government and politics from the University of Maryland, College Park. He is affiliated with the Urban Studies Program. He is the author and editor of two books: *Black Social Capital: The Politics of School Reform in Baltimore* (University Press of Kansas), which won the Policy Studies Organization's Aaron Wildavsky Award for the best book published in 1999, and *The Color of School Reform: Race, Politics and the Challenge of Urban Education* (Princeton University Press), which was named the best book in 1999 by the American Political Science Association's (APSA) Urban Politics Section. He is the editor of *Transforming the City: Community Organizing and the Challenge of Political Change* and *Power in the City: Clarence Stone and the Politics of Inequality*. He is also the author of numerous scholarly articles, essays, and reviews.

Rogers M. Smith is the Christopher H. Browne Distinguished Professor of Political Science at the University of Pennsylvania and chair of the Penn Program on Democracy, Citizenship, and Constitutionalism. He is the author or coauthor of numerous articles and six books, including *Still a House Divided: Race and Politics in Obama's America* with Desmond S. King (August 2011), *Stories of Peoplehood* (2003), *The Unsteady March: The Rise and Decline of Racial Equality in America* (1999), and *Civic Ideals: Conflicting Visions of Citizenship in U.S. History* (1997). *Civic Ideals* received six best book prizes and was a finalist for the 1998 Pulitzer Prize in History. Smith has received teaching awards from Yale University and the University of Pennsylvania. He was elected a fellow of the American Academy of Arts and Sciences Fellow in 2004 and of the American Academy of Political and Social Science in 2011.

Kenneth K. Wong is the first Walter and Leonore Annenberg Chair for Education Policy and is currently the chair of the Education Department at Brown University. While holding joint appointments with the Education Department and the Annenberg Institute for School Reform (AISR), Dr. Wong directs the master's program in urban education policy. The twelve-month program, designed to prepare students for professional careers involving policy development and analysis in urban public education, is a collaborative effort of the Education Department, AISR, the Taubman Center for Public Policy, and the Education Alliance.

Index

accountability, 130–131, 135–136, 139, 142, 154, 184

Adams, John, 213

adult citizenship classes, 71, 77, 80

African Americans: discrimination against, 84, 182, 185; disenfranchisement, 15, 163–165, 175–176; in economically distressed cities, 12–13, 181, 191; employment, 46; in Ferguson, Missouri, 6–7; and gun violence, 190; migration to cities, 37, 46, 83, 217; and patronage, 47; political power, 16–17, 183, 187, 194, 209; poverty, 54, 161, 172, 191; in prisons, 15, 160–163, 168, 169, 172; in rural counties, 168; use of term, 178n34; violence toward, 183, 190–191, 198n45; voting, 4, 8, 42–43, 51–52, 54

agenda setting, 130, 132, 135–136, 146–147, 149, 152, 157n37

AITF. *See* Anchor Institutions Task Force

Alabama, 175

Alinsky, Saul, 6

Allen, Ivan, 3, 17

American Fund for Public Service, 90n106

American Historical Association, 70, 81

Americanization, 66–67, 204

American Legion, 66

American Political Science Association, 69, 71

American Revolution, 181–182, 211, 215

Amsterdam, Daniel, 66–67

anchor institutions, 135–139, 144

Anchor Institutions Task Force (AITF), 136–137, 140

Anderson, Robert M., 86n16

Annie E. Casey Foundation, 13–14, 138, 151

Appalachia, 167

apportionment, 163–165

Argentina, 215

Aristotle, 23; *Politics*, 211

Arizona: immigration law (SB 1070), 197n27, 209, 219; Phoenix, 46, 219; prisons, 168; Tucson, 46

Arpaio, Joseph, 206

Ashley, Roscoe L., 74; *The New Civics*, 69–70

Asian Americans, 4, 218

Aspen Roundtable on Community Change, 143

Association of Community Organizations for Reform Now (ACORN), 188

Athens, 23

Atlanta, Georgia, 17, 67